NAKED IN A NIPA HUT:

I'M A CYBER-SEX GURL

and I wanna tell you my story...

Dr. Paul W. Mathews

First published in Australia in 2015 by
Warrior Publishers at Smashwords

E-book ISBN 978 13 1014 1461

Amazon paperback: 978 16 8984 8077

Warriorpublishers@outlook.com

NON-FICTION

CONTENTS

Acknowledgements

I would like to thank John Escobar for his unswerving patience and tolerance of a mad and angry anthropologist in helping, beyond the call of duty, in establishing contacts with some of the gurls herein and sustaining some semblance of fieldwork amongst a litany of lies.

Ironically, acknowledgement, if not thanks—and in fact, certainly no thanks—go to the even more insane Israelis whose fumbling and lies and deceit led to my telling the stories of ACMs, *for* ACMs, herein.

Serendipitously, their actions ultimately led me to meet a beautiful, wonderful gurl/girl, which led me to give her a chance in her life time, to sponsor her college degree—a gift for life—and to meet her blessed family.

I also want to thank Melinda and her friend Angel, and their families, who showed great warmth and acceptance of my presence and interference in their lives.

Leanne, too, I thank for helping me with insights, contacts, and, what I would hope, a continuing friendship.

Not least are those gurls who I have bugged to get their stories, on and off line, for tolerating my being *makulit*.

I also thank the reviewers of my earlier works; while I may present at times as defensive or scathing, their comments and views have been insightful and inspiring.

Dr. Paul W. Mathews

INTRODUCTION

In my earlier, pioneering book, *Asian Cam Models: Digital Virtual Virgin Prostitutes?* (2010), I set out to explore the ACM (Adult/Asian Cam Model) industry in the Philippines, specifically identifying the economic piecework relations of a new global industry. I also explored how the industry operated and the views of some ACMs garnered through netography and interviews. At that time nothing had been written about this phenomenon.

The book received little attention, but in fact some criticism from Filipinas and others who saw it as just another portrayal of Filipinas as objects of sexuality and sub-servience. Even a local Filipino radio station in Australia refused to consider doing a story on the topic.

In the meantime, the discourses of legal and social oppression and repression continued to unfold, culminating in the Cybercrime Act. But nowhere in that history were the voices of ACMs themselves. This current volume therefore attempts to give voice to those gurls and guys who, for whatever reason and howsoever, may identify for the moment as an ACM.

It was ironic that an Israeli TV documentary program spurred my return to this subject matter in 2013. They had wanted to portray the gurls' side of being an ACM and enlisted my help, initially unbeknown to me that their real motive was to expose a certain "Mr. Big" who ran some of the ACM sites, with an agenda to expose him as making millions of dollars from exploiting (young) "uneducated" poor girls of 2nd or 3rd world countries, such as the Philippines. Frankly, infuriated by the deception of both myself and the gurls who they did interview, I began to collect the histories of some ACMs whom I came to know through this unfortunate incident.

These are *their* stories.

In my original work I attempted to explore several issues, without any real attempt to answer the questions posed, but rather offer possible explanations, thoughts, comments, and directions for future research. These issues were diverse: the labour relations of ACMs; the impact that digital technology has had in providing employment for formally unskilled, (primarily) young female workers, while simultaneously exploring how economic, cultural and digital globalization may have adversely impacted on employment and labour relations; and some of the objective and subjective interpretations of ACM-ing. For the latter I included some brief case studies, achieved mainly through on-line conversations (netography).

In that book I began with questions, rather than hypotheses: How are we to construe ACM-ing?—as sex work, as prostitution in particular, as stripping, exhibition-ism, as pornography? The evidence, primarily from the gurls themselves, suggested they were none of these, but what they did was simply a job, work, and their actions as per-formance; and that they largely had no problem with doing this type of work.

Oddly, the current set of stories in this volume contradict the previous gurls' views; several, but not all, of the informants here in this volume clearly agree that ACM-ing is a form of sex work, and indeed, prostitution, or at "best'" they are porn stars.

As an adjunct to this issue of what constitutes sex work, the gurls took up this work of their own free will, exercising their agency, albeit within social, economic, sexual and gender constraints—but then, don't we all? Hence the media and NGO focus on trafficking—and its conflation with prostitution—was and still is largely misguided. To fuse the two concepts of trafficking and prostitution totalizes the experiences of all women working in the sex industry in a variety of situations involving different levels of personal will.

Although this subject area readily lends itself to issues of agency, and to sexual/gender objectification, I tended to steer away from such an analysis, fraught with difficulties, in my haste to document in the first instance the industry and the gurls' work and non-work lives. I raised questions in that first book, unable at that time to answer them, and almost no other material to draw upon other than publications of prostitution and other forms of sex work such as stripping, pornography, and exhibitionism—existing categories with which ACM-ing had some parallels but also from which it differed. How then could ACM-ing fit with these categories, or perhaps indeed challenge them, and challenge us to think of sex work in a different way?

I have since been brought to task to more fully explore if not answer these questions, yet oddly enough, throughout the criticisms there was a constant nag to allow the gurls themselves to answer the questions. Thus, this book, rather than privileging my white, male voice, gives voice to the gurls' views—at least some of them, we hope. Unfortunately, it is difficult to not interpolate, for their stories are recorded and transcribed rather than wholly autobiographical. To attenuate this somewhat, I did ask some of the informants whom I could still contact to read the transcripts of what I had written, and amend them accordingly. Tina and Leanne did so, with only Leanne suggesting two small changes, while Tina commented that I had captured her interview very well. I have tried to limit my interpellation into their narratives, but do so only of necessity, to try to structure to some degree what would otherwise be incoherent. Where I do offer comments or interpretations, these must be read as only possibilities, and not definitive explanations.

What really inspired me, however, was the second main issue I raised in the book: the economic exploitation of the work, ie, not only the contingent or situational labour relations, but exploitation by means of an economic principle of payment—piece rates. As I argued then, and develop herein also, piece-rate payment schemes are, in principle, *inherently* exploitative. Thus, while bosses and the site owners may benignly portray the employment opportunities available through this kind of piece-rates work, in reality it is a system of capitalist exploitation that shifts the burden and risk to the worker at the point of production.

A third issue also arose whilst writing the first book, and subsequently. This involved a range of methodological issues. My study was based on one "chat-room" (ACM) site, *AsianPlaymates*.[1] I had adopted the methods of observation, participant-observation or what Walstrom (2004a; 2004b) terms "participant-experiencer", and ad hoc—and therefore often fragmented—interviews over a period of more than 12 months.

The lack of guidance on this kind of work, my own lack of experience with (sex) chat sites and the obvious trickiness of conducting research in sexually charged environments made this project difficult to navigate, not least of which were moral and ethical concerns—of which I was acutely aware, but nevertheless I had to make decisions, for which I do take responsibility, but for which I do not apologize.

I will return to these issues in a later chapter. Suffice to say here that, in writing the current book, I did obtain informed consent from the participants—and indeed on some occasions enthusiasm.

Indeed, Part 2 of this current book will present, in a slightly condensed form, a paper on the topic of ACMs and the critiques of that paper, and my responses to those critiques to enable further elaboration of several issues.

Normally such a debate would come early in a book such as this, but I feel to do so would detract from the essential and primary purpose of this book: to put the ACMs at the forefront of discussions. After all, these are *their* stories, this is *their* book, of them, *for* them.

Thus this current book is organized into four parts: Following a brief note about what ACM-ing is and the methodologies employed in researching ACMs, **Part I** presents ten histories from ACMs. Subsequently, because the gathering of those stories was spurred by an unfortunate incident with an Israeli TV crew, I present how this unfolded, and the implications of media interference and misrepresentation.

Part II presents a structured academic rendition about ACM-ing, and several responses to that paper, and ultimately my responses to issues raised by several reviewers, as I mentioned above.

Part III is a first attempt to discusses the structure of the sex industry in the Philippines, some if its economics aspects, and where ACM-ing may be placed within that structure—assuming that ACM-ing is a form of sex-work. Assuming this, the question arose why some ACMs do not want to, or are unable to, move into other forms of sex-work such as massage parlours, bar-work or street prostitution. Conversely, why is it that few girls move from other forms of sex-work into being an ACM? Thus the issue of occupational mobility into, out of and within the sector is discussed.

Part IV briefly discusses—indeed speculates on— clients of ACMs. We know almost nothing about ACMs' clients. This is followed by a brief conclusion to the book and the general issues touched upon.

ACMs/ing

For those not familiar with ACM-ing I provide a very brief overview of the industry/activity, and a brief note on the methods employed for the writing of this and my previous book. These matters are expanded in a later chapter.

ACMs are gurls who present themselves live via internet cam (camera) to solicit customers to view the gurls naked or engaging in sexual activities in a private show, usually at $1 per minute. Of this amount they receive only 25 cents, as the site owner (the Company) takes 50% and the gurl's boss—should she have one—takes 25%. The ACMs' presentation is facilitated through several sites. *AsianPlaymates* is one such site.[2] Each ACM is required to meet a quota of prvt chat minutes (usually 100 minutes) each 15 days, and thus it is not uncommon for ACMs to work 10-12 hours a day. If they do not achieve this quota they do not get paid at all. However, if in the following 15 days they reach or surpass 100 minutes, then they will be paid their full credit. Thus, ideally, the gurls aim to achieve 200 minutes of prvt performance each month. However, because most of the young ACMs experience menstruation each month, perhaps lasting up to a week in some cases, during which time they may choose not work, they effectively have only 3 weeks in a month to reach their quota.

In accessing the *AsianPlaymates* site the client can log-on as a "guest" or register for free with a User/Screen name. Page one subsequently displays hundreds of photos of Filipina gurls of various ages, in different poses, each with their own screen name. Each model can have up to 7 screen names, so they can appear in several ACM categories on the site. At one count (in July 2014), 3,400 gurls were listed as ACMs on *AsianPlaymates*. Not all were currently active, however, since ACM-ing seems to have a high turnover of models. Certainly not all are available to chat at any one time; usually, there are about 200-300 gurls on line at any one time.

At page one, a customer clicks on a gurl's picture, which takes him/her to that particular gurl's public "studio" or "room", where one can chat with her (and possibly other clients).

If one takes a gurl "prvt", ie. into a private, one-on-one chat or performance session, one pays with a credit card via the site. One clicks on the gurl's hyperlink, which takes only the paying client and her into the prvt show, where the client can direct the gurl to perform sexually such as taking off her clothes, parading and dancing in front of the cam, laying down with close-ups of her vagina or breasts, posing in different positions, masturbating, or using a toy.

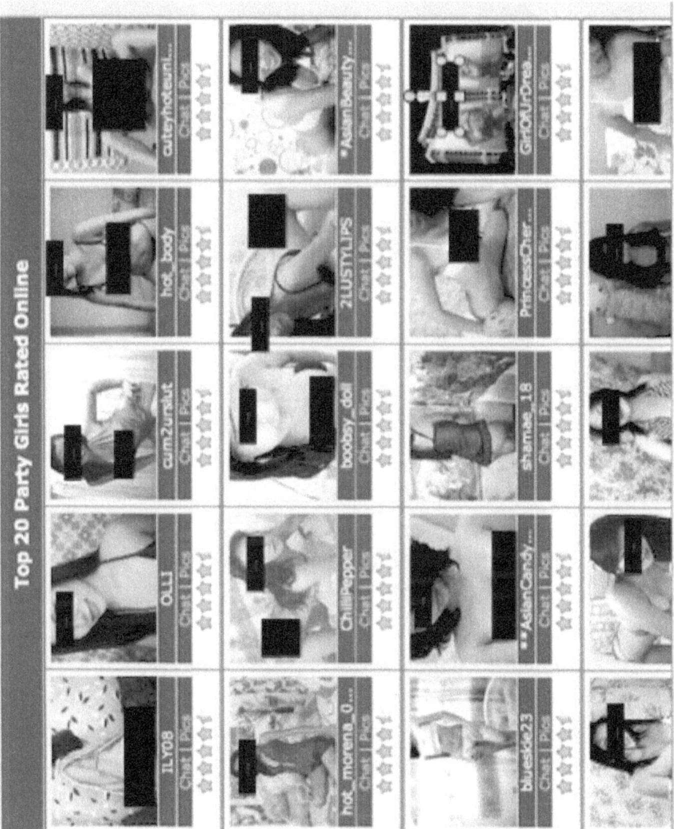

Page one, after logging on.

Methodology

Both my previous study and this current one are based, initially, on one "chat-room" (ACM) site, *AsianPlaymates*, which is part of a more comprehensive set of similar sites run by the same USA-based company. I also visited several similar sites run by other companies. Through chatting with several ACMs I arranged to interview in person some of them in November 2013 and March 2014. I subsequently maintained contact via YM with about four of them in the ensuing months.

As with my previous study, I undertook some *ad hoc* "interviews—or rather, chats—with several ACMs on *AsianPlaymates* from September 2013 to the current time (about August 2015), as well as contacting via email some ACMs whom I had formerly known. The main purpose of contacting these gurls was to arrange for me—and an Israeli TV film crew, that will be explained later—to interview the gurls in real. I also attempted to enlist some of these gurls in helping me find other ACMs whom I could interview. Thus, it was made clear to these gurls that I was an independent researcher, and the purpose of my interviewing them was to gain a better understanding of the industry overall, and in particular their life situation and *their* views about ACM-ing.

Through this means I became well acquainted with three gurls and two transgenders, and one ACM whom I had previously known. A few others, both former acquaintances and new contacts, were also willing to meet with me in real, but unfortunately, as it turned out, availability, time or distance did not allow for those meetings to eventuate.

Nevertheless, what was methodologically interesting was that real life meetings with these informants had clear advantages over on-line conversations and *ad hoc* interviews —or rather questions and answers. This requires further exploration, but several reasons in this case could be put forward:

Firstly, my physical presence in the Philippines, and actual physical co-existence in the same space and time, indicated to the ACMs that I was genuine, and not, like so many other customers, "performing"—promising to come but rarely doing so. It also privileged the gurls to be with a foreigner and to be taken seriously—seriously enough for me to travel to them, meet with them, eat with them, and so forth.

Secondly, unlike on-line where I remain an ephemeral persona without any tangibility, in real meetings I am, for them, an opportunity—for whatever they may have had in mind. Here I not only mean that I was able to sponsor them a meal or to provide money, but also I was possibly seen as a potential boyfriend or future spouse, or even just a person by whom their status could be elevated. Indeed, three female ACMs and one transgender indicated, or in the least hinted, at desires for me to be a boyfriend. Alex, for example, during a taxi ride quizzed me about my marital status and out rightly asked if I wouldn't want a nice Filipina (like her) as a wife. Melinda was frequently making similar overtures, while Paris, a *bakla* (transgender), was very keen to take me to a party as her "companion" and for me to visit her home—alone, without my female assistant.

~

Following are many, although not exhaustive, terms commonly used on the site I examined.

(: = sad
:) = happy/smiling
AC = Angeles City
ACM = Adult/Asian Cam Model
b4 = before
bakla = (male) transgender
bb = baby
bf/gf = boyfriend/girlfriend
bola, bola-bola, bolaX2 = (you) are teasing/making fun of me (Tagalog)
brb = be right back
butterfly = to go from one client to another or several
cam = (internet live video) camera
CC = credit card
DC = disconnected (ie. the transmission was disconnected

unexpectedly for technical reasons)
gr8 = great
grrrrr = angry
gtg = gotta go (leave)
hehehe = laugh/smile
hbu = how about you ?
hru = how are you ?
hun/hunni/honey = honey/baby/darling/sweetheart etc
ic/oic = I see/Oh, I see.
lol = laugh out loud (to laugh/smile)
lolz = laugh (out loud) in a teasing way
meet-ups = to meet a client in person/in real
ntmu = nice to meet you
ntmu2 = nice to meet you, too
nu = and you ?
ofc = of course
plzzzzzzz = please
prvt = private (show)
screen name = the name that a girl uses as an ACM (eg. *SweetChelsea, Cutelanie, inucentasia, fuckmyhole, Jazz, sexylicious*)
tc = take care
TG/TS = transgender/*bakla*
toys = vibrator, dildo, and other sexual aids
ty/tyu/tnx/thnx = thanks/thank you
u c = you see ?
ur/yur/yr = your (age, name, etc)
uu/oo = yes (Tagalog)
w8 = wait
wb = welcome back
wc = welcome (to my room)
ym = Yahoo (messenger)
yw = you're welcome
Beggar = a customer who does not log on using a screen name and hence us unable to take a gurl prvt; a customer who does log on with a screen name but who rarely if ever

takes a gurl prvt, or one who has no credit balance on the site. Sometimes these "beggars" do not even chat publicly for free with the gurls. Because we don't know anything about clients, we can only speculate that some take the position of "beggar"—a term used by the gurls themselves—in order to simply watch a gurl, perhaps in the hope she may reveal more of her body, or may chat with a gurl in an effort to entice her to reveal more of her body with promises that he will take her prvt if she does so. See the stories of Kate and Cristy for examples.

PART 1

Group Interview

You invented capitalism, and brought it to the Third World,
now you want to judge us who take advantage of it.

Before undertaking a series of individual interviews with Leanne, Kate and Ken, and Cristy, I engaged them in a preliminary group interview in order to obtain collective input as to how the ACM industry works and *their* general views, as well as their thoughts about whether or not they perceived ACM-ing as a form of sex work or, in particular, as prostitution.

All of the participants worked on the same site, *AsianPlaymates*. I began by guiding the conversation toward why they worked as ACMs. They all agreed that they work as ACMs because they "have" to, that if they didn't work then they could not support their families, they couldn't survive. While they also stressed that they make a choice to work as an ACM, they also noted that their choice is constrained by several factors, not least of which is that it's difficult to get other work because of their limited education and—ironically—appropriate skills.

The irony is that these ACMs *are* talented and smart, and have largely taught themselves to be performers and entrepreneurs. Because many of them have experienced disruptions to family relations, and have been ostracized by society *because* of the very work they do to survive, they have—despite these factors—learnt how to survive. These models *have* skills, skills that no formal education provides! While the ACMs I interviewed may have had limited formal education, I found them articulate, political, questioning, curious and perceptive. Some are also quite technically savvy: Leanne, for example, knows her way around both the hardware and software of PCs, and Jonaz had an interesting experience at college that highlights the irony of life: her teacher suggested an English typing competition amongst students, to which Jonaz responded with great enthusiasm; with her typing and English skills acquired through being an ACM she undoubtedly excelled in the competition!

Another constraint for these ACMs is the inconvenience of other kinds of work, and conversely the convenience of ACM-ing. Single mothers in particular are able to work inside their own house, or nearby, take care of the children at the same time, and do other household chores. As Leanne said, "If you work in a mall you have to leave kids some where, that's a problem, who will look after them if I am not there?" But even if they are not single mothers, but rather *bakla* (trangenders) or single girls, they may not have the education to get alternative work.

They agreed that they might be able to get a legal job, but the income is not enough for their expenses, especially if they have children. The basic salary is 460 pesos per day in Manila, but in the province it's maybe 300+ pesos. For example, work in a canteen pays only 100 pesos a day, which is *"enough only for my breakfast and lunch, I can't buy dinner, I cannot buy milk any more, or diapers...,"* Leanne said. One can get a basic salary of about 460 pesos if one has sufficient education, but its hard to get a legal, a good job, if one is not educated or is otherwise unqualified. These participants have tried to work in a mall or call-centre but the qualification required was too high, requiring fluent English and usually a College degree. *"We're not qualified"*, said Leanne.

The other structural problem for these particular ACMs is that they live in a relocation settlement, where there are few jobs to begin with. Perhaps their best option, then, is to commute daily to a job in Manila, which would cost them about 20-25% of their salary and require long, tiring hours of travel. Thus one can readily appreciate that the advent of ACM-ing is a boon; it provides employment, enables mostly *women* to work, and to work at home. When I asked if they couldn't work as an ACM, what would they do, there was silent resignation, with Leanne summing up their situation: *"Yeah, hard."*

They agreed that if they could find a nice job they would stop being an ACM, which Cristy summed up when I pressed them, would they in fact stop? *"If I have nice job and better salary, why not?"*

"Some models are lucky," said Cristy. *"Sometimes a customer will ask a gurl not to work as an ACM, and offer to support her. They respect her. For example, they will say in prvt that they don't like the gurl to be naked and want her to wear a dress, they want to respect them. Stop there* [at being an ACM or being naked ?], *they say they will support the gurl."* Cristy insisted on citing cases of men paying 10,000 pesos monthly (about $50-60 weekly) to support such gurls.

But we have no evidence of this other than hearsay, and we have no idea how long such an arrangement may be sustained. Nor do we know what happens when such support is terminated. However, I am personally acquainted with three men who have supported ACMs for several years.

Thus, as the models continued, some gurls hope they will find someone to support them, and tell the gurls to stop being an ACM. *"Some models, especially single gurls, work in cam because they want to marry a foreigner, like my friend, she married an Italian guy"*, said Cristy.

"So this is a way of meeting a foreigner?" I asked.

"Yes. If they are lucky."

I directed the conversation to an issue made in an earlier conversation with Leanne, about some people thinking ACM-ing is "easy money". Leanne mentioned in some ways it is "easy", in the sense of a convenient job, as noted above, and a model can earn more money than working in a legal job, sometimes, but it depends on the model. Otherwise, as they all agreed, it was not an easy job; they have to do what others want them to do, and *"we get tired waiting for customers...It's just comfortable."* Nevertheless, it's not really easy money because they have to work long hours, buy cosmetics, act/perform, people abuse them, they have to buy and wear sexy or good clothes, and they may choose not to work during menstruation. In addition, if the PC gets hot, as it tends to do so in hot weather over a 12-hour period, then the connection and operation can be slow, and the PC may have to be shut down. Heavy rain can also interfere with the internet connections; and of course brown-outs make it totally impossible. These and other factors cut into the time available for gurls to be on-line and hence earn money.

These comments led to questions about their earnings, and what they must do to maintain their popularity and hence income.

Asked how much they earn they unanimously said, *"It depends."* As Cristy explained: *"If you're making your own salary"*, ie. without a boss, *"then, for example, if one day you don't have any prvt you don't get any salary, but on the next day you get lucky....That could be 2,000 pesos a day. But if you have a boss and make 100 minutes, that's only 1,000. You make your own salary, so if you're lucky or not it depends on you and your performance."*

Here the models note the issue of working for one self, a piece-rate form of payment, and how one's income depends on "luck" and the model him/herself, their performance. This led onto asking if they need to develop their performance and choreography, with which they all agreed. They indicated that it was necessary to change their performance or presentation by wearing different clothing, appearing more attractive, and/or change their studios in terms of colours and décor, and putting different or more pictures in their portfolios, the rationale being that the more pictures a customer sees the more he will be likely to visit the gurl's room.

But they also noted that some other gurls are always in prvt simply because they are popular. A few examples were given of some gurls who are simply or naturally attractive or sexy, or have large breasts, and are in big demand for prvts. On the other hand, it was noted that some gurls simply show their vagina or breasts or dance naked, while one gurl who was singled out simply sleeps with the cam pointed at her vagina and underwear. But as Cristy continued, *"You have to learn how to perform and always change your performance and be smiling, happy, etc."*

I pointed that some gurls, such as Chelsea whom I had met several years previously, take the time to talk to guests who don't have screen names, while others don't bother, or just ask names, age, country etc, then ask to be taken prvt. While they agreed that this is a possible strategy, they abided by Cristy's comments that, *"Yes, but gurls have to ignore guests so they can focus on other customers who log in and might take us prvt."* I asked, however, couldn't they talk to more than one guest at a time, and thereby groom potential customers, and asked how would they know a guest is not going to take a gurl prvt—that even without a log-in/screen name, he could return as logged-in and take the gurl prvt?

Referring to one type of "beggar" clientele, Cristy explained: *"Because they ask too much, for example, 'stand up, take off your clothes', then take off your bra, they get a free show. We get to know them. They take up your time, and you kinda know they will not take you prvt. The time and effort is wasted. At least you don't waste your time. You'll know it once you're there"* [as an ACM].

I then moved on to what do customers do when asking the gurls to give such a "preview". *"Sometimes when they ask you to stand he's masturbating already, and when you stand up he's done, boom, so you don't get anything."*

They agreed that it is a gamble, of showing a little more

of their bodies to entice customers, to snare a prvt show, and that they have to be tough and understand the men. But in a prvt show, and indeed even in a public chat, the men are able, if they are willing, to show themselves on cam, so the gurls can actually see these guys playing with themselves.

"Yes, sometimes, if they want or ask, we can see them", they all chorused.

Curious about the gender of their clients,[3] I asked how they might know if a client is male or female, and how many female clients visit their rooms?

"Because they tell us", was the short answer. *"But we don't care, all we care is they have money."*

In prvt the ACM suggests the client play with his penis, but if it's a female she will say she is a female, so they usually tell the ACM if they are female. Also, if the client has a cam, then the model will see they are female or male.

Besides, the ACMs' concern is what they can do to please the female guest and, ultimately, get money. They simply don't care who the client is—a notion that very much runs counter to bourgeoisie notions of sexual relations within a romantic framework in which *who* one makes love to, and *why*, is paramount. In terms of the number of female clients they have had, Cristy could say she had only one, although Ken mentioned he had a few.

This led onto what the gurls actually do in prvt shows, or conversely what paying clients ask, expect or demand. Collectively they quickly provided a list of things that clients had asked for, using the term "fetishes" to explain that some clients want to treat a model as a "slave", ask her (or him) to hurt herself and/or cry, to eat cigarettes (and drink water while doing so) and to vomit and then eat more cigarettes, or simply to smoke cigarettes; also listed were poo and pee shows for which they used props to fool the client; to use (sex) toys—a common request; and animal shows such as having sex with a dog, or hurting an animal. However, the cam site management does not allow some of these fetishes to be performed.

More benign requests are that men simply want to chat, or tell a story about their life or a relationship. Leanne said that, "*Sometimes a gay will come in* [on-line] *and ask for advice about making his partner happy*", but the ACM will ask for prvt before giving any advice. Other customers may be planning to visit the Philippines and ask for information about the country and people, etc, or may try to arrange to meet an ACM—one can speculate here that such men may think, quite erroneously, that, because an ACM performs sexually on cam, she will also readily engage in sex in real.

Overall, the models all agreed many clients are crazy and ask for crazy things, but they don't care what a customer wants, as long as he/she pays. As Leanne summed it up: "*They're crazy, but happy.*"

Since the models seemed to focus on doing almost anything so long as they get paid, I tested what is probably a common perception—if the models would therefore also perform or even engage in further sexual activities in real? Thus I asked, if a customer came to the Philippines and asked them to perform in real in his (or her) hotel room, ie. strip and masturbate, etc, even if he doesn't touch them, would they do so?

Cristy: "*No, I wouldn't do it, because I can't fake it.*" The others concurred with this.

Cristy: "*But, it depends, if I know him deeply. I really have to know him deeply, so that I'm sure it's no touching, because anyone can say no touching, but once you're there and, you know.... How will you know he will not touch?*"

Leanne: "*We choose that work* [ACM-ing] *because others* [men] *in a bar will touch you and you don't know what to do... Besides, I don't drink....As an ACM no one can touch you, except ourselves.*"

Following on from this, the conversation was steered toward a final issue about whether or not they thought ACM-ing was some form of sex work. I present this more as a dialogue in order to give voice to the ACMs themselves. While Cristy and Leanne dominated the conversation, Ken and Kate also added their views or generally concurred with the other two.

Q. What do you think of bar girls or street prostitutes?
Leanne: "*They work hard.*"
Cristy: "*It's not for us to do that. It's not easy for me to just fuck a guy I don't know, it's not an easy job.*"

Q. Why is it so hard for you when so many other girls do it?
Cristy: "*Because we have a different choice... For example, we have dignity that at least a customer don't touch us. So, yes, we sell our body, yes, but no body can touch us.*"

Q. But don't you think showing your naked body, touching yourself on cam, is selling your body?
Cristy: "*Yes, we know that, but its not for touching, nobody can touch us.*"
Leanne: "*It's ok for us to show ourselves, do it on own* [body, touch themselves] *but not do it with a man we don't like.*"

Q. Bar girls and masseuses I have spoken to about ACM-ing say that ACMs are disgusting because they play with themselves. One said, 'why would I play with myself when I can have the real thing, have a man play with me?'
Leanne: "*I know, it's our choice. If you want to work in a bar and feel better there, then ok, go there.*"
Cristy: "*But other girls, if they want to work in the bars* [and] *after one night they will have the money, cash, they don't have to wait a week.*" [for their salary].
Leanne: "*Yes, that's why other girls choose to work in bars. Faster money.*"

Q. At what point would you work in a bar or do sex in real? If your PC was broken and your kids were hungry and you could not get a job, would you become a bar girl or street worker?

Leanne: *"Still not. I can work with a boss again, ask them to let me work there until I earn a lot."*

Cristy: "No, *I don't see myself working in a bar, because I know I can do some thing* [else], *other little job....if I don't have a choice, I just chose it...."*

The models were adamant that they would not engage in real sex, even for large amounts of money. Leanne pointed out that a mutual *relationship* was required, involving liking one another and respect:

Leanne: *"Other girls, yes. It's like, if it's someone important* [then] *they think they don't* [have to] *respect us, but if they* [have] *respect for us, as well as for our child and our mum...."*

Q. Some people would think that what your doing, ACM-ing, is prostitution....?

Cristy: *"Yes, yes it is, because it's selling bodies."*

Ken: *"Selling whole body."*

Q. So the only difference is the man cannot touch you?

Leanne: *"We don't have to drink in bars."*

Ken: *"It's safe for AIDS, cancer,...."*

Q. Some people would think there is no difference between what you do and what a bar girl does...?

Leanne: *"I'm a prostitute as well, but I'm the smarter one than the one working in a bar."*

Q. So an ACM *is* a prostitute?

Leanne: *"Yes, but not as worse* [bad] *as working the bars."*

Cristy: *"It's selling* [your] *body in real."*

Ken: "*If you work in a bar many people know you're a prostitute, but if you work on the cam....*"

Cristy: "*...you can hide your self, you're doing cyber inside the house. You can hide it.*"

Ken: "*No one can know....*"

Leanne: "*...you're working as a cam gurl; your neighbour can't know it.*"

Ken: "*But if you're working in a bar...*"

Leanne: "*...your neighbours can see you, wearing makeup, always going at night, they will already think you're working in a bar and that's bad* [immoral] *for them that your working in a bar. But we don't let our neighbours know we are working as a cam gurl, it's really illegal in the Phils.*" [Philippines].

At this point a long open discussion occurred about whether or not they saw themselves, as cam models, as prostitutes. They all reiterated that they were, even though a client cannot touch them, but are different from other prostitutes:

Leanne: "*We do admit we are prostitutes, but not in the worse way.*"

Q. So there are different levels?

Leanne: "*Yea! Yes, you got it! I admit that I am a prostitute. They can call me prostitute because of my job, but I can tell to them that I'm the smart prostitute than the prostitute on the street. I can earn money without anyone touching me.*"

To draw them out further on these issue, I explained to them that masseuses whom I interviewed in Manila, and who provide a special kind of massage "therapy" (*lingham*, in which the male client is masturbated), considered ACMs to be disgusting, that ACMs are prostitutes.

Cristy: "*Actually, we don't do things that they do, we don't fuck in real...*"
Leanne: "*We don't have to fuck a lot of guys...*"
Cristy: "*...to make them satisfied; yes, bar girls they also make them satisfied, it's the same job, but they do it in real, we do it in fantasy, in cyber world.*"
Leanne: "*We don't have to fuck a lot of dicks, in real, we just fuck ourselves, that's the difference. If you have a lot of dicks you can get......*"

Q. So what do think of these massage girls?
Leanne: "*It's the same...*"

Q. But they actually touch the man's penis, then they say they are not prostitutes...
Cristy: "*Still just the same. They are the kind of prostitute that don't admit they are.*"
Leanne: "*They hide it.*"
Cristy: "*They tell themselves it's therapy, but actually... We don't know if we don't come in* [to the parlour—wouldn't the same apply to bars?], *it's undercover.*"

Q. But they have a certificate, saying they are trained, they're professionals...?
Cristy: "*Yes, but underlying* [it] *they are some kind of prostitute.*"

Q. So there are different kinds of prostitution, different levels...?
All: "*Yes.*"

Q. But some people might say that prostitution is prostitution, it doesn't matter what the difference is, as long as you are doing something sexual for money then its prostitution...?
Cristy: "*Yes, but others don't know there are different*

kinds of prostitution."

Q. But I suggest ACM-ing is *not* prostitution because clients can't touch them, the gurl is not real, the "sex" is not real…?
Leanne: *"For you, but not for me."*

I suggested that ACM-ing is not prostitution, for several reasons: the sex is not and cannot be real because it is mediated by technology, that the gurl's image is simply that, an image on a computer screen. Secondly, the participants in this activity are separated by space—they can be on the other side of the world. This of course begs the question of the relevance of space in a sexual relationship, since spatial separation proscribes touching. Similarly, non-synchronous time may also determine if an activity can be construed as sexual, and hence in both cases if it can be construed as prostitution. On the other hand, an ACM is presenting her sexuality by displaying her naked body. However, if this were to be axiomatic, then every *Playboy* centerfold would be a prostitute. My comments not-withstanding, the models continued to assert their views:
Leanne: *"We think it's the same as bar girls, doing the same job like them, but* [we] *do it on the PC, so we think its prostitution."*

Q. But it's "ok" prostitution…?
Leanne: *"It's ok prostitution. It's a better* [kind of] *prostituting."*

Q. So there are different levels or types of prostitution?
Leanne: *"Yeah."*

Q. As I said before, some people would say prostitution is prostitution, it doesn't matter what you do, as you long as you sell sex, it's prostitution…?

Cristy: "*That is why you have to distinguish what is the different kinds of prostitution that would make you.....*"
Leanne: "*Prostitution is selling* [your] *body, is that it? We sell* [our] *body, so we do prostitution.*"

Q. Leanne asked for a brief definition of prostitution, which I gave as "the exchange of one's sexuality for money", and with which they agreed. So if you dance on a table, naked, and get money for it, that's prostitution.
Leanne: "*What if on cam?*"

Q. That's the problem, because it's not real.
Leanne: "*Yes, it's real.*"
Cristy: "*No, it's in cyber.*"
Leanne: "*Ok.*"
Perhaps what Leanne meant by "real" was that for her, on one side of the cam, it was real life, that she was really taking off her clothes and playing with herself, overlooking the fact that for such actions to be prostitution, for argument's sake, requires an equally real Other, real in time *and* space.
Another point Leanne seems to overlook is that she is in fact "confessing" to actually being a prostitute, despite protestations she is not like other prostitutes, but a prostitute nevertheless.

Q. Is a *Playboy* centerfold girl a prostitute?
All: "*No.*"

Q. But she is doing exactly the same as ACMs, showing her naked body, yet many people would not think centerfold girls are prostitutes, so why would they think ACM-ing is prostitution when both are doing the same thing? On the other hand, ACM-ing is a *moving* picture and in real time.

This latter point, that ACMs are moving pictures, and in

real time, caused the models to raise the question of what we would label a girl in a porn movie, arguing that she is a porn star, but not a prostitute.

Leanne: "*Unfair, ha!*"
Cristy: "*They are just a porn star, so we* [ACMs] *are just a porn star...? You could call us porn star? But that girl would not be a prostitute, they're just a porn star. So we're just a porn star, right?*"

While the models make a good point, they overlook that an ACM is an *interactive* "porn star", one that can be commanded to do certain performances at the behest of the audience rather than the Director; the audience becomes, on each occasion, a Director of a "porn star". What also differs is that ACM performances take place in the same virtual space and same time dimensions.

The gurls also overlook the fact that to label themselves as pornographic (stars), then the law could argue they are pornographers and they peddle pornography.

Taking up the legal argument, they realized that if the law was unable to define them as prostitutes, then it was at odds with the definition of prostitution and their own perceptions of their ACM-ing, as Cristy queries:

Cristy: "[So] *we're* not *prostitutes?... yet we are being paid for the exchange of our bodies but we're just a porn star...?*"
Leanne: "*We are a porn star because we are moving, like porn stars on the video.*"

Having become bored or confused—or both—over this issue, the models shifted the conversation to one of politics, legality and fairness:

Leanne: "*Actually, the problem is the government.*"

Q. Perhaps, but the government is pushed by politics, by

feminist views and NGOs...?
Cristy: "*Yes, yes.*"
Leanne: "*But in other countries it's legal.*"
Cristy: "*Even if it's illegal they can't control it.*"

Q. But sometimes the neighbours might not like you, and if they know you're a cam girl they might call the police...?
Leanne: "*That's the problem, our job now is illegal, but if your neighbour will complain about your job they will get the cops.*"

Q. But why will they complain?
Leanne: "*Why? We have to ask* them."
Cristy: "*Some may be jealous because you're earning more money, or some think they* [the ACMs] *are noisy because there are some cam models there, and it's immoral so it's not good for our kids... They say you're a cyber cam, but they don't have evidence that I am. They still have to prove that I am a cyber* [model]."

Q. So, they have to catch you in a private show?
Cristy: "*Yes.*"

Q. But the way Philippine policing works is that they just come in, see the computer, the cam, the room, etc, they take your PC....?
Cristy: "*Yes. They don't need to see you nude, or doing a private or working, they just need to see the toys, the software that you're using... then you're a cyber.*"

Q. And even if they can't prove it they can still take your PC etc, and you have to try to get it back...?
Cristy: "*Yes. But they have to have a search warrant.*"

Q. In the Philippines?

Cristy: "*Yes. If they enter your house without a search warrant then its worth nothing.*"

Q. Have you tested that?
Cristy: "*No, I don't want to.*"
Leanne: "*Why will the government get us in jail, we're helping the Philippines, as well, like OFWs* [overseas workers], *because of the dollars, OFWs bring dollars here, we also bring dollars here to help the Phils, make our peso high. We help the Phils, we go to America* [ie. CAM to/work for Americans]. *It's unfair. The more cyber the more money comes in, and since the cyber has been created the peso has gone high, so you have more work, lower debt.... My point is we help the Phils then the government want us to get in jail because of our job.*"[4]

Q. But a maid in Hong Kong is not selling her body.
Leanne: "*We just have to push them to understand why we're doing this job.*"
Cristy: "*Because they pretend it's immoral, Philippines is very conservative.*"
Leanne: "*That's why they can't accept our job.*"

Q. But you're a mother, as mothers/fathers, you don't seem to have a problem with ACM-ing...?
Cristy: "*Actually, I do have a problem with this, I don't want my daughters growing up knowing this is my job.*"

Q. So you don't mind doing the job, you don't think it's bad...?
Cristy: "*No, of course I think it's bad.*"
Leanne: "*We think it's* panget" [ugly, or repulsive, horrible].
Cristy: "*Actually, our job, but we just don't have a choice, we just want to do our job.*"

Q. But you said you *do* have a choice…?

Leanne: "*So we can save money, have a business, study, that's why we're here still.*"

Cristy: "*Now since we are working, earning money, we can save or continue studying, then we can have higher education, then go to the next job.*"

Leanne: "*Working in cam can help us to start…for a better life, it's ok for the non-educated people to start there.*"

Cristy: "*It's a stepping stone for us.*"

I think understanding these gurls is a stepping stone for *us!* Clearly these gurls had thought about these issues—*we haven't…*

OUR STORIES

I
LEANNE
Performance belies reality.

Over several weeks I would visit Leanne's room to chat, to keep her company for a while if she was not busy and therefore bored, and hopefully to make her laugh. I never took her prvt, and told her I was not interested in that. However, I would be interested in meeting with her as a person, and also to learn more about her life as an ACM. At first she was reluctant to meet with me "in real". But, as our correspondence developed over a few months, she would tell me of her life, family and troubles.

When I suggested we go to Olongapo, a city with beaches and resorts, for a few days on my next visit—a place where in fact she had gone to elementary school, and where, with her help as an assistant, I hoped to contact more ACMs—she agreed. A short time later I witnessed one of her clients suggesting something similar to her, but in a way that made her feel she was a prostitute. Leanne declared that the guy was rude and a jerk, and treated her as an easy "pick-up" gurl, as a "standby", whereas I had developed, so I thought, a relationship of trust and friendship, and our proposed sojourn was one of research and companionship—whatever that may have entailed and however that was interpreted by her.

As the time approached for me to arrive in Manila and meet her, she broke her code of performative conduct and confessed that, while she was happy to meet with me, she was not prepared to have sex with me (in Olongapo, we assume), or, for that matter, with any guy, because her heart had been broken too many times, and she simply didn't believe what guys told or promised her. Later she was also to inform me that she self-identified as a lesbian. She told me that her agreement to go with me to Olongapo was all performance: *"I'm an ACM, you know it's all about performing."* **[5]**

I responded that I understood her role, but she also needed to understand and accept me and that she be truthful, as friends should be, if we were to remain friends. The end result was that she apologized profusely, and we *did* meet in person. **[6]**

The real result is this book, that tells the *real* lives of ACMs as both virtual models and as *real* people.

Leanne turned 23, in early 2014. She has two children, aged 4 and 2, both girls. The children are frequently sick, usually the flu or stomach upset. Leanne does not and never did breastfeed her babies, so they like, and still depend a lot on, powdered milk, especially at night. *"If they don't have their milk at night they get makulit* (annoying), *and restless"*, she explained.

Leanne and her children live alone, in a rented house, having moved from her mother's house so she could have her "own life". Her mother lives nearby and sells vegetables in the local market, and she has a brother who is in 2nd year college. She lives quite close to several other ACMs, in a relocation settlement. It is an area that has few employment opportunities, few amenities apart from basic services, with small lots and houses that residents can buy from the government via an installment plan after meeting certain residency requirements.

Leanne became pregnant to her de facto partner (boyfriend), Atok, about 5 years previously, when he was 25 years old and she was 18. A short time after the birth of their first child he left her and lived with another girl; then he returned to Leanne. She accepted his return because he was, after all, the father of her first child, and she wanted to "protect" the child's name, she wanted a *whole* family, not a broken one. However, Atok was often unemployed, drank heavily, and was "always looking at other girls" (*chic-boy*).

After a short time he got her pregnant with a second child, then he left again, to take up residency with a new girlfriend/partner in the same neighbourhood, living in his parents' house. For Leanne this was the final break, she would not entertain taking him back again. During this second pregnancy Leanne was financially supported by a male foreigner, who was a frequent virtual visitor to her ACM studio.

By working as an ACM for the last 4 years, Leanne has managed to finish high school and commence College to become a teacher. She expects to graduate in about 4 years, at age 27. On the one hand she sees ACM-ing as a "stepping-stone", and a College degree as "*an escape from ACM-ing*"; on the other hand, when her boss and friend asked her to be an ACM, she felt it was OK to do so, and that taking off her clothes on cam was "*no problem, I'm open minded. I'm not a virgin, so it was ok for me.*" She went on to explain that "*I don't have to deal with men directly, to touch them, it's like having cyber sex without the sex. It's only on-line, not real. I don't do sex in real, even for money.*"

But her years of work and life have never been smooth. She first started working for a boss, Cristy, who also was—and remains—her good friend. More recently she left that employment to start her own ACM business; but Cristy asked Leanne to return to work for her in order to pay a debt. Leanne had no option but to comply because she may have need to borrow again from her former boss. She also had no option but to borrow, and borrow from Cristy: in the relocation settlement in which she lives and works she could not borrow from others because there almost everyone is poor. Other than some ACM bosses, very few people have any substantive money; it's a place where 100 pesos ($2) makes you a king or queen.

But having made the break, she already had an old computer and became her own boss, which would double her income. However, her immediate problem was setting up a room in her house that assured her of privacy in her work. Her goal was to buy some wood to partition a room in her house into a work studio; but unable to get the money she settled for makeshift curtains.

Henceforth a litany of further problems ensued. First, the PC she used was not very fast, and constantly breaking down. On one occasion she got a power-surge, which almost destroyed the PC. She managed to get it repaired, to some extent, but it was haphazard in its operation.

In the meantime, Leanne was constantly short of money for food, and especially for milk for her children; this was especially so if she had not achieved her quota each period (the 15th and 30th of each month). It was not uncommon for her to contact me via YM to ask for money for one reason or another: to repair her PC, for food, milk, rent, the electric bill, etc. She had already pawned her widescreen TV, her *sala* (lounge), and eventually her cell phone. In her own words:

> "I have pawn it [the cell phone] in a small pawnshop here coz my friends had no money too lend me but it has interest. they price it at 400 peso but had interest of 80 peso. I have no choice.

> Bought small milk already 250 pesos, dinner 50, got 100 peso left until tomorrow. I will get my phone back maybe next cut off na lng i will use the money what ur going to lend me for food again."

To add to her woes, she also became sick with what appears to be vertigo, and which prevented her from working as much as she needed. Again she requested that I help her with the costs of her medical tests and medication. She clearly needed a rest. When I suggested that the father of her children look after them for a while, so she could have a break, she indicated yet another problem.

A few years previously her de facto's father had sexually assaulted Leanne, and hence her reluctance to leave her children in Atok's household in which his father lived. Hence, with Leanne's mother working, she had no one with whom she could leave her children and therefore could not get even a short break from child minding and household chores.

To add to this, gossip (*tsimis*) was rife that Leanne was both an ACM and—therefore—a slut or prostitute (*puta*). In fact, it was her former de facto's father who accused Leanne of being an ACM and therefore not a good mother to her children. What followed was a convoluted kinship dispute about her "father-in-law's" sexual assault upon her a few years previously. The incident arose because the current de facto partner of Atok approached Leanne with the story that the father-in-law had also sexually assaulted *her*. It was at that time that Leanne decided to bring into the open the story of her own sexual assault. However, the opposing family, including Atok, stood united against her, and the girl who initiated the complaint with Leanne reneged on her story. Thus Leanne's attempt to expose her former father-in-law's alleged licentiousness and protect the current partner of Atok resulted in Leanne being ostracized and criticized. Not surprisingly, then, having been hurt several times by different males, she didn't trust men and did not want to be emotionally or sexually involved with men in the foreseeable future.

There was however an ironic—one might say, poetic—twist to these chain of events: Having been accused by Atok's father of being an ACM and a "loose" woman, that father's niece soon after became an ACM herself. Indeed, he accused Leanne of being an ACM because she wanted "easy money". Clearly he had no idea of what being an ACM entailed. ACM-ing is hardly "easy money", as we have seen. It involves long hours, often of boredom, with no guarantee of any income, and requires a lot of skill in terms of deploying technology, performance and choreography, and responding to a myriad of men's flirtations and questions, and all in a foreign language, as well as the possibility of being cheated by bosses and clients, raided by the police, not being able to work during menstruation, having to work when sick, in addition to social stigma. Easy money? Pure humbug!

In short, if ACM-ing was such easy money, then why was Leanne not only poor and struggling to support two children without any help from their father, but was now also publicly ostracized? Such stress only added to her pre-existing medical condition, which also affected her ability to work. Indeed, her vertigo posed dangers of her fainting and falling down steps, which did occur on one occasion.

Leanne existed on a day-to-day basis of borrowing money, repaying others with borrowed money, so as to enable her to borrow again at a later time. She had borrowed 3,000 pesos from me to treat her medical condition, even sending me a picture of the hospital to prove she was genuine.

Following that, she told me of her next pending commitments: that she needed food for her children, diapers, the rent was due soon, as were the electricity and internet bills, she needed to pay for one daughter's schooling needs and repay some other debts, pay for her end-of-year exams, and could not afford to buy medicine, which would enable her to work. In addition, her grandmother (*lola*) had just been taken to hospital in a coma; no doubt Leanne would need to contribute to medical expenses and, at worst, funeral expenses. (Her *lola* was in fact discharged from the hospital because her family could no longer pay for medical treatment; she lay at home in a semi-coma, with only slim hope that she would reach her 87th birthday, just one month hence. She died shortly after.)

In telling me this saga of events and needs Leanne frequently referred to suicide.[7] She was sick, tired, stressed, unable to work as much as she needed, in debt, and her youngest daughter was again sick. She encapsulated her life situation by saying: "*I hate being like this, always debts and problems.*"

But, having improved in her own health in the following few weeks, and passing her exams and now eligible to enroll in College, she again contacted me and, in a very performative way (*sip-sip*) asked if she could borrow 6,000 pesos to enable her to enroll in College the next day. What she offered in return, apart from promises of repaying the debt to me, which now amounted to almost 10,000 pesos, was a free prvt show of her and a female friend engaged in sexual activity.

I pointed out that, apart from my disinterest in watching such a show or even seeing her naked, my seeing her engage in sexual activities or even naked could alter our relationship of friendship; she replied that it was sex with another girl vis-à-vis a male, and it was all performance, just a show.

Ironically, it was in fact through such a performance that I came to know Leanne as a person, as the opening to this portfolio reveals.

Even more ironic, perhaps, indeed poetic, was that Leanne was, in 2014, voted in as class captain in her College class! Rather than make assertions, let us explore this—but not to imply that I question Leanne. Here is an impover-ished, rather (formally) uneducated gurl who, by her own admission is a prostitute, a lesbian, working as an ACM, with 2 children born out of wedlock..... Personally I have no qualms with this. Do *you*?

Irony aside, Leanne's dramas continued to unfold. Having started out at College at the beginning of June, she found in a few weeks that, in reality, College left little time for her to be an ACM. Even if she did manage to meet her quota, she might have to wait a month before getting paid, a fortnight at best. Thus by late June she again contacted me, hoping I could lend her some money for the "extras" that her Course demanded. She agreed with me that education was expensive; it was not just the semester fees for enrollment or the uniforms she may have to purchase, but costs associated with extra "curricular" activities—excursions, travel, exam fees, etc. It struck me that education in the Philippines had changed very little in the last 25 years by continually placing additional demands on students such that only those who could afford these "extras" could get an education; and, of course, it is only those who are already reasonably well-off, with parents who themselves are probably educated, who will be educated, thus perpetuating socio-economic in-equality. Students like Leanne, and like Jonaz (see below), would never be able to afford to elevate themselves from poverty without outside help.

About 8 weeks into the first semester the difficulties and stress for Leanne continued to mount. At the end of August 2014 she contacted me again via YM. She had already told me in a previous conversation that she was now working with her mother in the market and had little or no time for being an ACM; besides, she had not been able to pay her internet connection fee, and was thus using her mother's PC and connection. But, I wondered, if she lived with her mother and was using her internet access, then why could she not use that for ACM work...?

Nevertheless, in her late August conversation via YM she reveals a number of issues and further requests. She begins by saying she had discovered a means of earning an income by becoming self-employed through selling coffee and vitamins (as far as I could gather the gist of what she was saying), and had attended the company's seminars and had heard unfaltering testimonials from others. All she wanted was some capital to start up her business and suggested that even I could be directly involved. I looked up the website/company she referred to and it was immediately apparent that the scheme was a pyramid scheme, technically illegal in the Philippines (among many other countries). More importantly, it clearly appealed to poor people, like Leanne, and their desperation to earn money if not totally escape poverty, and to their business naivety, and thus took advantage of their vulnerability. My explanation of all this to her was not well received.

Leanne then jumped about in the conversation, raising a few more issues, one of which, sadly, was that, in her attempt to be educated she encountered the situation of not being able to tell people her job (as an ACM) and thus where she got money from. Classmates, too, she said, were becoming suspicious of her, and she was greatly concerned about what would happen if the school found out that she is, or had been, an ACM.

Following, therefore, is an abbreviated transcript of our YM conversation, to not only allow Leanne to speak for herself, but also because it brings to the fore several issues that I briefly comment on.

Leanne: hi paul
Me: WB. what u been doing ?
Leanne: im ok paul also in school, u?...and Jonaz...hru both?
Me: ok....dalawa [both of us]...Jonaz is flooded again
Leanne: i feel sirry for Jonaz shes in a bad place

Me: yup

Leanne: the typhoon will keep coming in here in phils...untill november maybe

Me: yikes

Leanne: thats phils....rainy from june....maybe untill october only lol...i will pray hehe

Me: Well, no rain, no rice

Leanne: paul i found a nice business to do....but its capital is kinda big

Me: oh yea...

Leanne: u can research and look for it as well and maybe Jonaz can as well....its like marketting....actualy it is....like buy and sell

Me: buy/sell what...where ? online ?

Leanne: not online...yeah u can see it online...its the royale company

Me: chocolate ?

Leanne: were they sell glutationes and vitamines coffes and etc....u wanna take a look?

Me: sure

Leanne: u can search for royale product paul...ive been attending their seminars

Me: ic

Leanne: royale is now international...and i thought they are all fake that they are just saying that they are earning

5000 to hundred thousands weekly

Me: yeah sure...if that was true everyone would do it dba [wouldn't they?]

Leanne: but i saw those proof of people from just being a janitor....now a multi millionaire...and many of them na

Me: U gotta be level headed in all this

Leanne: i didnt believe online before soo i try to go their and sees many people now are trying the business buying their product then sell...my mom and dad raised me from business....i know how it works na

Me: I will look at Royale

Leanne: 

Me: and my education and experience tell me to be careful

Leanne: ok paul

Me: I will look ok...that's all I will do for the moment

Leanne: 

Leanne: the best testimonies are u can see on you tube or in at facebook

Me: L... I have seen a million testimonies about these get rich quick schemes...slow down

Leanne: yeah 

Leanne: i have met some of them in person na

Me: its never as simple as they say...and it is a risk

Leanne: ofc if ur negative....u cant reach the goal

Me: no, I am not negative, I am careful and practical

Leanne: u can do the business there as well....i did loading small store sell vegies on the market by my own but still poor...coz small income....soo i tried the cyber world

Me: and you STILL poor

Leanne: hahaha

Me: u gotta have capital, hard work, long hrs, and good promo

Leanne: u said its not the end...yeah... can i borrow haha

Me: slow down...I will look in 5 mins

Leanne: i did research almost 1week haha....and sell my cousin as a product too...its effective...i dont believe on what i dont see in real...thats y i get inspired...after i meet...the peoples in royale company

Me: yes yes that's good, yr inspired and positive...but u also have to be practical and careful naman

Leanne: excited as well actually....heheh...i did cyber

Me: okoko...can i look at it first na

Leanne: already u think I'm not practical paul?...is Jonaz a business minded girl too?

Me: mmmmm. dunno. I think so

Leanne: i just think i can do the job even at school...sell on students and prof's

Me: sounds like pyramid selling...i will look in a minute

Leanne: i can tell to u na how its going except from selling and earning on your own product u can earn on those people who have joined in ur group—its a group business too not just individual there are weekly cut offs the group gets points on the items sold or even individual get points on the items sold the company is giving a check converting that points to cash giving it weekly and also they give incentives and bonuses

Me: yup...its pyramid selling

Leanne: for example i have two person got inspired on me and then join me to sell the products i will earn on them forever hehe...as long as they are buying and selling the products...bigger group i made bigger money

Me: yes Leanne...it is pyramid selling...Amway, cleaning products, was very big in the Phils and USA...its illegal in Aust

Leanne: i see 😦 ... but y?

Me: bc its exploitation and fraud [I tried to explain, in simple terms].

Leanne: fraud??????

Me: yup

Leanne: how come?

Me: the company is legal...but the method is fraudulent

Leanne: i dont think there's fraud ?...only if a people trusted to send u money and u promised to send the product to them and do not...that will be fraud ? kinda?

Me: yes, but there's other kinds

Leanne: royale business club Philippines

Me: Which means it is "Multi Level Marketing" which is always a scheme to part you & your money. The only ones to make money is the company itself. My advice is to stay away from it. If it is so great then why are they trying to get you to invest your time & money instead of selling their products themselves?

Leanne: the people are earnings u can see...they are also trying to teach people how to do business...just be open minded...ofc the company want to earn too and also the people who believed on them...thought u see the people who earn already!

Leanne: ?

Me: Multi Level Marketing = pyramid selling

Leanne: its legal here ryt

Me: no. It's illegal in many many countries, including the Phils...Sorry L, but everything u have said, says Pyramid...Sorry L,

Leanne: ill stay poor nalang...im just looking for answer

Me: I know u wanna be ok for money, but afraid life aint like that for us millions of ppl

Leanne: how can i stay on collage...i cannot continue na to the next semester

Me: yes I know. But think this way, if I didn't tell u the truth---and I AM yr friend dba---you would end up even more poor

Leanne: the cyber sex is more illegal here in Phils paul...which one is best do u think?

Me: yes, hun, probably bc the ppl at the top of the pyramid are wealthy ppl who make money from poor ppl joining the scheme [ie. it is because wealthy people control the pyramid selling that it is not adequately policed, whereas ACM is very much a grassroots phenomenon from which wealthy people in the Philippines can not make a profit].

Me: the best, cyber sex na...bc at least a gurl can get 25%, or have own PC and get 50%...but its still a piece-rates system in principle

Leanne: yah the one that they called prostis here and want to sent in jail

Leanne: i cant even imagine my girls can see me naked on the room and asking me wat im doing

Me: but what if yr mom saw u naked and doing cyber ?

Leanne: u forget paul, wat we told u before, were just doing cyber not just to be in bars and also a stepping stone to get out of that job

Me: yes i know hun, I didn't forget

Leanne: we dint like it really...they are illegal...their company as u said...cyber is not...were am i safe?

Leanne: i cant even tell to people wat is my job...where i get money...i had many classmates now and their suspecting me...if the school know im a cyber girl...what will happen to me?...and first the job is hard to do na...with my schedule...

that y im looking for other things to do 

Me: I know Leanne

Leanne: to survive

Me: And I am on yr side, remember

Leanne: I like to try the business, paul  than cyber

Me: Leanne, its a dream

Leanne: everyone had

Me: They target ppl like u who want to be rich

Leanne: I had kids and rent to pay and school

Me: I know I know

Leanne: I cant stay on 300 [pesos] earning a day

Me: But this scheme will not make you rich hun, sorry

Leanne: I dont mean to be rich, i dont want to be rich, i just want to give my kids need...

Me: I know L

Leanne: ...and school needs

Me: And yr doing the right thing by getting an education

Leanne: i told u bfore I don't want to be rich...thats y im not even trying spend money on the lotto...ofc i had a dream too...and my goal is not to become a poor

Me: I fully understand

Leanne: paul will u help me have the business?...or try

Me: not a pyramid business hun...no way, sorry

Leanne: i have no one to ask nmn...u know...give me a chance nmn or else i really need to stop collage na....

pyramiding is better than crab mentality...give me a chance nmn or else i really need to stop collage na...i had many utang na except on u...what i do????

Me: just try to get a little bit of work when u can...and do the best u can

Leanne: i see...u want me to stay in cyber...which is illegal here

Me: if u have to, until u graduate...or I win lotto

Leanne: i dont want to go back there...its making me a bad person...telling a lie...to lots of people...showing my body

Me: but u said its only performance dba

Leanne: yeah...but the performance....people here...

Me: u didn't seem to have a problem when we talked in March naman

Leanne: dont understand

Me: just tell them you work with yr mum, and yr ex-bf helps with the kids...and I pay u to do some editing work naman...that will make them happy

Leanne: a lie again

Me: yup...but only until u graduate...and a lie for a good reason

Leanne: what now u will help me get my connection back?

Me: *ano*? [What !?]

Leanne: u just said anything not just with that pyramiding...and better want me to do cyber how can i do cyber had capital...too...connection ofc...i had pc nmn na

Me: Can I tell u something hun, I really don't have any money.

Leanne: the nerve of me, ryt... im stuck in a crazy mind na

Me: i know u r Leanne, and I really wish I could help...so yr not the only 1 with utang [debt]

Leanne: if i let u fuck me at olongapo maybe im not like this now

Me: but u said u would not fuck for money

Leanne: im just stating the fact

Me: I dont know [if we *would* have sex and if that would lead me to supporting her]. **[8]**

Leanne: thats life...sorry to disturb u paul

Me: Leanne, yr a nice girl, and I like you, but really, I have money problems too...honest, if I was rich or win lotto, I would help you...if there was a way to help u have yr own business, REAL one, then I would help if I could...if u wanted to start a *sari* [small grocery store] then MAYBE...

Leanne: i dont have capital for any business...ryt now

Me: I know, but if my situation changes, and u had an idea for a real business....

Leanne: impossible for me...end of the world

Me: its not the end, you made it this far, you've done all the right things, just keep pushing....

By this point Leanne was not responding for any number of reasons, such as having fallen asleep, become depressed, other things she had to do, or had forgotten to log off...

She had put me in a difficult position: by not financially supporting her hair-brain pyramid business scheme, she takes a moral stance contrary to what she had previously enunciated many times about it all being performance, suggesting now that *I* condone ACM-ing which *she* has moralized.

But the really sad thing about this conversation—apart from Leanne appearing to give up, to give up hope, her despair, her perpetual entrapment of poverty, her vain attempts to take control of her life and not understated she needs to reconcile her desires with her means, etc—is that, for every Leanne, there are 10,000+ other Leannes.

But this conversation did not end here, for the next evening she again came onto YM, taking a more negative stance, and even hinting, again, of her own death. As the conversation quickly developed, and her despair became readily apparent, I tried to distract her a little, trying to make her smile perhaps, and move slowly to finding out what had happened in the last 24 hours, in order to give her some support, as much as I could on-line:

Me: hru
Leanne: dont ask that question anymore pls...i hate the word hru
Me: ok...How was yr day ?
Leanne: next question

Me: ok, so how do i ask, "Did u have a good day?"
Leanne: [dead].
Me: Oh i see. so u YM from heaven now na
Leanne: no...im using wifi from hell

Me: omg I charge extra for wifi from hell

Leanne:
Me: lol. what's up L ?
Leanne: give me sum drink like gin...thats wat i need
Me: ok, I send now by FEDEX
Leanne: add some hurry
Me: I can email it to u, as a jpeg

Leanne: what?? i drink it from PC?????
Me: okok...sorry

Leanne:
Me: what's up Leanne

Leanne:
Me: what's happened hun

Leanne: none   [nothing].
Me: hihihi i like that one

Leanne: i luv this one
Me: i mean its cute

Leanne:

Me: howz the kids

Leanne: i will put them on the trashcan...never mind...sorry...i dont understand...

Me: ok so what's happened today L...they makulit ba [annoying/misbehaving?]

Leanne: ......

Me: Leanne...u wanna tell me...

Leanne: tired of telling

Me: Leanne...u said the other day, if yr negative you cant reach yr goal...u have survived and come a long way...raised 2 kids, finish high school, started in college...just take one day at a time, things will change...

Again, by this point, Leanne had dropped out of the conversation, which showed her continuing despair, apparently not helped by her two kids being *makulit*. Her brief comments or responses, including her desire to have some gin, and her emoticons, all suggest perhaps a consistent depressed state. Her reference to being "dead"—and not for the first time—and YM-ing from Hell vis-à-vis Heaven perhaps suggests that she feels like dying, and that she is a bad person and hence deserving of Hell.

As I continued to write this book throughout August 2014 Leanne was in frequent YM contact. By August 3 she informed me that she had not been to college for the past week, and was not expecting to go in the following week, saying that 300 pesos income a day was not enough (the minimum wage income per day being 460 pesos), and that the money spent on travel to and from college would be better spent on her kids' needs, such as food (150 pesos a day), diapers, milk, etc. I asked if her mother or ex-partner (the father of her two children) could help, but she simply replied. "*We are all the same, poor.*" She had given up— given up on going to college, almost on life.

And yet these fucking insulated pedestal-prone middle

class moralists and feminists, the Catholic church that expounds the giving of alms, the white and Filipino, make all kinds of gestures of moral despair and condemnations of ACMs and other sex workers, when in fact the despair is with the likes of Leanne and the condemnation should be *of* the State and the Church, and civic society.

Certainly it is easy for me to criticize such moralistic critics, without offering a solution, but in so doing I could fall into the very same apathy of hand-wringing. But in fact I do offer a solution—or rather, Leanne and Jonaz do. If each of these moralizers were *really* genuine (*talaga*) in actually *doing* something, they would create a Foundation for the advancement of such gurls, just as Jeff has done in giving Jonaz an opportunity for education. These gurls *have* taken the initiative, with my help, by forming *The Foundation for Single Pinay Moms in College* (formerly on-line); where is the *real* support from *other* women and *others* whose moralizing energy would be better spent with practical support!?

And simply, and I mean simply, without all the moralizing gook, with the practicalities of life in the slums, what has the fucking catholic church done, is doing? Because Filipinas can't get divorced, they live in "sin", which men (and women) see as an opportunity to live in and with "sin", of not marrying, of evading responsibilities to each other and their joint children.[9] Are we to blame and moralize about these women, when in fact it is the fucking pedophilic church and corrupt government, among others, to blame?!!!!

She who casts the first stone......

The saga continued...

I had not heard from Leanne for a few weeks. Almost at the end of August she contacted me, saying she had been evicted from her house because she was unable to pay the rent, and, could not pay two water bills, about which the owner was insisting she front a barangay council to settle the matter. She didn't ask for money that day, and I told her to go to the meeting and negotiate, to "perform", as I knew well she could—throw herself on the mercy of their emotions by outlining she is a single mother, with a *chicboy* partner who left her and doesn't help support his kids, that she's gong to college to improve her self, etc.

Two days later she again came onto YM, and again didn't ask directly for money, but sent me pictures of two water bills, due that day! The total was about 1,200 pesos (less than $50). Her landlady was not concerned about the rent due to her, but about Leanne paying the water bills to ensure the water was not cut off; and she kept some of Leanne's property, including her PC, as assurance. Thus Leanne had moved back to her mother's house, but was unable to work as an ACM because she could not get her PC until she paid for the water. She also hinted that she was again having trouble with the operation of her PC, that it could need fixing, again.

Needless to say that I "lent" her the $50. In the meantime, Leanne had skipped another week of college, but was determined to go—indeed, had to go—the following week because it was the mid-term exams.

By this stage I had decided enough was enough. There was no way I could substantiate her claims and situation, and perhaps the best way to deal with this cycle of debt and poverty—assuming it was true—would be to remove her partial dependency on me, but also thinking she would find another person from whom she could extract some help. But having seen at first-hand homeless women with children on the street, that spectre of Leanne and her kids also haunted me. I told her, and vowed, I would never send her any more money.

The next day she told me she had recovered her possessions—including her PC—from her former landlady, and would start working as an ACM again....

Needless to say the litany of events—or rather, disasters—continued. As time wore on, her PC could barely cope with Leanne's demands on it, and she could not cope with the financial demands of college. By mid second-semester she had suspended her studies, but remained hopeful she might be able to catch up with a summer Course. Meantime, a single, male cousin had fallen gravely ill (with what appeared to be renal failure), and Leanne took it upon herself to try to help him, as well as be concerned for his young son should the cousin (likely) die....

Nevertheless, the litany of events still continued—too many to recite here. Suffice to say that by February 2015 Leanne had dropped out of college, and her PC was dead, completely. She was cagey about how she was supporting herself and what she intended to do, merely noting the she was helping her mother sell vegetables in the market.

Several months later Leanne sent me an automated request to add her to my Linkedin account; her profile there showed she had taken up the Royale pyramid selling plan. A few months further on we had a brief YM conversation, in which she said she had quit that work, because her two underling workers were not selling anything, and so Leanne was not making any money.

In September 2015 she unexpectedly YM'd me, at first quite conversant about general things, and saying she was only working with her mother selling vegetables. She also said she had to give one of her kids to the child's father, as Leanne couldn't afford to pay the expenses of two children. Apart from my being sad that she had done so, and seemed to have had to, I was acutely concerned that the child's grandfather, who had attempted to sexually assault Leanne, might also attempt some similar action against Leanne's daughter.

She went on to say that she felt unwell, that mostly her neck, shoulders and back ached, that she was highly stressed—as she commonly was. While had sympathy for her plight, there was little I could other than try to console and advise her.

Leanne's contact with me went on for another 2-3 days, at the end of which she asked me to "lend" her 1,500 pesos for the electricity bill. Despite her earnest pleadings, I refused. It came about that, although Leanne's mother had had the money, she was pressed to pay Leanne's brother's College tuition fees—what choices people have to make. She also said that she did not want to go back to being an ACM because, as she had indicated earlier, it was living a lie, it was a performance.

The next day she told me the electricity had been cut, but I could still lend her even just 1,200 pesos, to restore the service. I refused.

II
CRISTY

Cristy is 23 years old, a high school graduate, and lives near Leanne. She has 2 daughters and a current boyfriend—who is not the father of her children—with whom she lives in a rented house. She pays all the bills and supports her children without any help; her boyfriend does not help with these, but does domestic chores. She's comfortable with this because she loves and wants her boyfriend, who knows she is an ACM.

Cristy started 6 years previously, at age 17. She used her cousin's ID, who was her boss, until she turned 18 years of age. Prior to being an ACM she worked in a canteen, but was dismissed because she was breastfeeding her daughter. The employer's view was not ostensibly a moral one of her exposing her breasts to feed her daughter, but, as Cristy explained, "they said its not good for her daughter". There are two aspects to this, the first being that breastfeeding *ipso facto* was not good for children. The second aspect was that breastfeeding would tire Cristy and therefore she would not be able to cope with having the child. Cristy exclaimed,

"*They are crazy!*" and noted something that the employers overlooked: "*How can I support my kids if I get fired...?*"

Having become an ACM, she saved her money and invested in buying her own PC and becoming her own boss. "*When I was pregnant with my second kid, I had to live and work on my own so I had to save and invest to have my own salary and cut out the boss.*" As she got larger with her pregnancy she stopped being an ACM herself and got other gurls to work for her. Her first model was Leanne.

As we saw, Leanne left Cristy to become her own boss after two years. Although this came as a surprise to Cristy, she understood Leanne's need to earn more money, and was willing to help her, especially since they had been friends for almost 10 years. She understood that Leanne was only doing what Cristy herself had done in becoming her own boss, and the problems Leanne faced in finding work and raising two children.

She wasn't sure that she had been a good boss, although she and Leanne concurred that Cristy, although strict, had a good relationship with her models. While she took 30% of the net income (ie. after the Company had taken its 50% share), she also paid for the electricity and internet, effectively therefore netting 25%

While she currently works as an ACM from time to time, she also does other things. She doesn't plan to get more models to work for her in the immediate future. Her longer term plan is to quit the job as soon as her children grow up; but in the meantime she needs money, particularly for her to go to college, after which she will quit. Essentially, then, ACM-ing is purely for the money, a means to an end. But as she had said previously, it's not always easy money, but convenient work.

It certainly is not always easy money, for Cristy, like the other ACMs, often encounters strange customers. But she was quick to point out that she didn't care what the customers wanted, "*You just act, perform, like an actress, even if you don't like doing it, you have to smile and act to convince him you like it.*" She agreed with my summation that customers think that, because the ACM is a woman, a Filipina, the customers are in control, but all the time the ACM is in control. Cristy giggled and repeated, with a wink, "*They have little dirty secrets, under the table....*" She continued to emphasize that the "*men are getting cheated.*" She agreed that many Western men think Filipinos are stupid, etc, but what the ACM is doing is *acting* like a stupid "*Filo fucking machine, but it's really the Americans who are stupid. The American people would believe us* [the ACMs' performances] *but actually we're just acting. So who's stupid?*"

In the end, the ACMs walk away with the money, and the customers are fooled.

But what is fake?—they still show their bodies. Certainly the performance, the acting of being pleasured through a performative sexual act, albeit virtual, is fake, as are the many ruses they employ to pander to the various fetishes customers may hold. But what is not and cannot be fake is the raw exposure of her naked body to a stranger.

<h3 style="text-align:center">III</h3>

<h3 style="text-align:center">KATE & KEN</h3>

Kate and Ken are married, and live near Leanne. They have one young daughter. Kate is 20 years old and Ken is 22. Both have only a high school education. They each used to work for a boss, but saved money and bought their own PCs.

While each has his/her own screen name and perform individual prvt shows, they also work together, as a "couple" and have a combined screen name depicting that. Their studios are adjacent to one another, so when a customer wants a couple they simply move across into one studio.

I interviewed them together, as they requested.

Born in Manila, Ken's mother died when he was 15

years old; he was "mad at himself" and so turned to drugs, but changed himself, seeking work anywhere. He became a tourist guide in an exclusive resort in Bikol and then a salesman in Bulacan. When that contract finished he took up ACM-ing, as there was no other work. He has been an ACM for 2.5 years, having had his own ACM show as a single male for 1.5 years before teaming up with Kate.

His aim is to help his brothers and father, as well as his wife and daughter. If he were lucky enough to get a big salary or if someone would support him he would like to get *legal* work. He believes in himself, having a standard to prove himself as a capable man to others. But at the moment he has no money and thus can't say when he might stop being an ACM. Money is the reason he does this work. No one can ever tell him that because he's a man he has to work, because he's willing to do any work, even if it's illegal. He works not for other people but to support his family.

"They say to me to grow up, you're not a kid, just work... We don't want to depend on them, we have a daughter, a family..."

Both Ken's and Kate's families know they work as ACMs, "*but they* [are] *quiet, they understand, because we want to go our own ways to have a family.*"

Kate is from a distant province. She is one of 6 children; her father died when she was young. She always wanted to be a nurse, but had no money for college.

She was 16 years old when her female friend asked her if she wanted to work as an ACM. Her friend provided her with fake ID. She knew she had to take her clothes off and touch herself, but at first she was shy, because she didn't like her boss to see her, to show her bra, and there were so many "beggars" looking at her. But that was a long time ago, and it's now ok for her to show herself naked. She also gave some free shows when she first started, because she didn't know how to deal with the situation. Some guests would ask her to show her nipples and she would, because they said they would take her prvt if she did; so she would show her breasts, but after that the customers would leave without taking her prvt.

It seems the issue here is that customers want to get "sex" for nothing, perhaps in the belief that they shouldn't have to pay for sex, or that paying for sex makes them feel like they have gone to a prostitute,[10] or that if they can get free sex their sense of masculinity and sexual prowess is reinforced, or simply they are "smart" enough to con a woman, a Filipina, a "dumb-ass bitch."

Commenting on the customers and what they do in prvt shows, Ken and Kate said customers like to watch them fuck, or for Kate to suck Ken's penis and for him to cum inside her mouth, or watch him masturbate or for Kate to masturbate him, that they want to see him cum. When Kate does her single show they want to see her pussy and also watch her cum. As Ken said, "*It's easy to get prvts because customers are attracted to couples who can fuck, suck and do fetishes.*" Kate also does fetishes in her single show.

Given that they are married such sexual activities with each other are not a problem for them, and therefore not "fake"; it's really about making money and performing by doing what they might do anyway. But sometimes they do fake a performance, such as when a customer wants to watch them fuck for only a short time, but Kate and Ken need a long time to get a big salary, so they want a slow show. What they mean in this case by "fake" is they deliberately take their time to reach climax, thus engaging the customer as long as possible.

Many customers ask to watch anal sex, but again they fake it, because they don't want to hurt themselves. Some guests believe it, others claim it to be fake and drop out of the prvt show. Faking anal sex is by means of deploying the camera in such a way as to make the image obscure and/or inserting Ken's penis into Kate's vagina instead of her anus. As Kate said, "*It looks real on cam.*"

At times customers can be rude and denigrating, although Kate and Ken said they do not experience racial slurs. Rather, comments are more directed at Kate, as a female, suggesting in a derogatory way that she's a bar girl, a prostitute, that they want to meet and fuck her, that she is their slave. The couple don't care about these slurs because their focus is very much on making money, so they ignore comments, even though they think some customers are *"crazy, bad, liars, beggars and cheaters."*

For example, Ken once had a 16 year old female student in the USA take him prvt; her desire was to watch Ken masturbate while she talked "dirty". She then asked if she could meet Ken and fuck him, and she wanted him to arrange for him to get 16 of his male friends to have group sex with her in real. Of course he didn't believe her, as she was like many who simply *say* they will come to the Philippines. Ken said that he didn't care that she did not come, that he just wanted her money in prvt shows.

They think customers cheat other Filipina ACMs, but Kate and Ken have learnt to know the cheaters so they don't get cheated any more. They are focused on getting private shows, so they tell customers that if they will not take them prvt then *"they should get out of our room."*

Notable here is that Ken and Kate, amongst many other ACMs with whom I have chatted, view their room/studio as a personal, private space, even though it is open to the entire world, but over which they have control as to who they will allow in.

They both think many customers are stupid, but they don't care. If customers say Ken or Kate are handsome, cute or whatever, it's ok for them; they are focused on getting the prvt show and hence the money. It's all acting, simply because they want and need the money. *"If the customers believe it, then we have good acting, a nice performance; if they don't see a fake show then we feel it's a good job done."*

Finally, Ken and Kate asked that I not make any

judgement against them for their work, because they do it for the money, and asked what I would say to myself if I had no work and had to work as an ACM ?

Kate also commented that other people make judgements about them and their work, yet there are many girlie bars in the Philippines, so why don't the police raid them?

IV
MELINDA

If your family does not have a sex worker or OCW, then you don't eat 3 meals a day.

Melinda is in a similar situation to Leanne, perhaps not surprising given that she lives not far from her in the same relocation settlement, deficient in amenities and employment opportunities.

Melinda is barely 24, and has one daughter, aged 5. They live with Melinda's parents and 4 siblings; a sixth sibling, an older brother, lives nearby with his own family; an older sister similarly lives nearby with her own family. Her father raises up to 18 pigs in a rather makeshift piggery at the back of their small, 46 square metre, house, tucked away among similar wall-to-wall houses in a laneway barely wide enough for two people to pass. Melinda emphasized that the breeding of pigs was for the main purpose of providing for her brothers' education, and indeed a substantial sum from the sale of the pigs was ear-marked for one son's graduation later that year. No mention was made of sharing the income with Melinda, who, despite her frail frame and health condition, provided a lot of manual work in caring for the pigs and doing other household chores, as well as working late at night as an ACM, the money from which she almost wholly contributed to the household.

Despite their poverty and crammed living conditions, Melinda's family and the community around them seemed happy. Indeed, Melinda's friend, Angela, said as much: she likes to visit Melinda's house and neighborhood because, even though they are all poor, they are happy. It is a view that encapsulates the Filipino character.

Despite this ostensible happiness, life for Melinda and her family was difficult. Several years previously, at age 18, Melinda became pregnant by her boyfriend; her parents said she had to choose between her boyfriend and her family; she was heartbroken, in the end having to give up her boyfriend—who subsequently married another girl. Melinda suggested that it was probably because she was the only remaining girl in the household that her parents did not want her to marry her boyfriend, so she would stay at home with her parents and look after them. On several occasions she also strongly announced that she wanted to have a husband/family of her own and fall in love again.

Melinda works hard to help support her parents and to pay for her brothers' college, but feels that none of them appreciate her labour, sacrifice, and most of all herself as a person. While she loves her father and usually gets on well with him, she is often at odds with her mother. At times Melinda talked to me about giving up and, like Leanne, of killing herself.

I met Melinda on-line, by chance, in October 2013. She had been an ACM for only 11 days, having previously worked as a pole dancer in Olongapo city, amongst other passing occupations.

She then took up work as an ACM from home using a laptop that her elder brother lent her. However, her connection to the cam site was through an account a boss owned. That boss lived only a few doors away from Melinda. Most people in the neighbourhood are aware of the ACM industry, although it's not certain if they know exactly what the gurls do on cam. The boss charged Melinda only 5% of gross earnings because Melinda worked at home with her own laptop and paid her own electricity and internet fees. However, the money was channeled through the boss' account and thus left open the possibility of the boss withholding the salary or even cheating. This is exactly what happened, and so Melinda decided to leave that boss and work independently. But like Leanne, there emerged a litany of disasters that affected that opportunity, and indeed Melinda's ability to work at all.

First, she asked if she could borrow 5,000 pesos from me to help her father with the piggery, particularly since 2 pigs were currently sick and required medical intervention. She promised to repay the money when the pigs were sold or through her own earnings as an ACM, at which she could earn 5,000 pesos every 15 days, so she claimed. I provided her the money on that basis, but also with a request that she work for me by retyping PDF files into Word documents. In the end she did about 20 pages of about 200.

Then a litany of requests began to flow in from her, asking for smaller amounts of 1,000 or 1,500 for medicine for her sick daughter, school fees, a birthday party for her child, 2,000 for new dentures, and so on, all with the promise to do the work for me or repay me. As bad luck would have it, her nephews went into her studio and broke the PC; she managed to repair it, but again it became broken, and in the end simply not operational.

I visited the Philippines in March 2014 with the intention of interviewing Melinda about her life, and perhaps even making a documentary film about ACMs. As part of that I had planned to visit her house, and the relocation settlement generally, to get some footage, as well as sponsor her birthday party in conjunction with her daughter's birthday and also that of her friend, Angela, (a former ACM), all of whose birthdays fell within the same month. These plans never came to fruition, for on Melinda's very birthday, she came to Quezon City to meet me. When she appeared she was obviously very sick, and her aunt took her to hospital. She stayed there for about 10 days, during which time I visited her and, of course, provided some money for her needs.

After her discharge she slowly recovered, while staying with her aunt in Quezon City. Her aunt also offered her a job as a sales person, which she eventually took up, but with plans to also work as an ACM in her spare time and, hopefully, with her own PC. In the interim she developed a severe case of tinea, but was unable to afford a visit to the Doctor or to buy effective cream.

Several months later she left the sales position with her aunt and returned home to work again as an ACM, somehow having bought her own second-hand PC, and thus not working for a boss.

Returning to November 2013, I first met Melinda in real by virtue of an Israeli TV-documentary crew that wanted to make a documentary about the "real" lives of ACMs, not only in the Philippines but also other places such as Romania —as explained more fully in a following section.

I visited Melinda's home on a first occasion and built rapport with her family and community. She confirmed her agreement to be interviewed by the Israeli TV crew, whom I brought there 2 days later and who successfully interviewed both Melinda and Angela.

However, there is a sinister side to this event, explained in a following section.

V

JONAZ

Naked notes from a nipa hut.

Jonaz is 19 years old and lives in a remote provincial barrio with her two parents and 4 brothers. It is a 20-minute tricycle ride to the nearest town, that costs about 50 pesos one way. She has grown up very poor, with barely enough to eat each day, and living in a leaky nipa hut that has been, from time to time, flooded. She is a petite, smallish girl, an image that is transformed, through the help of cosmetics, into a robust, healthy, attractive gurl on cam.

She started working as an ACM just after her 18th birthday, when she had barely completed high school. Her aunt had an old computer and asked if Jonaz would work for her. She worked from her own home—using a makeshift wireless aerial that posed connection problems in bad weather—having bought timber veneer to close-in her own bedroom/studio, and which she decorated with colorful material to conceal the nipa walls.

She paid her aunt 25% of gross earnings each month. She also paid about 1,000 pesos for the internet connection, and another 1,000 per month for the electricity for the whole house. When she first started as an ACM she could earn about 5,000 pesos ($125) every 15 days, but, as for other ACMs on this site, business dropped off substantially. The site was updated in late 2013; partly because of this, and possibly because of low custom over the post-Christmas period and growing competition from other sites (some of which charge only 49 cents a minute), Jonaz can barely make 3,000 pesos ($65-$75) in 15 days, even though—having been given a second-hand PC—she now works for herself, without a boss.

While parents or other relatives may have knowledge of, and give consent to, the gurls' activities, they may not be fully cognizant of what those activities involve. In the case of Jonaz, for example, her parents assumed she just *chatted* to customers, despite being scantily dressed in underwear. However, Jonaz was reasonably sure that her elder brother knew the real situation of providing virtual sex.

During the first few months that Jonaz and I knew each other on-line her father worked, although not always fulltime. But, on one occasion he became sick; despite having medical insurance that covered most of his treatment, the medical expenses that the family had to pay still amounted to 17,000 pesos. At the same time, Jonaz's eldest brother also lost his job. Thus the sole support of the family of 7—including the education costs of 4 brothers—fell to Jonaz, who was trying to save money to fulfill her own ambition of going to college; needless to say, when her father fell sick and became unemployed for a long period her meager savings were quickly used up.

Despite having been an ACM for almost a year when I met her on-line, she had never actually spoken in real to a foreigner, which she looked forward to, provided it was in the "right situation". On one occasion she became involved in a long conversation—which I was able to capture—with a customer, Jeff. He wanted to get to know her and meet her in real, but also with a view of possibly having sex with her by taking her to a beach resort a few hours' drive north of Manila. She makes several outstanding points in her responses, some of which I italicize for emphasis, in a truncated and English-corrected version of the captured conversation, which also includes appropriate emoticons:

Jeff: ….We can make love at night….
Jonaz: ahahhhahaa [with a big smile/giggle].
Jonaz: u cant *because im not your girl friend or wife* lol (laugh out loud/smile).
Jeff: its up to u. i told u i will be honest with u… I wanna have a fun time on holiday with a nice girl, and want to make love to her….if u have a problem with that, its ok.

Jonaz: yeah i know *but im not a prostitute*
Jeff: I know yr not a prostitute hun… I never thought of u like that.

Jonaz: *but u want sex me with no status relation*
Jeff: I just thought if we can have a nice holiday together, we can be like bf/gf for a while…mmm... Well, I will come back to the Philippines again this yr, maybe for longer time.
Jonaz: *ok*

Jeff: I want to be friends also… U know, I can go to a bar and get a puta [loose woman or prostitute], but I don't know her…I thought we could be friends first here on this site, then go together…that's why I ask u many questions, to know you [as a person].

Jonaz: oo [yes].

Jonaz: i want to give u a chance *dear* but not in there [the beach resort]… near in my place only?… can u?

Jeff: Where?

Jonaz: Palladium hotel u stay and i come to u there…in XXX [a town near her home].

Jeff: oh ok. And then, at the hotel? then what?

Jonaz: knowing each other, *make love* HAHA.

Jeff: how about Makati, in Manila? Rizal Hotel, u stay one night? we eat and go to some bars, enjoy the night life?

Jonaz: no [emphatically]

Jeff: ok. I understand, but I am confused… U dont want to go to the resort and sex, but u will go to your town and sex?

Jonaz: *i need to know u* lol. *not easy to have sex to u.*

Jeff: ok, I dont want sex with a girl if she not ok with it.

Jonaz: i go eat

While it is obvious that Jonaz does not identify, or want to be identified as, a prostitute, of having sex with a man she doesn't know in exchange, possibly, for money, she also "flirts" with Jeff, with whom she has had several previous chats over the preceding week, indicating that she needs to validate a sexual relationship with him in terms of their non-sexual status. When he indicates that he is not just a fly-in-fly-out sex tourist but would be returning to the Philippines for a longer stay, suggestive that their relationship could be more enduring, she seems to condescend with "ok". However, in contradistinction, any hint of going to a bar or hotel with which she is not familiar or that may portray her as a "wanton" woman is emphatically dismissed. But at the same time, she is open to the idea of meeting, of getting to "know each other", however briefly, and contemplating the *possibility* of sex. Interestingly, she did in fact meet up with Jeff after several months, and they began a serious, and sexual, relationship.

Moreover, she does not raise what may appear to us a conflict or contradiction: she is willing to display her naked body on-line for money, but not engage in physical sexual contact for money. I was unable to explore this issue with her, for she was reluctant to discuss her work. From the little she did say it was evident she saw ACM-ing, for her, as a job, and her chats as performance. Later she would assure her boyfriend, Jeff, that she didn't mind doing the performance, that it was only her job, and differentiating that from her off-line life she therefore would not allow Jeff to take her prvt. Even so, when she did finally have to give up being an ACM she was happy to do so.

Jeff undertook to pay for her College tuition for two years, thinking that would involve merely the semester fees of about 7,000 pesos twice a year, some small amount for travel and lunch expenses. As it turned out, other costs quickly occurred.

First, Jonaz required three uniforms for her particular Course in Hospitality, one of which was a PE uniform. We may be at a loss to understand why PE—and military training—is a necessary part of a Hospitality or Secretarial Course.

Second, Jonaz had to attend classes 6 days a week, often for 12 hours a day, inclusive of travel. This of course made it impossible for her to do any ACM work, which had been part of the initial plan and would enable her to contribute at least something to her family's household expenses. While Jeff was pleased that Jonaz could no longer do ACM-ing, saying that it was not right for his girlfriend to be seen naked by other men, even if only on cam, it also meant that he now had to supplement the family's income in lieu of Jonaz's lost salary.

More expenses, however, were also incurred. Her Course required "extras", as was the case for Leanne. Jonaz required books, photocopying costs, a blender, ingredients for cooking classes, a bag, etc. In addition, while her father was willing and able at times to pay for the household electricity, his view was that he should not pay for the internet connection, now that it was not generating any income— even though it was the sole means by which Jonaz and Jeff maintained contact and by which he sent her money.

What is clearly discernible from Jonaz's situation and attempt to elevate her socio-economic position is that it is almost impossible to do so under the current Philippine education system. It is all well and good for moralizing middle-class Filipinos and NGOs and others to push for the outlawing of ACM-ing or other forms of sex-work; but they offer no alternative. Here, in the case of Jonaz, as with Leanne, we see clearly these girls doing exactly what the NGOs advocate—getting an education, attempting to improve their lot—but, if it were not for outside assistance, failing miserably. The cost of education and the additional "incidentals" does not help.

Jonaz reported to me that her PE class, for which she had to buy a special uniform, consisted essentially of providing free labour by having to clean up the college campus.... Baking classes were also a wonder: having cooked several dozen muffins or several cakes, at their own expense, most were taken home *by the teacher!*

And the following conversation snippet highlights the "extras" that students have to pay if they are not to lose face…and pass:

Jonaz: hun...

Jeff: yes

Jonaz: walang pera kami [we have no money]

Jeff: why?

Jonaz: the 500 left is we eat in fast food two times 

Jeff: Who? Who is "we"? Your friends?

Jonaz: all of my section lahat [all my] classmate...bcouse teachers day

Jeff: I see. I understand hun... and u dont wanna be shy [embarrassed] dba [right?]

But, even if such gurls were to get some outside help to enroll in and maintain a formal educational regime, and to meet the "formal" incidentals, as noted above, they can run into other, deeper issues that may mitigate their experience of education and social improvement. One of the constraining factors is that of social and cultural capital—the finesse of social life: being at college requires associating with classmates and engaging in peer social activities (eating at fast-food restaurants, going to the movies, discos/ karaokes, parties, engaging in sports or shopping, visiting the homes of one's classmates, etc, or simply exercising responsible freedom away from familial constraints). Those who can afford to go to college often already have the social and cultural (as well as financial) capital; but if you come from a poor family in the barrio, where your parents have barely an elementary education, your ability to call on and build your capital is constrained and, in the case of Jonaz, even undermined by parents who do not understand the value of peer interaction and networking at college. To add insult to injury, there can be embarrassment in bringing home one's classmates to a dilapidated environment and a situation where one cannot even offer *merienda*. Thus while college can provide the basis for the development of social and cultural capital, it also demands a certain *existing* level of that capital *and a capacity* to use and develop it.

As this book goes to press Jonaz has almost completed her college course, but not without significant effect on the family's financial situation and Jonaz's health.

Jonaz and I remained in some contact, so when I mentioned to her how far she had progressed, from being a cam gurl to almost a college graduate, she winced, saying she had almost forgotten about having been a cam model and never wanted to do it again.

VI
ANN
"I hate being poor..."

Ann (alias *Avril*) was poor by most standards: lack of money; no saleable assets; no "capital" other than her sexuality and youth; limited social capital and education; unsure of where she would sleep at night; and while she did have a "job", she was unsure if that would last and even if she would be paid at all. She complained about the scarcity and blandness of food (mainly fish and rice that she ate almost every day), and the need to socially forage for food each day. Also, her father and grandmother were sick, and soon her grandmother died, putting an extra burden onto Ann to travel home for the funeral and help pay for it. She asked to borrow money from me to meet this commitment, commenting that she didn't like to ask, but had no one else and no other choice. I sent her the money, but not for the reasons she had espoused, but rather for the chilling comment she subsequently made and with which I could fully empathize: *"I hate being like this...... I hate being poor."*

Ann was 21 years old and lived and worked in Angeles City (AC)—about 90 minutes north of Manila—although she was originally from Leyte, where her parents still lived. She had not completed college due to lack of finances; and that if she had the opportunity she wanted to own a *large* grocery store When I first met her she claimed that her grandmother (*lola*) was in hospital due to a heart attack, and needed money to help pay medical bills.

Ann worked under different screen names, changing from one name to the next because she said some names were unlucky, which affected her ability to attract customers. The fact was that, despite Ann being quite attractive, she did not present herself very well compared to many other ACMs: she used little or no cosmetics, wore her hair short at a time when it was noted that many customers were commenting on other girls' long beautiful hair; and despite her smile being a winning feature, she did not smile often. She also wore rather plain clothes and did not reveal much of herself in any alluring way, nor have a scripted choreography.

She eventually lost her job with her then current boss. Apparently she lived in the studio, with one other girl, for which they shared rent of about P3,500 a month. The studio was in the boss' house, where the boss' husband and son also lived. At other times Ann lived with friends and a cousin in another part of town.

On several occasions the boss' husband had got drunk and had become verbally and physically abusive, demanding that Ann earn more money.

Nevertheless, Ann often failed to meet her quota, and soon after I had met Ann on-line she said she would not get paid at all because she had failed to meet that month's quota.

Within a few weeks of the first instance of which I was aware of her boss' husband berating her, Ann's boss indicated that two new girls, kin of the boss, were to soon arrive and take Ann's and her co-worker's places. This soon occurred and Ann lost her job. She was out of work for a month before coming back on screen under a different name for a few days a week, using a friend's computer and studio.

At about this time I travelled to AC and met Ann. She now worked for her aunt and we were welcomed into her home and allowed to see her studio, and we met co-workers and several other members of the household; it was all presented as a place and form of work, and of real, ordinary people. Throughout my on- and off-line conversations Ann was insistent that she did not identify her work as sexual, but as entrepreneurial.

About a month later Ann was given an old PC by a foreigner, but by this time was back working for her former boss who, according to a vague and at times confusing explanation by Ann, would help her set up her own studio with two other girls. At first it seemed that Ann was pursuing her plans and had become more self-confident, adept and salacious, working on two sites simultaneously, baring more of her body to potential customers, wearing cosmetics and sporting longer hair, and even presenting with what appeared to be a black dildo (which was in fact a deodorant stick). She also became more popular, with a "star" rating of 4.5 of a possible 5 stars—which would move her into the top 20 ACM girls.

Although Ann's explanations were often fleeting and unclear, she informed me that she received more money through the second site on which she appeared, or at least less expenses were involved for her. Several months later I discovered Ann on yet another, third, site.

A few weeks after initially meeting Ann she indicated that her father was ill; and, not long after her *lola* was discharged from hospital, she died. Ann then made a special plea to me to send her money so she could go home to Leyte for the wake and funeral. Knowing that this was a very important but sad occasion in Filipino life and culture, I provided her with the minimum traveling expenses (P3,000).

The day after she arrived in Leyte she emailed me asking to "borrow" P4,000 for her *lola's* burial expenses, saying that her family and kin, whom had been asked to contribute, were all very poor, insisting that she would return to AC soon and work very hard to repay me. While I did not doubt her sincerity in this, it created both a financial and moral/ethical dilemma, for if I were to now add another monetary cost to my relationship with Ann, it would possibly lead to further, perhaps endless, requests; and I was mindful that she had yet to return to AC which would again cost money. Providing her money in time of need would also create a dependency relationship and an enormous *utang na loob* (moral debt). I would also need to justify this help in relation to not helping other girls who had asked, such as *Vina* wanting to return home to take care of her sick baby.

In the end I decided to err on the side of generosity and so I sent Ann about P3,000 for her *lola's* funeral. As I rather expected, she then asked for another P3,000 so she could return to AC to work and to pay her debts in Leyte, as well as saying that her two girls, whom now seemed to work for her in AC, had no food. In light of the fact that she already owed me money and had her own PC with which to start up her own business, I thought it prudent to get Ann back to AC so she could do what she had initially planned; thus I sent her another P2,000.

Within a day of arriving in AC she apparently had an argument with her cousin, with whom she lived, and was evicted from the residence. She emailed me three times from a coffee shop, she said, in desperation, asking me to "lend" her P8,000 for a place to live and to set up her own ACM business. Having forewarned her that I would not send any more money, I refused to do so on this occasion. A few days later I received three more emails, indicating that she now operated under a new screen name. When I contacted her there she explained that she was now working for her original boss, but was hungry because she had no prvts. I suspect that she was able to work for her original boss on the basis that Ann supplied her own computer, thus allowing her boss, who had only to pay for the electricity and shared internet connection, to have more than one girl working for her. As I spoke to Ann through the ACM site she again pleaded that I send her just a small amount of money because she was hungry and had no prvts.

Within the next few weeks she again emailed me and conversed on site, asking for P3,500 to P15,000, telling me that her cousin, who had already evicted her, was giving up the apartment and moving back to Leyte, and therefore Ann and "her two girls", as she referred to her co-workers, had no where to live. Although she seemed very genuine in her plight, there occurred an inconsistency in her story: Ann had already said that she had been evicted from her cousin's apartment and she was now living with a friend, but was embarrassed about that situation, and therefore had asked for P8,000 to establish her own living space; now, in this latest revelation, it seemed that she was in fact at—or back at—her cousin's apartment, and needed P15,000 to pay the down-payment on an apartment of her own.

As a result of this and of her not receiving any more money from me, in one conversation via the ACM-connection, there developed the theme of my not trusting her, and it seemed that the warmth and trust of our relation-ship had withered.

I also noted over several weeks of viewing her on the site that Ann had dramatically changed her presentation, at one time even displaying her bare breasts in order to attract customers, and, it would appear, somewhat to no avail.

As the story continued, in subsequent days Ann again emailed me asking, now, for only P7,000 so she could establish a dwelling and work place. I had previously suggested to her that she arrange to take over her cousin's apartment with her two "co-workers" and pay the landlord by installments. She subsequently replied that she was now thinking of selling the PC, and returning to Leyte if she could not find a place to live—which essentially meant that if I did not send her money for a home and for work she would sell the only capital—apart from her body[11] —that could potentially generate income for her, and that such an opportunity to be self-sufficient, however "sordid" that may seem to some people, would probably never be repeated.

By now it would seem obvious to the veteran Filipinist, and even the general reader, that Ann was "milking" me for all she could get. But was she? If so, she was doing quite a reasonable job of it, and, if so, then it throws into question the whole moral/feminist do-gooder argument about how these girls are exploited: they choose the job, they play it, they know how to manipulate.

As Flowers (1998: 45) suggests, the immunization, or training, that ACM-ing and/or other forms of sex-work provides teaches five basic skills: lying, playing along with offensive fantasies, reading and manipulating a stranger's desire, storytelling, and fearlessly breaking taboos—as we may have witnessed in several of the ACMs' stories.

So, who is being exploited here?

Knowing the Philippines very well, I could well understand the litany of events—the disasters—that befall Filipinos. While you and I, as comfortable middle-class Westerners or Filipinos, may be able to deal with these various events described, perhaps by simply pulling out our Credit Card (CC), when one is working with zero capital, little potential, and only social capital that is at best tenuous amongst like-situated Filipinos, when everyone is poor, as Leanne noted, then a litany of events—a sick *lola*, exploited by bosses, an ill father, the death of *lola*, the need to travel, followed by eviction, and so forth—is disastrous. In such a situation what else can one call upon other than social and cultural capital and, in Ann's case, the only physical capital, a PC, other than her body, she possessed?

To continue: about two weeks after her attempt to solicit these large sums of money from me, and my refusal to oblige, I wrote Ann an email, thinking she was by now in Leyte. To my surprise she replied a day later stating she was still in AC and still working as an ACM under her last screen-name from 10am to 3pm (perhaps regularly and on most days).

As the saga continued, in the following months I learnt that Ann worked on at least two sites, possibly three; and that while her photo appeared on the *AsianPlaymates* site, clicking on that brought me to another girl, whom it turned out was her cousin. Soon after, I encountered Ann herself on the second site; she proceeded to tell me that she was now pregnant to her boyfriend—who, according to Ann, had absconded when he had learnt about the pregnancy. By this time I was not to be surprised by any turn of events, nor of the fact that Ann had lied to me before, as she freely admitted, about not having a boyfriend.

A few weeks later Ann sent me an email, explaining she was still working as an ACM, and stating "*I am not angry with you*" (*sic*). By chance I came across her on the site early one morning, bare-breasted, and she informed me that she was ok; in fact, she was using the PC that had been given to her and working for herself.

A few more weeks rolled by and again by chance I espied her picture amongst the *AsianPlaymates* roll-call of currently available ACMs. Clicking on Ann's picture, however, brought me face to face with another girl who, quite rudely, told me at first that she did not know Ann, but subsequently indicated that Ann was in fact present, but down stairs. I later wrote an email to Ann saying that I had hoped to see and speak with her. Over the next few weeks I received three emails in reply, the first saying that she, Ann, was OK; the second said she would not be working during the following week or two as she had to go to a southern province for reasons not stated; and the third email, about a week later, informed me that she had been in hospital with a miscarriage. I of course sent my condolences, to which she replied that she had had to pawn for P5,000 the PC that had been given her in order to pay her medical expenses.

The saga, no doubt, continued...although there may be a happier side to the outcome to date. Ann's Facebook page shows her healthy and happy amongst friends, back in her home town in Leyte, and most recently she is studying.

So what do the mad moralists say about this?

VII
PARIS

My research assistant, Jena, and I met Paris in a quiet café in Cubao, late one afternoon. She was an attractive person, fair skin, long brownish/blonde hair, slim, perhaps a little thin, dressed casually but well, with some cosmetics, and with signs of small breasts. The interview of about 90 minutes was conducted in both Tagalog and English. Paris seemed nervous for the first 45 minutes or so, and spoke with a very feminine voice. Paris had been an ACM for about 4 years, but had also worked cooking hamburgers and in a salon.

~

My nickname is Paris. I'm only a high school graduate, but I think I'm pretty smart, and know how to survive. I've had to learn to survive, because I come from a poor family in Manila, with five brothers, and because I am gay, or what is called in the Philippines a bakla. These days, however, we are called TGs, transgenders. But I don't care about that, so long as I am respected for who I am. I am happy as a bakla.

Even though I had feelings of being a TG in high school, only when I graduated did I come out. But my parents didn't like it, so to be independent from my parents I went to live with a friend in Pampanga. There I was a kind of maid. My friend worked as an ACM and my job was to keep the house and studio clean and tidy, and do all the other things a maid does.

After a few months I decided to work as an ACM. I applied for official identification from our Post Office, to give to the ACM site verification as to who I am and that I am over 18 years old. At that time I was just 18 years old. I worked there with my friend for almost 3 years.

But during that time there were many raids on ACM studios, because the government and police thought that cybersex was bad and illegal, or gurls and TGs were trafficked, or kids were involved. That is so wrong, as you can see from my story. I decided myself to be an ACM, and never were there any kids allowed in the studio.

I was afraid of the raids, so I went back to my parents in Manila. They finally accepted me as a bakla, and I was able to help them financially. Soon I moved to my aunty's house, where I live alone, and look after her house while she is away, overseas, for a long time. At first I worked for a female boss who had a husband and kids; they were quite respectable and lived in the same street. Eventually I bought my own PC and was my own boss. When the site was good, on the old site, and the connection was good, I could earn up to 15,000 pesos in 15 days. My earnings were not always so high, but I could manage my own money. But if I didn't get my quota then I would have no salary at all! I don't mind the work, but sometimes it gives me a problem, if I don't meet the quota.

About sex and ACMs, I think that if a gay guy pays for sex with a boy they are just playing, not serious about a relationship. I have been with 6 foreigners; they just want to have sex and pay for it. Some day I hope to meet a guy who will take me away from this work.

There's a lot of clients out there who want to see me, as a bakla, there has to be if I make 15,000 pesos. Many clients ask for me to please their fetish, for example, some have paid me to just watch while I paint my finger nails, others want COS-play, so I have to have a few uniforms or dresses handy. Others want to see me masturbate or watch them do it, and worse is others want to see me pee or shit and then drink or eat it. But I have tricks for that: I have a hidden glass of beer or something that looks like pee and I swap it for the pee I do; and for poo, I have a chocolate bar that I can make look like poo.

I hope one day I can get real and bigger boobs, but I don't trust the surgery, about implants. I have heard bad stories. But maybe in another country such as Thailand it would be better. But it's also very expensive.

~

Paris, in telling his story, seemed to resent his former boss' situation, who had a comfortable, perhaps middle-class, life, but who was *kuripot* (stingy). I could not help be amused by the irony of this situation: a respectable middle-class family fostering an ACM!

VIII
ALEX

Alex was about 19 years old when I first encountered her on-line in 2010. She lived in metro Manila with her mother. She was a very young looking, and a quite cute and sexy girl (by subjective evaluation), who was new to ACM-ing in early 2010. I didn't follow up Alex at that time, other than to occasionally chat with her for a few days and get her YM address. What struck me at the time was how inexperienced she was as a cam gurl, perhaps even naïve in some ways. I vividly recall, however, that several guests were visiting her room, and she commented to me, with some apparent self-pleasure, about how amazing it was that so many (male) customers were looking at her.

But she was clearly a smart gurl, who quickly learnt the value of ACM-ing, so much so that she became quite popular, but also choosey as to whom she would chat. After about a year she disappeared from the ACM site.

About 3 years later I contacted Alex in the hope she would agree to be interviewed by an Israeli TV crew in a few weeks. Although she could not remember me, she did agree to the possibility of being interviewed, but indicated that she now had a 2-year old son whom she would have to bring to the meeting if she could not find someone to care for him. Hence it became evident that her disappearance from the ACM site was because she had become pregnant and she had been busy caring for her infant. But she also had returned to work as an ACM, with her own PC and, as I was to later discover, earning as much as 20,000 pesos a month.

At the interview, conducted by Ms. N. and filmed by Mr. G., with myself present, she was asked a range of questions. In particular, in an hour-long interview, the theme of sexual exploitation, objectification, victimization and trauma reoccurred. At one point Ms. N., the inept interviewer, asked —in English so poor that I had to translate her questions into English for Alex—about her experiences of being verbally abused and denigrated regarding her sexuality and gender. When Alex responded quite flatly by saying no, that she couldn't recall any such events or feelings, and if guests became abusive she would simply cut them off, Ms. N. reworded the question to elicit a "proper" answer. This was more along the lines of asking Alex to provide some examples of what she did not like about some of the customers and how they treated her. Alex launched into a vey articulate and passionate soliloquy about how she was at times offended by some clients referring to her as "just a Filipina", poor and uneducated, and the Philippines as a wretched place, in a derogatory sense, that will never succeed in the world, and how Filipinos would do anything for money. I was in awe at her calm tirade against such racist and, for her, anti-nationalist Westerners. She said she often retorted to their racist abuse by asking them, if they thought Filipinas were just "shit" then why did they, the guests, visit her room and pay to see her? Then she would simply disconnect (DC) them.

Overall Alex provided a superb and genuine interview, about how she came to be an ACM in order to support her mother and other relatives, and, after the birth of her son, she worked hard to provide him with a good life, without a father. Unfortunately for the Israelis she did not provide them with the feminist gender-bashing responses they had hoped for.

At barely 22 years of age, Alex was simply amazing: articulate, intelligent, diligent, hardworking, serious and dedicated—and I have no qualms in saying she was also attractive and cute. She had certainly come a long way since I had initially met her 2-3 years previously, when she had appeared naïve and quite innocent.

IX
RAY

In this interview, which took place in a garnered, surprisingly quiet, corner of a fast food restaurant in a provincial town, Ray was accompanied by Leanne and Cristy, and also by the following interviewee, Tina. These two new informants were introduced by Leanne, who also engaged in the interviews with comments and questions.

Both Ray and Tina were keen to be interviewed and, despite my contrary advice, keen to use their real names and even photographs of themselves in this publication. Despite their wishes, I have changed their names herein, as their anonymity is paramount.

Ray is 24 years old, living in the same area as Leanne. He currently identifies as bisexual. At 16 he identified as a TG, but at 18+ identified himself as bisexual—gay and straight. Ray is broad shouldered and masculine looking, tempered with a mild feminine appearance and mannerism, but not flamboyant in dress or manner as many TGs often present.

He has a high school education, and previously worked as a service crew in a fast food establishment and in telemarketing. Ray grew up in Quezon City. His father died when Ray was 5 years old and he was initially looked after by his grandmother. He has one elder sister, and a brother and sister from his stepfather. He currently lives with his friends, a boyfriend and some cousins and aunties.

Both his family and the people he currently lives with accept him as gay/bisexual and know he is a cam model, with which they now do not have a problem. However, as Ray explains, *"Before, because they* [his family] *don't want me to be cam model before, but I will decide for myself, because I want first of all to help myself, second, to help my mum, my brothers, sisters…"*, which he currently does. Similarly, his current household knows he is a cam model and seem to have come to terms with that, as Ray further explains: *"Before, they have a problem for me because they're dream for me is to be a successful business man or something, but I don't have money to take my college so that's why I decide to become a cam model."*

He began as an ACM in 2006, at age 16, by faking his ID. As an ACM he first worked for a boss until 2010, but now is his own boss and has 4 models—2 gurls and 2 ladyboys—working for him; he gets 40-50% from his workers, 50% on Fridays, but does not get any proportion from their Western Union remits from customers. Overall, his ACM income is 5k-10k pesos in 15 days, but he doesn't work every day because some days he takes care of his (young) cousin.

When Ray revealed his current situation I began by asking him to explain his role as a "boss", in which he tends to belabour his role as helping his models.

[I'm] *"Not really a boss because I was helping them, because I was a model before, so I know* [what it's like to be a model and working for a boss], *that's why I'm helping them because I know what it was like before."*

Q. How did you come to be a cam model?
"By my friend, he was helping me before, because when I finished my studies in high school it was hard to pay college because we don't have money, so my friend suggested I should be a cam [model], *which is good for me, because of that—a cam model, a cam boy or cam gay—I was helping my family. And by now, as a boss, I was helping other people like me, as a model before. I consider them, my models, not really my models, as my friends, because it's too hard to be a model before, that's why I understand them even though they're not telling me sometimes that they are*

sending by their guests [receiving money via WesternUnion from some guests], *but I understand, that's why."*

Q. How do you feel about being a cam model?
"Sometimes I was crying because my salary is not enough for me, just to help myself and my family, but I am [was] coaching myself to be a boss, which I am a boss right now, because I don't want to work for how [so] many years, so what I mean, I was working from 2006 until 2010 so I was working as a model for 4 years. It's too hard to be a model for those particular years, so that's why I decide to earn money, so maybe I can pay my bills, to pay for my apartment, especially my everyday expenses, for me as an independent of my family, because I rented...."

Q. Which cam model category are you in, on the ACM site?
"When I was 16 I was under TG, then, when I decided to be a bisexual I was under the category of gays and guys, sometimes [I'm] on the straight category, it depends..."

Q. Do you identify as bisexual, gay, TG...?
"It depends. I was [am] doing a beauty pageant until now, when I was Miss XXX during our beauty pageant..."

Q. But you identify as gay?
"Bi. Because I have my boyfriend, and he is bisexual too, and he became a cam model, too, before. I am living with my boyfriend."

Q. What are some of the things that customers ask you to do?"
"Sometimes cum in five minutes because they cheapest, that's why I didn't do that, because as a cam model you know to yourself how to cum because if you will cum quickly, so definitely your cock will not be hard for so many hours.

So if a guest is taking you in prvt, but [how] *to enjoy taking you in prvt if your cock is not getting hard? But sometimes they are telling me to drink my pee, but I didn't do that,* [I substitute another drink]*...I'm pretending that's my pee. So that's why after doing what they want I ask for tips."*

Q. What do you think of the customers who ask you to do these things?
"Super crazy, a bitch, because they're pretending I would do that for $2 for two minutes, that I will drink my own pee. What the fuck! They are hoping I will do that, but I don't do that."

Q. Do they say bad things about you?
"No.....Yes, if I don't do what they want, because some times I can't, that's why they say I'm a bitch, I'm dirty..."

Q. Do you think you're a prostitute?
"Yes, before, but now, since I stop working on ACM, I am no longer."

Q. When you were an ACM, you were a prostitute?
"When I was working." [yes].

Q. So when your models are working with you now, do you think they are prostitutes?
"I think no, because I am treating them as a friend, not a model, not a prostitute, I am helping them. It depends on the person to what they think and its..."

Q. So when you were working you thought you were a prostitute?
"Yes."

Q. But you don't treat your friends/models as prostitutes?

"*Yes.*" [that's correct].

Q. It's up to them to decide?
"*Yes.*"

Q. Have you had any customers who have come here to the Philippines to meet you?
"*Yes, four times.*"

Q. Did you go with them?
"*Yes, for a couple of days.*"

Q. Did you have sex with them?
"*Yes! I'm not denying it, because I like it.*" [This was before he had a boyfriend].

Q. Did you like these guys?
"*Yes.*"

Q. So do you see *that* being a prostitute and getting money for sex or more of being a companion?
"*It depends, depending on the customer.*"

Q. Yes, but the 4 customers you had? Was it a friendship and they gave you money, or was it sex and they gave you money?
"*They gave me money because he was satisfied with what I was doing.*"

Q. In bed?
"*Yes!....*"

Q. What would you like to do for work if you were not a cam model?
"*As a service crew.*" [in a fast food restaurant].

Q. So what is your plan for the future, to be a cam model, or ....?

"No. That's why I was telling you [before], *that I am working, say one time or two times a week, because I used to be a cam model, there's so many people, they were good to me so I am good to them, too, that's why I have many friends, more foreigners abroad."*

Ray's explanation about ACMs being or not being prostitutes introduces a new element, that of self-identification. While he admits as identifying as a prostitute when he was a cam model, he does not impose this on others, even other types of sex workers, and least of all his own models whom he considers to be friends. But he goes further, in a very liberal framework that perhaps we could all learn from, of acknowledging that even if his models or other sex workers were to proclaim self identification as prostitutes, then he accepts that.

Other than that, much of what he says about helping others, of being friends with customers, and even a casual lover in real to four of his customers, revolves around friendship, companionship, mutuality, reciprocity and altruism. While this may appear as some form of denial or justification, such a perspective that Ray holds may not be uncommon.

X
TINA

Tina—who wished to be referred to as a female—lives in the same area as Ray, Leanne and several of the other ACMs noted above. She identifies as transgender, and commonly dresses and acts in a feminine manner. She is a slim, rather petite and attractive transgender (TG). She revealed that she has small breasts as a result of taking hormones and wants to have a full sex change, that it's the dream of all TGs to have a real vagina.

She has a high school education, and lives with her mother, niece, nephew and brothers. Her father works in Manila and goes home once a week on weekends.

Tina grew up in Manila, with 3 brothers and 3 sisters, she being the youngest of the 7 children. She identified as a TG at age 13, but said transgenderism was not inborn because, at age 11-12, as a boy, she had a girlfriend. Her family was "happy" for her being a TG.

Tina commenced as an ACM in August 2012, and does this work for her own financial support and to support her brothers' college education.

I began by asking Tina about how she came to be a cam model:

"Before, I worked under a big (sic) *boss, renting her studio and PC."* By "big" she meant that her boss before was Cristy's model (Sara), who herself became a boss, so Tina subsequently worked for Sara. But is often the case, it was more complex: Tina actually worked "for" Cristy (the "big" boss) for a few months, but in fact only used Cristy's PC and room and simply used Sara's account, and therefore was paid by Sara and was not actually employed by Cristy. *Capisce?*

Q. Who told you about being a cam gurl?

"I had heard a lot from my friends, but I choose to become one, I found Sara and Cristy, at age 17, 3 years ago, and faked my documents."

Tina now works for herself, using her own PC and studio. When she worked for Sara her income was about 3k-4k pesos every 15 days, but now, as self-employed she gets about 8k pesos.

Q. Why did you become an ACM?

"To help my family, for my [own] *financial needs, to support my brother/s to study at college."*

Q. How do you feel about working as an ACM?

"Its nice working there because I can earn a lot of money than normal (sic) *work."*

Q. What about feelings, how do you *feel* working in this kind of work?

"They get me down, they tell I am a dirty bitch, like that, [I'm] *nothing, working that kind of work—the neighbours, who know I am a CAM....neighbours call me prostitute,* [because I] *show my body in cam just for money. A lot of customers are nice, they understand what my job is, others say I am a whore, bitch, dirty, prostitute."*

When I asked Tina if she considered herself to be a prostitute, she emphatically replied in the negative.

Q. But you're selling your body for money...?

"Yes, I know that, I am selling my body in front of the camera for just money, but for me being a prostitute is doing it in real, but showing my body in front of the cam is not being a prostitute."

She went on to say there is a difference between a guy/girl who has "real" sex, that they are a prostitute, and those who do not have "real" sex.

Q. But you are selling your body, virtually, digitally, on screen, and you're not a prostitute, I persisted?

Leanne: *"Do you think the girl in the bar selling their body are prostitutes?"*

Tina: *"I think so."*

Leanne: *"But you are not?"*

Tina: *"I am not, because I am not doing it for real."*

Q. But you're still selling your body....?

"Yes, I am selling my body, but my customer cannot touch me, only myself [can touch me]."

Q. So what do you think of girls who go to hotels or

work in a bar? Do you think they're bad?

"Well, some work that kind of work for a reason, so I think they do that kind of work for a good reason, so I don't think they are bad, but other persons [friends, neighbours] *they think they are doing it as a bad thing."*

While Tina insists that she, as a cam gurl, is not a prostitute because her "sex" is not real and customers cannot touch her, physically at least, she also acknowledges that other girls, such as bar girls, whom she does consider to be prostitutes, are not "bad" because, like her (?), they undertake the work for "good' reasons; but the friends and neighbours of such girls may think they are bad. We have witnessed similar comments from Leanne and Cristy to the effect that they are more concerned with what neighbours and kin might say or do about their work, although also recognizing that, while ACM-ing is not "bad", it is not the most desirable job *because of moral undertones.* But such morality comes in fact from the socialization of sexuality, as we witness with neighbours' gossip.

Q. What are some of the things that customers ask you to do?

"To get my cock hard and to want it [sex]*, ask me to show my ass, something like that, and to put my two fingers, three fingers, four fingers in it, and sometimes they ask me to use a dildo, which is a big size like nine* [inches]*, something like that, then they ask me to cum and ask me to eat my own cum."*

Q. And you do all these things?
"Yes, of course, because they ask me."

Q. You must get a lot of guys to visit your room, to take you prvt, to make your money; so, what do you think of these men ?
"Oh, I think they want to have some fun with me. I think

they just only want some fun that's why they do that,...they spending money by taking a model in private, for fun."

Q. So do you think it's just fun for them or do you think they are secret gays?

"They are gays, too, because they do not take a transgender like me in prvt if they're not gays. Because if they are straight guys then don't take a TG like me in prvt they just prefer only girls."

Leanne: *"But...I had a guest before, who was a straight guy, but he took a TG as well."*

Q. How do you know he's straight?

Leanne: *"He was my guest! And he told me he just came from a TG's room, and took him in prvt."*

Tina: *"Maybe he took that transgender you're talking about, maybe he wanted some experience, with a Trans* [TG], *even if he's a straight guy, maybe have a fling, because I have encountered that before, he was a straight guy, but I asked him, 'why did you take me prvt if you're a straight guy?' He answered me that he 'need and wanted some experience about a TG like you.'"*

Q. The problem is, however, that they can tell you anything. You can't always see them [or know what they have done a few minutes earlier, as in Leanne's example, or yesterday or last week, or whenever]. They can tell you that they are gay or straight, or male or female, any age. So basically they can lie to you, and so we don't *know.*

Leanne: *"But one time, there's a young boy, just 15 years old, and he got his father's credit card, and he showed it.....*

Q. So you would take his money even if he was only 15?

Leanne: *"He gave it, about 30 minutes, and I did not do anything except show my boobs."*

Q. So the things your customers ask you to do, you don't mind doing, I asked Tina? You just think of the money?

"Yeah, just think of the money."

Q. Do you hope to meet any of these customers some time?

"Yes, I do. I do met [have met] *some of them."*

Q. So you've met some of them already ?
"Yes."

Q. And you have gone out with them, to a hotel ?
"Yes, actually."

Q. And they pay you for sex?

"No, no, just only for fun, but some of them gave me money for my time, because I said to them I'm going to have time off [to meet them], *they have to pay me for my time, they have to pay me for that, but I don't do anything for him, I just have to make him satisfied."*

Q. So if any of these men offered you money for sex would you do that?

"I don't think so, maybe if he offer me a higher price, something like twenty-thousand [pesos], *maybe I will do for him."*

Q. Does your family know that you work as a cam model?

"Yes they know that."

Q. And do they know that you take off your clothes and play with yourself; they know what you do?

"Of course they know."

Q. So they know everything?
"Yes."

Q. So they know you get naked and....?

"*Yes.*"

Q. Do they have a problem with that ?
"*No, they don't have.*"

Q. So they don't think you're "bad"?
"*Oh, I think, they think....about me... First of all Filipinos is open minded for the kind of work...*"

Q. Yes, but your neighbours don't think you're very nice
"*Oh yes, that's true, but you know that, when I play my music it's so very very loud, that's why they get mad at me, they throw some stone on the upper, the rooftop, to make me stop.....*"

Q. So why don't you turn the music down so you will get on well with your neighbours?
"*Oh, you know what, on Fridays I play that music very very loud to enjoy myself performing, but they ask me....[to turn it down].*"
Leanne: "*Every time I visit her she's always dancing and.....*"
"*Oh yeah, I'm shaking my ass....*"

Q. What do you think about the case of the American sailor allegedly killing the TG, Jenny, in Olongapo, recently?
There followed some confusion over the story that both Leanne and Tina told.[12]

Q. How do you people feel about this, do you think this American guy is bad, crazy...?
They agreed he was not really bad, but Tina added: "*I feel really bad when I heard Jennifer was killed by a US military [person] because of that issue. Well let's say that Jennifer made a mistake, but I think the US military [person] will not kill [should not have killed] Jennifer.*"

Q. So you think things would have been different if Jennifer had been a real girl and not a transgender ?
"Well, um, I feel bad as well, because we have [a] *thing about nationality, we're Filipino, so I think..."*

Q. So its not about gender or sex, but nationality?
"Yes", they all agreed.

We Are Well Past Plan B
When fieldwork is not fieldwork.
When enlightenment is fifty shades of shadow.

A certain Mr. Matan Gez, claiming to be a Director of a TV documentary series on KESHET-UVDA TV, based in Israel, contacted me via email in late 2013, after finding my publications about ACMs. He and his crew had been working for several months on cybersex, mostly in Europe, with the aim of producing a 60-minute documentary, ostensibly about the real lives of ACMs. They were planning to visit the Philippines to complete their research and material gathering, and enlisted my—unpaid—help in contacting gurls there and persuading some to be interviewed.

This I managed to do in a very short time; Melinda and Angela were two of the interviewees. I had arranged for these interviews to be undertaken on a Sunday at about noon or early afternoon, and expected the Israeli TV crew— consisting, in fact, of only Mr. G (the "real" Director and cameraman) and Ms. N (a somewhat incompetent journalist/ interviewer)—to sponsor some *merienda* (snacks) and take some interest in the economic environment in which these gurls worked. They were accompanied by an equally incompetent and insensitive Filipina freelance journalist by the unlikely name of Sunshine who, having grown up in the USA, could not even speak Taglish.

As it turned out, this misfit crew of Israelis and Co.

arrived to pick up myself and my Filipino assistant, John, at 4pm instead of 1pm; and with heavy traffic to Melinda's house we arrived with barely enough light to film any thing—including the sun that shone from their collective ass.

It was at this point that a whole array of lies told by the Israelis became apparent. Why they were so late on this particular day was because they had been to another part of Manila, in particular, a women's refuge centre that catered, in part, to ACMs who had been "traumatized". It became apparent that the story they were after from these various ACMs was one of exploitation, trafficking, harm, trauma and abuse. Targeting a refuge centre gave them that very needed material, contrary to other interviews that I had organized.

But there was an even more sinister motive to showing the negative effects of ACM-ing: the Israelis were determined to expose a certain "Mr. Big" behind the ACM sites, said to be a Croatian or Romanian operating from the USA, and earning millions of dollars from this business of "exploiting" thousands of poor Filipinas, and other gurls.

The irony of this was that the Israeli's themselves were now exploiting the plight of Filipina ACMs as they embarked on some kind of moral crusade to do an exposé of Mr. Big, and were exploiting myself and John in order to facilitate that. They failed to acknowledge that their actions could endanger the lives and livelihoods of not only the ACMs interviewed but also all ACMs.

Perhaps it *is* true that this "Mr. Big" has made money out of ACM-ing; but he has also provided jobs for thousands of gurls who would otherwise have no income, as we have seen in the foregoing case studies. But this begs the question of whether Mr. Big is any different from other capitalists, or even the Israeli film crew? Is he any different from multi-national corporations that pay low wages and exploit the need for employment in third world countries? Or is there a moral issue here, one of sexuality?

In other words, the Israelis seemed to have held a moral

position, which does not hold up in the Philippines context, and I suggest in other countries, simply because the gurls, as they clearly stated in interviews and their histories, see no moral issue; they see no problem in displaying their sexuality on cam, because gurls *choose* to be ACMs, to do what they do, and separate that role/performance from their real self. The gurls themselves said this, but the Israeli crew did not like that kind of response. These gurls do not feel exploited in terms of gender or sexuality, as Alex clearly states in her interview: when asked about personal experiences of degradation as cam-model, she waived the national flag and objected to clients denigrating *Filipinas* and the *Philippines*; when pressed for perceptions of sexual exploitation, she simply said no, she did not feel like a product, a victim, a sexual object, she was doing a job, a performance. For her, being an ACM and displaying her naked body was not a problem. The problem seemed to be that of the Israelis and that of the Western world generally, including the pseudo-moralistic middle-class and NGOs in the Philippines. It is in fact the Israelis and others who have the problem with sexuality and nakedness, with gurls selling "sex". Having invented capitalism, and brought it to the Third World, Westernizers and the Westernized now want to judge those who take advantage of it!

In asking these kinds of questions of the gurls, what the Israelis did was vent their own moralistic position and, in that process, actually *create* a problem for the gurls when no problem for them previously existed. The moral problem, then, is in the *Westernized* mind, not that of the ACMs.

But if the Israelis were genuinely concerned about exploitation, then the real focus should be on the real and immediate exploitation that bosses, at the coal face, can and do deploy by cheating the gurls, or by imposing direct demands/quotas, etc. *There* is the exploitation. Mr. Big has given opportunity for work, while bosses (with some exceptions) at the local level bastardize that opportunity and directly exploit the gurls.

Having said that, one could argue there *is* exploitation on the part of Mr. Big, but not in terms of making money, as any capitalist aims to do, by "employing" *ipso facto* ACMs. Rather, the exploitation occurs in two, economic, ways:

The first is the excessive 50% of gross earnings taken by the company that owns the site. There never has been any negotiation of this proportion, nor indeed could there ever be; and thus this excessive proportion, without any apparent justification, is simply imposed on the basis that the gurls are so desperate for work they would accept it. But such a large chunk from gross earnings has a profound affect on the net earnings of the gurls when one considers they must often share the remaining 50% with a boss, and/or pay electricity and/or internet fees monthly. In other words, it is questionable if the company's 50% cut is justifiable, or simply greed.

The second and more subtle but indeed more insidious means of exploitation is that ACMs operate on a piece-rate basis.

A piece-rate system of payment consists, in its simplest form, of remuneration to workers on the basis of *the number of "products"* they produce in a given period of time vis-à-vis a wage that is dependent on the *time* at the work place. In its more complex forms, quotas may be imposed by the capitalist (boss), penalties applied for failing to meet quotas, rates and quotas varied arbitrarily, and poor quality products rejected and thus not included in a quota. In some cases the supply of materials and tools—and their use—is subject to capitalist control or have to be paid for by the worker. "Work at home" schemes, such as marketers for Amazon, are modern examples that are subject to many of these conditions, such as supplying one's own capital (a computer, internet connection fees, electricity) or meeting quotas, and which also can be readily illustrated with case studies of ACMs.

In this regard there are two questions:

1. Are piece-rates exploitative of the worker only in given situations?

or,

2. Are piece rates *inherently* exploitative? Is there something *intrinsic* about a system of piece-rates that is exploitative for the worker?

My argument is that there is indeed an *intrinsic principle* of exploitation in any system of piece-rates, of which both the site and the boss take advantage. Regardless of the situational conditions, it is the piece-worker who, within the existing normative framework of capitalism, bears the burden and risk of production. This arises because the management of labour through a piece-rate system of payment *shifts the risk of production, at the point of production, to labour.*

Ultimately, a piece-rates system puts the burden of the worker's ability and productivity onto the worker, and the need for him/her to control his/her *own* input and hence output, and in so doing places the risk of performance (productivity) on to the worker vis-à-vis capital (boss).

In the normative order of capitalism, what piece-rates as a system of remuneration to labour does is shift that risk to labour. Capital not only violates this normative order, or established principle of capitalism, but does so by false pretenses—by presenting piece-rates work as opportunity, when in fact other facets of capitalism such as control of the production process and other capital still provides the capitalist with an advantage, that he/she is able to utilize situationally.

While the worker in a piece-rate system my believe that he/she has a share in the surplus value of their own labour power (as capital), the fact is that both social and economic inequalities place greater risk on the piece-rate worker than the counterpart capitalist who supplies only the machinery, land and other disposable capital, at minimal risk.

Essentially, then, piece-rates "represent the conversion

of time wages into a form which attempts....to enlist the worker as a willing accomplice in his own exploitation" (Braverman, H. 1974: *Labor and Monopoly Capital*. NY: Monthly Review Press. Pp. 62-63).

For the piece-worker, in practical terms, piece-rates *seem* to make sense and *appear* to provide opportunity. It is this "sense" to which piece-rates appeal—which is well illustrated in the case of ACMs. But it is simply an economic façade for exploitation. The piece-work system of payment introduces the *semblance* that the worker obtains a specified share of the product, when in fact he/she takes most of the risk—and in the case of ACMs, only 25% of the product share, despite the ACM herself being the product!

There are serious implications that arise from this situation and the payment system under which these girls labour. If she fails to reach her quota—which can be as minimal as 100 minutes per fortnight—then she *may* forfeit *all* of her income, at least temporarily for that period of 15 days. That is, she is not paid a proportional amount of the quota: it is all or nothing for that period.

In effect, in one period of 15 days an ACM may spend 96 hours (5,760 minutes) at work and have, for example, only 80 minutes of paid private shows (0.4% of her total time); consequently, she may get *no* payment at all for that period, until the end of the next period, 15 days hence. Even if she were to meet her quota of 100 minutes per fortnight (0.5% of her time) she brings in a *gross* amount of $100; 50% of this goes to the site, 25% to the boss (paid by the company directly into the boss' bank account and thus giving complete control of income to the boss); the ACM receives 25%, *not* the 50% that the promotions promise. This equals a net amount of $25 a fortnight, ($1 = P40). On an individual-show basis, she would get on average a net $3-4.

While work conditions and rates vary from one ACM to another, the fact is that the ACM does not get paid *for the hours "worked"*; that is, she is not paid for the time she is at the work site, but only for the "pieces" of work she actually "produces".

Situational conditions and exploitation are largely possible because it is the ACM who is taking the risk in production. Thus while the company and the boss have almost nothing to lose, because they can employ other labour or use the capital for other purposes, the ACM now has to bear the risk of production to meet her own needs (ie. returns to labour), as well as, incidentally but by no means insignificant, situational obligations.

Thus, regardless of the situational condition of the piece-worker, she/he bears the burden and risk of production by having to monitor her/his own labour-as-capital. In simple terms, piece-workers take it upon themselves to ensure their own survival, and in so doing risk failure at the very point of production, at the coal-face of the labour-capital process. Failure to appropriately monitor their own work capacity and work ethic, and to ensure output greater than their labour input, brings forth the risk of under-employment or un-employment.

So while the Israelis and others may have a moral view about sexual exploitation, which may well be argued either way, they have missed very much the economic exploitation. Perhaps it is that Mr. Big *is* exploiting gurls by using their natural sexuality and gender, but more fundamentally he could not exploit that in such a way without also exploiting the economic principles that capitalism has established and that he utilizes.[13]

In the end we need to ask who is exploiting who, and how? To tell the true stories of economic and social hardship that ACMs encounter in trying to survive would not sell the Israeli's TV program. To bring Mr. Big down through some kind of social or moral justice via a sensationalist docu-mentary, however, would not only sell a TV program and make the world feel righteous, but also further the Israeli's own careers. *That* is exploitation of the gurls, solely for the

Israeli's own ends.

What did they give these gurls and their families in return? How will they benefit? Perhaps as a result of this exposé the sites will shut down, or the gurls will be raided by the police, and so they will be out of a job....and they weren't even paid for their exploitation by the Israelis!

But to add insult to that injurious exploitation, the Israelis did not even have the courtesy to even attempt to abide by certain cultural norms and expectations in the Philippines. Apart from the unnecessary and constant lies by commission or omission I encountered from the very beginning, the Israelis displayed blatant cultural insensitivity and disrespect toward Filipinos and Philippine culture. No regard was given to these or the economic circumstances that facilitated ACMs' exploitation, other than the black/white dichotomy that the gurls were poor and therefore *had* to do it. In subscribing to such myopic views they were simply perpetuating the righteous versus the poor and down trodden without actually doing anything about it. Perhaps they should change their TV show to be entitled "Sensationalist Crap".

Let me list the litany of lies and deceit and cultural insensitivities this group of Israeli media presented. All these raise issues of highly problematic ethics in the purpose and conduct of the project:

1. Because of the basic lie told to me regarding the purpose of the Israeli documentary I developed certain relationships with ACMs in the belief that the Israelis wanted to tell the story of the ACMs, ie. their economic circumstances, how the industry worked, and their moral and sexual views of ACM-ing. The fact that the project was an exposé of a certain "Mr. Big", and of some kind of "mafia", caused me to reassess my relationships with the ACMs. Because I didn't know the truth, I ended up having to lie to the gurls, even though for me their dignity and integrity was first and foremost, as people, as Filipinos. So many times I

had to change my story to these gurls to accommodate the Israelis' lies, and continually build their trust in me to achieve the Israeli goals,which I still hoped would include some truth and to which I continued to try to direct the events.

2. At first I was told Matan Gez was the director and he would be the key person to visit the Philippines and direct the production process. This then changed to Ms. N and a "cameraman". The "cameraman" turned out to be the "director", Mr. G., who I subsequently learned was in fact only a reporter accountable to a more senior director. So the questions remain about who has authority, who is account-able, who should I and the gurls believe and trust?

3. On first contact in Manila, Friday night, Matan called me from Israel to ask for help in getting gurls in Taguig, with whom they had been in contact without informing me. Naively, he expected these gurls to come to a 5-star hotel in Makati and speak to the crew. Ms. N. said she would give me their phone numbers. The next day she said Matan did not have any contacts in Taguig. The following day, Sunday, I discover that the crew had been to Taguig and had interviewed gurls there.

4. I was also informed that the Israelis had a "fixer" in Manila. What they didn't tell me was that she was a local journalist, who couldn't even speak Taglish, and that they were intent on visiting a crisis/rescue centre in the city—to get the sad stories of exploited gurls that would support their aim of showing how Mr. Big was exploitative of ACMs and that ACM-ing was demeaning and victimizing. More disturbing was that this "fixer"/journalist was also intent on writing up the "sad plight" of ACMs for local media and thereby risking the welfare of ACMs and the industry on which they relied for survival.

5. When I asked the crew who they were interviewing on the Saturday of a long weekend/holiday, they replied "Government officials". This was a blatant lie, since one

would need *very* high political connections to get government officials to even talk to you, and especially on a holiday. Pure bullshit.

6. Regarding the high cultural insensitivity and disrespect displayed by the Israeli team toward Filipinos and Philippine culture, I am astounded. Despite my prior and ongoing advice, they failed to understand that certain cultural protocols should be followed. Although ACMs may not be high-ranking government officials, they and their culture deserve respect and due consideration from visitors. They found this out the hard way when they discovered that their ACM informants from Taguig would not meet with them and they required *my* help to push forward such meetings. Unlike the Israeli team, I did not sit in a grand hotel and present such ostentatiousness that ACMs can only dream of and thus rub in their face their poverty; nor did I simply wait for ACMs to come to me; I went to *their* homes, as an equal (as much as circumstances would allow), and let it be known *hindi ako mata pobre* (I am not ashamed to be with poor people).

7. The worst case the Israeli team created was with Melinda and Angela. These gurls had prepared *merienda* (snacks/afternoon tea) for our visit, even though they were poor. They probably borrowed the money for that. Because the Israelis were so late the gurls had to eat the *merienda* themselves and thus had nothing for us; not being able to provide even a snack for us was shameful for them. Moreover, because they had spent money for that, they had nothing left for their own dinner, so went to bed hungry. Of course the Israelis had no idea this was happening because they were so insensitive to what was going on around them.

8. Next, having arrived late, out jumps the Israeli team with cameras and gear, barging into the community, without even taking the time, as is customary, of meeting the gurls, their parents and kin, friends and neighbours. They just barged in with cameras blaring with full focus on what *they*

wanted, with no consideration of what the gurls wanted and required. If the Israeli team had even bothered to look at me and watch what I did they may have followed suit. I met the gurls and Melinda's father, gave them hugs, talked, gave them cigarettes, and strolled as a friend to their house, stopping to chat with neighbours. While the interviews were underway I talked to Mel's father, neighbours, etc, and had a few drinks with them, to build community rapport and goodwill, especially if something bad happened, as it eventually did.

In addition, the Israelis were so fucking selfish they could not even see that Melinda's father had given permission to use his house, interview his daughter, intrude into his life, and all he wanted was to show his pride and joy, his piggies. Why? Because he is the head of the household, he is the man, and raising pigs is a skill, and a source of income and his masculinity. But the Israelis couldn't even be bothered to spend 5 minutes acknowledging his self worth. Instead, by ignoring Melinda's father the Israelis simply made him look unimportant in the eyes of the community.

Nor were the Israelis even aware that Mel's mother was getting angry because they took so long interviewing the two gurls and thus kept Mel's mother out of her *own* home. In addition, the Israelis didn't even bother to offer Mel and Angela some small payment for the intrusion created.

The only reason Melinda agreed to allow the Israelis to go there was because Mel felt she had an obligation (*utang*) to *me*. John and I had gone there 2 days earlier, talked to the parents, neighbours and visited the piggery and praised the father. And the only reason I took the Israeli team there, even though 3 hours late, was because I had an obligation to Mel and her community; they were excited at the opportunity to show how they lived, to tell their stories, but which was totally ignored by the Israelis.

I also had an obligation to the gurls and their families and community. They met the Israelis because they trusted me. But because of the Israelis' lies, I betrayed their trust. These gurls welcomed us into their lives, experienced further deprivation in entertaining us, and yet the Israelis treated them, and John and I, with no understanding or sympathy.

9. As a result of the Israeli team barging into this community Mel's former boss got angry at her whole family; so the family's reputation and position became a problem. The boss told Mel to inform the Israelis that they cannot use any material they got from Mel. This is the only way she and her parents could regain some dignity in the community and rebuild trust, friendships and position.

Overall, I found the Israelis' behaviour and attitude disgustingly outrageous, selfish, insensitive and outright racist and arrogant. Further, the project was not only poorly conducted but also not thought out; the Israelis did no research about the culture, local politics, or possible effects.

It is a warning for academics to not work with or trust the media. As I said to Ms. N., "*You ain't seen angry yet, and we are well past Plan B.*"

The irony of the Israelis' insensitivity is that I have ended up presenting, as much as possible in their own voices, the *true* story of Filipina ACMs, and doing an exposé of how bad the Israelis treated their seduced informants.

The only good thing as far as I am concerned that came out of this mess was that I met several nice girls and their families, who I am subsequently able and willing to help. What have the Israelis done for them?—Fucking nothing, other than create problems for them!

So what do we mean by "Mr. Big"? Someone who is "big", powerful or wealthy enough to exercise power over underlings, the poor and down trodden. So isn't Mr. Big the Israelis…?

Personally, I always find it amazing how Israelis treat disrespectfully others; given their own history of persecution one would think they would be sympathetic to others in similar situations.

PART 2

THE WORK OF ACMS
—explanations, questions, comments and responses

Preamble:

In 2013-14 I published a paper, *Noli me Tangere* (Touch me not): *When is sex-work not sex-work?*, with John Escobar and Louie Navarro,[14] in *Sabangan* (Crossroads), a new Journal of the Women's University of the Philippines. The paper drew heavily on my 2010 book, although some new material was incorporated. This inaugural Issue of *Sabangan* was structured by presenting our paper, followed by six commentaries by various pertinent scholarly reviewers, and subsequently our responses to those comments.

Here, in this section, I will present a condensed version of that paper, so as to not repeat what has previously been written, and several of the more pertinent comments and replies, not as a defence of my work on ACMs, but as a means of structuring some of the very important issues the reviewers raised and some of which this *current* book has attempted to address, or which require further elaboration.

The basic argument of that paper was that ACMs are commonly construed as trafficked pornographers, exhibitionists, strippers, or as (digital) prostitutes. But the gurls themselves do not necessarily identify their work as prostitution or, more broadly, as another form of sex-work. Certainly they do not consider themselves to be trafficked. Our focus in the paper was on the gurls' denial of their work as sex-work—now a very problematic argument given the preceding accounts herein by several ACMs. We also focused on their agency—their choice to enter this profession as a form of work, within structural restraints. We thus *explored* how ACM-ing as a form of cybersex extends

100

our understanding of sex-work, and challenges popular and political notions of non-agency. We also addressed, briefly, the problems associated with using internet communication technologies (ICTs) as a tool in research.

It was essentially a first foray into this topic area, and in our haste to report our findings, thoughts and the issues we do not deny overlooking both empirical and theoretical aspects, as well as legal issues. We make no apology for such omissions or commissions, as we wanted to get this topic and the problems it threw up into the public domain.

~

Introduction (to *Noli me Tangere* (Touch me not): *When is sex-work not sex-work?*)

Sex-work has principally been of interest to researchers usually in the context of public health, sexual exploitation, trafficking, or eradication policies. A great volume of research on sex-work has focused on socio-economic and sexual inequality or psychological factors as root causes of sex-work (cf. Weldon, 2006; O'Neil, 1997), or with sex trafficking. Much of the latter draws on the notion of impoverished third world girls being coerced by one means or another into some form of sex-work, while the former approaches equally posit the taking up of sex-work as somehow related to disadvantaged conditions or personal attributes. These dominant discourses emphasize poverty, inequality and exploitation as the main features of sex-work. Economics of course plays a role in sex-workers' entry to the industry and their continuation of sex-work (Benoit & Millar, 2001; McKeganey, 2006; O'Neill & Campbell, 2006; Willman-Navarro, 2006). Clearly, sex-work is an income-generating activity. Therefore, economic analysis could provide a useful tool for examining sex-work and the various types of economic incentives that may be determinants. However, prejudices are common in such studies on sex-work, with a bias towards supply-based analyses that tend to focus on how economic conditions push and pull people into sex-work.

Such an economic-agency bent presupposes that sex-workers are not only rational beings, as they are, but also economic ones; in this way sex-work resembles other forms of market-based work. Several autobiographies by sex-workers also tend to follow the same socio-economic discourses and thus lend credence to such views.[15] Sex-workers undertake their activity for some kind of remuneration, regardless of how important that may be for taking up the activity; that much we know. But what we are often left with is anecdotal evidence of how much sex-workers earn and thus why, implicitly at least, they engage in sex-work, and hence we are left with a purely economic rationale. In short, such studies document the obvious and appeal to the popular, or to the morality-laden situational exploitation that supposedly occurs among sex-workers.

Hence, sex-work is founded on economic necessity, like all work, but moralized by some sleight of hand. Within these discourses it is assumed that necessity rather than choice is the key determinant for women, and especially third world women; it is suggestive that Filipinas cannot make a rational choice because they have limited education, or are somehow irrational, psychologically disturbed, situationally coerced, or structurally constrained.

Agustin, however, in her various writings argues that, although women take up sex-work for the money or because of a lack of alternatives for them, they do so by and large consciously, making the choice to do so, and with the ultimate goal of supporting a family, saving for the future, etc. For Agustin, however, agency is more than economic decision-making; is also about identifying, determining, who I am.

Overall, the abundance of sex-work studies falls within a dichotomy of coercion/necessity/morality versus agency. In other words, whatever the reason people become sex-workers, they are deemed morally if not otherwise exploited, and thus we have the traditionalist view of morality and economic necessity vis-à-vis sex-work as another form of work, but always with a sense of unease that it is a different kind of work—a sense driven by some notion of desperation and/or immorality, rather than using the best of one's expertise (cf. Holden, 2005; Bernstein, 2007.)

In contrast to the plethora of scholarship on prostitution and other forms of sex-work, there is no academic literature on ACMs, other than my own (Mathews, 2010; cf. Senft, 2008, who has barely 2 pages of snippets in her book that deal specifically with paid sites like *AsianPlaymates*). Thus it is necessary to draw upon other literature on the diversification of types and changing views of what sex-work is.

While the ACM industry affords opportunity to explore several issues, it also problematizes the nature of sex-work because it is virtual and hence mediated, and many ACMs with whom we spoke did not identify ACM-ing as sex-work. Filipina ACMs can largely fit Agustin's model, in that they voluntarily decide to take up the work and for clear and often noble economic reasons, as well as incorporating the idea that agency is a determinant of whom they are; but they also differ, in that the determination of Self does not include a notion of their work as sex. The mediation of technology helps in this determination. Whereas some women enact agency by professionalizing their work and sense of self (Bernstein, 2007), Filipinas enact agency by technologizing their work and determining their self as separate from what others perceive as sex and thus who they are.[16] As Pertierra (2003: 2) points out, new technologies and their potential remains an open possibility. The new ACM "cottage industry" uses the new digital technology to sexually connect the local and the global economies (glocalization). This deployment, and indeed appropriation of 21st century technology, has effected changes in sexual cultures, identities and the meaning of commoditization.

Thus in what follows, we outline our methodology, then provide a brief contextual introduction to ACMs, how the ACM industry works and its system of piece-rate payments. The following sections then explore how ACMs identity their activity as work, what constitutes sex-work, and the issues of agency and trafficking. The paper draws on my previous 2010 publication, as well as on-line discussions and off-line interviews after its publication from mid 2010 to 2014.

Methodology

Taking the view that research is not about toeing the line, but about knowing where the line is and daring to cross it, this study was based, initially, on one "chat-room" (ACM) site, *AsianPlaymates*. I also visited several similar sites run by other companies.

The initial phase of the study involved becoming familiar with the site as a guest; subsequently I registered with my own logon name, initially mostly observing and reading dialogues on the site. I spent several weeks familiarizing myself with the site before I began to engage more with the ACMs and their customers, and subsequently ask questions of the ACMs and engage in public dialogues. This stage was necessary to enable me to understand how the site functioned, to see the range of activities and interactions taking place there, and experience what it was like to be a participant in the site. It allowed me to study the site's organization—its format, publicly accessible profiles, monitoring systems, forms of public exchange and so on.

The second phase of the study—participant observation, or "participant-experiencer" (Walstrom, 2004a; 2004b)— allowed me to engage with users and extend my knowledge of the site and its use. The use of the term "experiencer" rather than "observer" is helpful because on-line there may be no or limited opportunity to directly observe some of the other participants; the researcher can, however, experience what it is like to participate in the interactions by reading and posting messages accordingly (Garcia, Standlee, Bechkoff & Cui, 2009: 58).

In this phase I responded to users, raised issues and questions, and, occasionally, when there were only myself and one or two other customers on-line, I tried to engage in one-to-one discussions. This stage of the research allowed me to experience communicating *within* the environment. I found that many of the ACMs and customers with whom I tried to communicate about the site or about themselves were reluctant to do so.

To *customers* I never revealed my identity as a researcher, as it was evident that the underlying facets of the site were not only its anonymity but also its sexuality and entertainment. Rather, when it was possible I slipped into the general chat some innocuous questions such as where they lived (although this was often offered by customers when the ACM asked), how long they had visited the site, their job, etc.

To some of the ACMs with whom I became familiar I *did* reveal my identity as a researcher, and raised the possibility of my doing research on their activities. Some agreed to meet in person at a later stage for an interview, but generally most were disinterested.

The obvious trickiness of conducting research in sexually charged environments made this project difficult to navigate, not least of which were moral and ethical concerns. In particular, this piece of research involved being on a sex site for the ostensible purpose of engaging in sex, and involved talking to participants in an atmosphere where talk is often explicitly sexual, and indeed functions as sex. In conjunction with this was the problem of language, and thus the study opened up all kinds of potential for mis-communication.

Another particular difficulty was how to approach site users. Both ACMs and customers were clearly at work or play, respectively, and thus engaging them without causing offence or irritation or detracting from the ACMs' prospect to earn an income was at times difficult. Equally so was how to steer a respectful and ethical way through exchanges which might be read as (potential) sexual encounters by participants.

Maintaining a strong sense of detachment and researcher identity during the very lengthy periods I spent on the site and during sometimes rather intimate exchanges was also difficult. I engaged in, and felt that I must engage in, a level of empathy as a human, and contrary to the persona of pure researcher—if there can be such a thing. On several occasions I found myself presented with visibly distraught ACMs who merely wanted consoling and counseling, a friend to talk to, and perhaps some recognition of them as people rather than sex objects. On this basis I became friends with several young gurls.[17]

The third phase of the study was no less problematic: of finally meeting face-to-face (or in "real") some of the ACMs with whom I had arranged interviews, accessing their studios, assuring them and their bosses of my benign intentions and of my moral neutrality, and that no legal problems would ensue. It was at this point that my co-authors and researchers facilitated interviews, data collection and engaged in fruitful discussions.

Despite the numerous difficulties encountered, we collected some valuable and detailed information, insofar it at least provided a starting point for more substantial research.

To this point I might be accused simply of voyeurism, and that "real" research requires face-to-face interviews and real-time observation. I make no apologies for what may appear to be a voyeuristic approach; the very nature of the ACM business in fact requires some degree of engagement with voyeurism, or the appearance of voyeurism. But the same could also be said of research into prostitution, strippers or pornography (cf. Frank, 2007), or even secret/sexual rituals. However, this apparent voyeurism has been tempered to some extent by sustained contact with particular ACMs over 12 months;[18] and, by using the very medium by which they operate, I have achieved some kind of "interview" with several of them. Although these were often achieved on a piece-bit basis, essentially this is no different from ethnographies based on fieldwork in which conversations occur over time and knowledge is increment-ally accumulated. Indeed, given changing circumstances and technology, one could argue that internet-interviewing, as I undertook, is as valid (cf. Attwood, 2009). Indeed, "virtual reality" is not a reality separate from other aspects of human action and experience, but rather a part of it (Garcia et al, 2009: 54).

Of course, technologically mediated environments may profoundly change the nature of the information obtained through participant-observation/experience research. Most computer-mediated communication (CMC) research has a textual bias, focusing on the written word rather than on the full range of modalities available, although visual, aural and kinetic aspects of CMC may be integrated into online environments (ibid: 61), as is the case with ACM-ing.

In offline participant-observation, ethnographers routine-ly experience and analyze participants' verbal messages in conjunction with their facial expressions, tone of voice and body language, along with the impression given by participants' appearance, clothing, and setting. Online netographers, too, also need to integrate visual aspects of their interactions into their observations and analysis and to treat visual data (eg. the use of backdrops, colours, teddy bears and dolls, clothing or, in the case of ACMs, *lack* of clothing) as important aspects of the online location, interaction, and the participant's self identity. This may require developing a new set of skills and data collection methods (ibid: 62).

Clearly, the methodology I employed—variously dubbed nethography, nethnography, netnography or netography—does have certain limitations. But within a preliminary study of the issues, such a deficiency in methodology does not constitute an apology, but rather a call for further research and the refinement of appropriate methods.[19]

Working Gurls

In accessing the *AsianPlaymates* site the client can log-on as a "guest" or register for free with a User/Screen name (eg. *fireman, guiterman, sinlover, bigdick, hornyguy*). He can adopt any persona, age, status, nationality or even gender that he wishes, and can operate under several log-on names, free to randomly or selectively click on any gurl's picture.

Page one subsequently displays hundreds of photos of Filipina gurls of various ages, in different poses, each with their own screen name, as we have seen. These photos and accompanying screen names usually depict a single gurl in each frame. The gurls adopt screen names that range from the innocuous—such as *SweetChelsea, Angelface, Wicked-Angel, SinBabe, Digital Miss*—to the outrageous: *PinaySlut, LetMeBeyur_Slut*. Many of them include the number 69 in their screen name (eg. *Sexilicious69*), while many others include the word "fetish" (eg. *FetishSlut* or *CumFetish*) or "Sweet" (eg. *SweetAngel*), and we counted 98 screen names that included "hot" (eg. *HotPinay*), and 87 with "4U" (eg. *Sexygurl4U, xxcum4Uxx*). All these are designed to promote the sexuality of the gurls, to portray a willingness, in fact a *desire*, on their part to engage in and offer "sex", to provoke interest as much as their portfolio photos may do so. They are designed to provoke the customers' imagination and fantasy. The site is open 24/7.

Welcome to my room...

On this first page of the site a customer clicks on a gurl's picture, which takes him[20] to that particular gurl's "studio" or "room". One then encounters the gurl herself, live, on camera (cam), in a public arena which displays the screen names of all customers who are logged on to that particular gurl, and their conversations with her and other clientele.[21] While the client can see the gurl, she may not be able to see the client; this depends on his technology.[22] At this point the gurl will often initiate a somewhat standard conversation, using cyber-text, greeting the clients (*hi, ntmu,* [23] or *welcome to my room*), asking his country of origin, age, marital status, name, etc. One's chat with the ACM may be interspersed by conversations with several other clients, and therefore can be confusing at times as to whom the ACM is addressing her questions or remarks.

As a client, you are not the only one viewing this particular gurl; [24] depending on her popularity, there may be two, three or many other clients simultaneously viewing her, whose screen names and comments one can view, and with whom, as a client yourself, you can textually converse. Some of the clients may bombard this gurl with comments, questions, suggestions and commands of any description; others may remain quiet. Often there is pressure on the gurl to reveal more of her body for at least a partial "free show". Common also are abusive, denigrating and quite naïve remarks, and sexual suggestions and references.

As clients view and chat with the gurl, she simultaneously may be chatting with clients on a second and even third site, or on the same site under a different screen name, as well as via Yahoo Messenger (YM), having given her Yahoo address to selected clients. Thus a visual observation of the gurl's eyes and other body language quickly reveals she is skipping from one site, one conversation, to another.

Some of these gurls may, as part of their repertoire, or as a spontaneous enticement, or as succumbing to pressure as well as a need to attract clients, reveal various private parts of their body, engage in tantalizing sexy dances, or textual innuendos. Some routinely show their exposed breasts, while a few gurls, such as *Jazzy* and *Sheena*, may provide a "free show".

Paying for Prvt

If one takes a gurl "prvt", one pays with a credit card via the site. One then clicks on another hyperlink on the gurl's screen, which takes only the paying client and her into a prvt show. In my extensive conversations with ACMs they revealed that a paying client in a prvt show can direct the gurl to perform sexually, such as taking off her clothes, parading and dancing in front of the cam, laying down with close-ups of her vagina or breasts, posing in different positions, masturbating, or using a toy. Essentially, it is similar to having a prostitute in one's hotel room and commanding her to act out the client's desires; the only difference is the client cannot touch her (*noli me tangere*), and can only virtually communicate from a distance. Several of the gurls confirmed that, generally, they expect their paying clients to masturbate during a prvt show. When asked what they, the gurls will do, they said that they often chat to a potential client with assurances that she will make him cum, and that she will also cum.

The show may last from a few minutes to anything that the client is prepared to pay for. While a client or gurl may terminate the show at any time, the gurls will attempt to keep the client in prvt for as long as possible; the axiom that "time is money" is literally true in this situation. We have no certainty of how long a prvt show may last, in terms of average or range. A few gurls complained that clients had taken them prvt for only 7-10 minutes, saying the clients were *kuripot* (stingy). Other gurls reported prvt shows lasting 20 to 40 minutes.

Several gurls also informed us that many customers also engage in private Yahoo Messenger conversations with gurls. This enables gurls to bypass the 50% commission payments to the Company, and to establish a more personalized relationship with clients. Subsequently, gurls may ask the men, as "friends", to send them money or goods, or offer them an opportunity for a prvt show via Yahoo, paid in advance via WesternUnion or similar services.

Naked in a Nipa Hut: Studios and Sex

The gurls' prvt shows, and the public chats, all take place with the gurls located in "studio" settings. The ACMs draw on a wide range of settings, costumes, props and poses in constructing their displays. These vary from the very mundane—bare, brick and wood frame walls, unpainted and stained, poorly hung curtains, bare floor and worn cushions—to the elaborate bedroom suite with a façade backdrop, a neat bed and linen, and, almost invariably, a teddy bear or several.[25]

Example of a rather drab studio, with a poorly hung curtain.

Whatever the setting, most ACMs try to at least draw, to varying degrees of success, upon established signifiers of the erotic or the feminine (Kibby & Costello, 2001: 361): overall setting and backdrop, costumes, fancy or enticing bed, the invariable teddy bear or doll, and poses and actions elaborated for erotic purposes. They thus not only capitalize on their youth through use of the teddy bear as a prop, but also pander to customers' fantasies by projecting themselves as subservient, juvenile females who need care or mentoring.

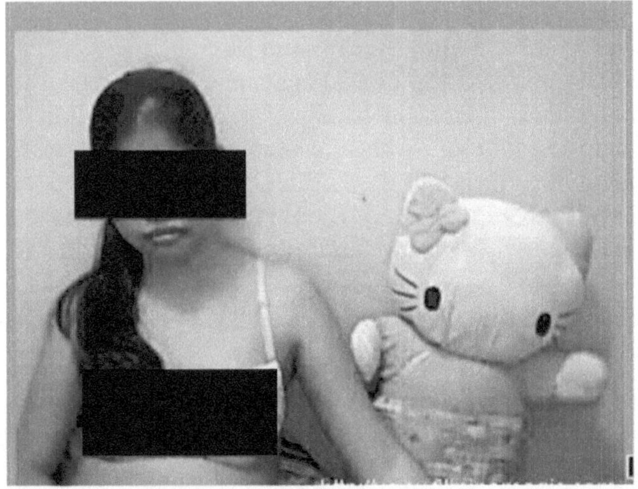

A plain studio, with, invariably, a teddy-bear/soft toy.

Another example of a rather plain studio.

An example of an elaborate studio.

A well decorated room with numerous teddy bears.

(The curtains, however, conceal rather dilapidated nipa walls. Indeed, the ornate presentation of this particular room, as with others that I have witnessed, belies the reality of their context. On cam one would never think that such a room was located in a very run-down nipa hut in a remote rural barangay (see the following picture), and of the ACM inhabitants as normal girls one sees in the streets, schools and malls). **[26]**

One cam gurl's house.

Another cam gurl's house, in a relocation settlement.

Some of these modest studios are just one of several in a house controlled by a boss; co-workers may be as little as 5 feet away. It is common to espy shadows of other people passing through, and even an actual person transiting the space; and it is common for the gurl to look at and talk to another person close by. In regard to privacy, particularly when a gurl is in a prvt show, naked and even masturbating, some gurls said they didn't mind, and indeed often a co-worker would use the keyboard while the ACM gurl on show would perform her sexual activities.

Other gurls, such as Chelsea, operated under slightly different arrangements. She worked from home, and her boss was her aunt. Her studio was in effect a well-decorated and neat bedroom of the household.

Chelsea's room.

While many of these gurls, by their own admission, were or had been sexually active, some also presented themselves, ostensibly, as virgins, and indeed a few of them perhaps were. Apart from declaring themselves as virgins, these gurls would refuse to insert even a digit into their vagina. This raises the possibility of one being a *virgin*, digital *prostitute*, if one were to think of ACMs as prostitutes.

It's a Job

"We are here for work, that's why I need prvt, to earn money", said Marylou, alias *virginpussy69*, *"....hope you understand how I sacrifice."* Marylou's insightful comment was in response to several potential customers looking at and talking to her on-line, but none of them taking her prvt. Slowly they dropped off-line, which left just her and I to talk. She complained that many customers come to her room for fun, but she was here "for work", implying that if the men were serious about having fun, they would take her prvt. Marylou it would seem had not yet fathomed the two sides of the same coin; just as a waitress or entertainer is "here for work", their work depends on the customers wanting—and having—fun. Marylou encapsulates, if not fully comprehends, that one person's fun involves another person's work, around which all of capitalism revolves.

But at the same time, her comments point to several issues easily overlooked. Foremost is that ACM-ing is work, it's a job, just as many (other?) sex-workers would call their activities work, and which they take seriously. Marylou was in fact visibly annoyed not just by this apparent contradiction, but more so by the fact that the fun-makers did not take her work, and hence her and her efforts, seriously. What she highlights is that clients seem to go for girls who seem to be "having fun" and enjoying themselves, such as *Jazzy*, which contrasts to how these "working gurls" consider ACM-ing as a job like any other.

Secondly, Marylou finally asked me, *"What about you? You wanna take me prvt?"* When I told her no, that, as with other ACMs, I just wanted to be friends, she was puzzled. Rightly so, because she was in her studio to work and earn money; what did friendship have to do with it? Friendship meant entering into her non-work life, somehow connecting the two worlds of work and non-work. But Marylou was here for work; I was simply a customer, not a friend; and if I were to become a friend it would blur her two worlds, her two identities.

Clearly not all ACMs are like Marylou. Chelsea, for example, took a different approach and clearly cultivated the kind of friendly relations that not only could potentially lead to something which would improve her life, and life chances, but which also personalized her work as non-sexual by engaging in and putting effort into emotional labour (Hochschild, 1983). By this means, like other sex-workers in the Philippines (Mathews, 1987) Chelsea employed various strategies to develop more personalized relationships with clients. Thus, rather than performing as a passive object for the consumption of others, she demanded recognition as a living subject (Senft, 2008: 5), and hence engaged in more personal relationships.

To paraphrase Schweitzer (2000: 74), somehow Chelsea, as with other ACMs, intuitively recognized that she is both the "lived" body of the self and the "object" body seen by the other. When the client empathized with the performing ACM, with the "lived" body, the relationship became more than just money for genitalia. In that case, it became an aesthetic experience, about an appreciation of the perform-ance, about an appreciation of the creation of the "object" body. However, when all the client notices is the "object" body, without any understanding of or engagement with the "lived" body creating it, then the performance becomes little more than an economic transaction, where dollars equal performance.

Thus the gurls may attempt to de-objectify themselves, often romanticizing or normalizing their activity and building dialogical relationships with clients, which helps to de-identify their work as sex, and themselves as sex-workers. Rather, their self is constructed as a performing self, as a worker, or as a friend. Just as girls who went to Japan called themselves "entertainers", ACMs call them-selves performers and, as noted previously, employ choreo-graphies, settings and strategies to enable their performance.

In other words, their work does not determine *who* they are.

Avril (alias Ann), too, did not identify her work as sexual, but as entrepreneurial. She worked for her aunt and we were welcomed into her home and allowed to see her studio, and we met co-workers and several other members of the household; it was all presented as a place and form of work and of real, ordinary people.

Similarly, we met 18 year old Carla in Manila; she was accompanied by her two aunts, who explained that Carla's boss was another aunt and that her mother knew of Carla's activities. They reasoned that it was better for Carla to be an ACM than hang about the streets with boys and do nothing but flirt. They readily perceived Carla's potential clandestine activities as sex, or even sex-work; but they perceived ACM-ing as a job, to keep her off the streets and away from sex.

Chelsea also worked as a manicurist, and saw her ACM work simply as yet another "side line". *GurlofyurDreams*, a veteran of ACM-ing for more than 5 years (and whose father was a lawyer), had once been a model and was currently studying veterinary science. She identified as many things, past and future, and blatantly insisted that ACM-ing was a job. Katrina, having been a private schoolteacher and now simply waiting for her public-school licence, said she was a teacher, and ACM-ing was a mere means to provide herself and family with income. Yet another gurl had been a sales-lady, while several other gurls were students. None of these gurls identified themselves as an ACM in terms of a core identity, but as a performance for money.

But it was a performance not just for the Other, the client, but perhaps as much for themselves. *Sheena* and *Jazzy*, for example, seemed to relish the attention that their sexual presentation provided them. Indeed, one ACM, *Crazy -Princess*, who was not initially popular, even commented with some apparent self-pleasure about how amazing it was that so many customers were looking at her. Others, such as *Gurlofurdreams*, a rather sassy and independent ACM, proclaimed openly in her portfolio pictures about how she felt about her self (eg. *I'm not conceited, I'm simply aware of my sexy lil self!* or: *I may not be your gurlfriend, but I'll fuck you until she arrives*). Even Chelsea, who, despite protestations of being "old" at age 27 and her self-acclaimed lack of beauty, was quietly pleased that her self was appreciated. Conversely, one ACM asked me if she was *panget* (ugly), explaining that perhaps it was because she was unattractive that clients did not visit her room. (I genuinely assured her that she was not unattractive).

Hugh-Jones, Gough and Littlewood (2005), in their study of female non-clinical exhibitionists, similarly found amongst their subjects that "*knowing that people enjoy looking at me makes me appreciate the way I look too*", and they, the audience, were "*really admiring me.... I accept the fact that women are sex objects, but to be admired also is a big bonus to my or anyone's self-esteem.*" What providing a fantasy to clientele does is to outline the ideas of attractiveness, which girls ultimately use to measure the social value of their inner selves.

Also prominent in their comments was their control of the situation: it is the very fact that a girl decides when, and to whom she exhibits that allows her to feel in a position of relative power. Here is not only agency to engage in such activities, but also to act within situations.

While we don't want to suggest that ACMs are exhibitionists, the fact that they *are* looked at, admired, and desired, as well as having *some* degree of control over whom they display themselves to, and how, can provide them with some self-pleasure and allow them to take some satisfaction in the attention they receive. In this sense, perhaps, ACM-ing can be personally and sexually liberating, while, paradoxically, also affirming sexual and gender inequality.[27]

When sex-work is not sex-work

GurlofyurDreams, Chelsea, *Avril*, Katrina, Carla, Marylou and many others we talked to insisted that ACM-ing was a job, and that they were not sex-workers or "loose" women (*puta*), and especially not prostitutes. A prostitute was narrowly conceived as a person who had a physical sexual relationship with a client, who paid specifically for the engagement. However, *puta* conveyed a broader notion of the Western idea of sex-work or promiscuity. The problem then lies in defining what "sexual" activity is sex-work.

When I asked some of these gurls why they did not work as night angels in bars or on the streets where they might earn more money, there was clear disdain for those women who did so. Many expressed the fact that stripping and/or masturbating for an unseen customer was ok, at least they didn't have to have sex with him (*noli me tangere*), or touch him. I once asked an ACM if she would be interviewed as part of this research and be in a documentary film; misunderstanding my explanation, she said no, "*I don't want to be in a porn movie because I'm not a prostitute.*" Yet, when we asked the views of non-ACM women about ACMs, they expressed disdain, commonly referring to them as *puta*.

If sex-work is defined simply as an exchange of money for sexual services, then we need to define what a "service" is and what is "sexual" about it. As common sense would tell us, what ACMs provide is something sexual, in the form of a presentation of their sexualized bodies, nudity, sexuality, for which they receive money; but they do not explicitly engage in a reciprocal, *tangible* sexual act. However, they *do* provide their sexualized body as a "service", although they are not physically present, and unable to be physically touched. Although I do not have to be physically present, or have any real-time contact with a client whose paper I am editing, I am providing a service, and thus I am an editor—or at least *performing* as an editor. Thus, based on this logic, ACMs do provide a service, one that is sexual because they do present and use their sexual being, in exchange for money, and therefore are sex-workers....so one would think.

But, do they "serve" *sexuality* to a customer, or merely (re)present it? Is this merely an issue of semantics? Does sex-work then require physical presence and/or contact? What role does technology play in this bridging, or un-bridging, of the physical with the image? While common sense might suggest that "real" prostitution requires physical presence and touch vis-à-vis the virtual, this risks contributing to the production of a sort of *false* intimacy. What makes something artificial or not "real"? The process of manufacturing it? The intermediation of technology? This line of reasoning implies a possible "natural" intimacy or realness. Rather, the disembodiment of intimacy, the unfolding of personal relationships in the absence of face to face interaction, suggest how it will be possible to be human and intimate in the 21st Century.

But then, what are the legal and other implications of accepting this virtual intimacy as real?—legislation, for example, would be able to legitimately categorize ACMs as prostitutes.

But, if ACMs constitute pornography as per the Philippine law RA9208 which refers to ACM-ing as internet *pornography*,[28] can these gurls also be, *simultaneously*, prostitutes? Is prostitution pornographic, given that pornography has "evolved from being the actions of prostitutes to the *depictions* of prostitutes" (Kibby & Costello, 2001: 357)? Or can pornography be construed as prostitution, or more broadly as sex-work?

No one would seriously consider a *Playboy* picture of a naked girl as prostitution; so what is the difference between a moving, real-time image on a screen, and a *Playboy* image? Yet, some of us might consider a girl who, in "real" life, strips off her clothes, dances, cavorts and caresses herself in front of another person, without any physical contact, in exchange for money, as a prostitute. Others may see her as a stripper. While in public discourse there is often a conflation of stripping and prostitution, empirically and legally, the two activities can be separated. For example, attempts were made in the 1970s to outlaw pornography in California by prosecuting porn stars for prostitution. The Courts made a legal distinction between someone who took part in a sexual relationship for money (prostitution) versus someone who took on the act of merely a *portraying* role, where a sexual relationship is engaged in as part of their acting. en.wikipedia.org/wiki/Pornographic_actor#Legal_challenges **[29]**

It would seem that, in California at least, for a sexual service to be construed as prostitution, it must be "real", unmediated, and involve some form of tangible sexual interaction, and, importantly sex must be sold directly rather than as a portrayal of sex, as ACM-ing may be construed. Yet, it would also seem, and perhaps common sense would tell us, that parading one's naked body on-line and/or with contortions of sexual activity to a stranger in exchange for money *is* sex-work, of *some* form.

However, most ACMs would deny that it is. When I asked *Avril* why she did not get another job, such as a bar girl, one that perhaps would give her a better income and security, she replied that she did not like bar girls (ie. the idea of being one) because she did not like to fuck with different men. She proceeded to explain that as an ACM it was ok for men to look at her but they could not touch or fuck her. Thus, for *Avril*, touching/fucking, *tangible* sex, constituted prostitution. But it was still not clear if the sexual display of her body also constituted prostitution or sex-work of another kind. Could there be *degrees* of prostitution, or other work that could be construed as sex-work? A "sexy" waitress in a skimpy skirt and bikini top that displays ample signs of her sexuality is a waitress; yet she could well be employed and attired accordingly to present and perform her sexuality as a promotional strategy. Is she a sex-worker?

What, then, does sex-work, and in particular prostitution, and the ACMs' display of their nudity, their sexuality, have in common that could possibly construe ACM-ing as sex-work? Beyond the simple definition provided above—as an exchange of money for sexual services—is the common element that money has been substituted for personal relationships (Schweitzer, 2000: 71), and it is only in personal relationships that sex, sexuality, sexual "services" are exchanged. Whereas prostitutes exchange their tangible sexuality for money, ACMs exchange their *intangible* sexuality, their nudity, their (moving) image, for money, and in both cases the money substitutes for normative personal relationships. However, as we have seen, Chelsea, *Avril, GurlofyurDreams* and others often did attempt to develop normative personal relationships with clients.

All this notwithstanding, so what if ACMs are prostitutes, pornographers or even strippers or exhibitionists? To even begin to try to define them under any of these categories is, firstly, to deny other possibilities; and secondly, it is to fall into the moralistic hetero-normative, public/private, Madonna/whore dualism that underpins most views of sexuality and sexual display.

The gurls' perceptions of cybersex-work are no doubt informed by such mainstream views of sex-work—ie. it is wrong, licentious, vulgar, depraved, disgraceful, and degrading, etc. It is a mainstream view that generally sees women subject to domination and exploitation in patriarchal culture. Thus women engaged in cybersex-work, even if they enter this work out of their own volition, are seen as victims of gender-based violence that is endemic in a society where women are systematically discriminated against, exploited, marginalized, oppressed and subordinated.

Our examples makes it clear that the primary motive for engaging in cybersex-work is financial. The decision to do so is a rational choice and un-coerced, made on the basis of weighing the pros and cons of this work, with the "pro" outweighing any of the "cons", particularly loss of dignity and self-respect, and internal conflict—which reflect the socialized mainstream views of sex, sexuality and women. The availability and use of ICTs may make this form of sex-work more acceptable to the worker, and the decision to engage in it an easier one—there is no physical contact with the customer, which impersonalizes the sexual acts; the customer's location is remote; it can be performed in the privacy of one's room, or the work can be accomplished in the presence of others performing the same or similar acts which serves to normalize it and endow the gurl that she is neither alone nor deviant. These facilitate detachment and protection from what may be considered the adverse physical and psychological effects of actual as opposed to virtual sex-work, and thus facilitate the denial of cybersex-work as non-sexual.

ICT takes sex-work to a different level, and makes cybersex-work what it is—performed in real time, remotely and impersonally. ICT obviates many of the undesirable aspects of actual sex-work such as physical contact and the risk of physical violence, sexually-transmitted diseases, and unwanted pregnancies; much of the emotional effects such as humiliation, stress, trauma, and anguish from the actual performance of sex acts; and the non-payment of fees. ICTs expedite contracting with customers literally on a 24/7 basis, and for the independent cybersex-worker they allow control over where, when, and how often she wants to work. If she is not pleased with a customer, she has the option to simply drop him. As in the foregoing case studies, ICT also allows the cybersex-worker to ask for money from regular customers without having to perform any sexual acts.

Further, it is not really a difficult job,[30] and it can pay well at times. Thus ICT makes virtual sex-work an attractive and tempting choice—and "choice", here, is the key word.

Trafficking ?

The United Nations defines human trafficking as the "recruitment, transportation, transfer, harbouring or receipt of persons, by means of the threat or use of force or other forms of coercion, of abduction, of fraud, of deception, of the abuse of power or of a position of vulnerability or of the giving or receiving of payments or benefits to achieve the consent of a person having control over another person, for the purpose of exploitation." (http://en.wikipedia.org/wiki/Human_trafficking)

But for ACMs, where is the recruitment, transportation, transfer, harbouring or receipt of persons by force, threat, deception, etc? Several of the ACMs we came to know ***willingly sought out*** such employment, were aware of the remuneration system, and were free to leave the employment. At worst, gurls who work as ACMs may be in positions of economic vulnerability; but so too is every piece-rate and wage-worker. Several ACMs we spoke to worked at home, or could return to their home province, or seek other employment. Where is *non*-choice in all this? And where is the "slavery" or "forced labour" if the ACMs are getting paid? And where is the "prostitution", or even the "pornography" which Philippine law has not yet clearly defined? **[31]**

The Philippines' media, moralists and legal authorities have of course made much of ACMs, branding ACM-ing as cybersex, as sex, and connect this within traditional discourses as sexual exploitation. There is little point in belabouring a debate with the moralists, to whom the media subscribe, as it would simply replicate previous controversies about prostitution, child sexuality, pornography, sex tourism, "mail-order" brides, overseas workers, and the like. But what *is* worth noting, and critiquing, is the discourse and tenuous position of the legislation about "trafficking" and "prostitution", as a 2009 newspaper report illustrates:

"The reason why the models usually allow *themselves to be trafficked in the Internet for cyber sex is because they don't have alternatives", a police informant said. "A lot of the kids should be in school, but they don't have the money.*

They are pitiful. During raids, you discover that they are actually on drugs. It's the only way they can do cyber sex," *he says.* (Our emphasis).

Here the discourse moves in two directions: first the police officer indicates that the ACMs "allow" themselves to be trafficked—and of course trafficking equals prostitution; what else could it mean? But choice is not part of the definition of "trafficking", so how can these gurls be "trafficked"? Second, he now links ACM-ing with another crime, drug use, as if to say, as in the classical discourse about prostitutes, that the two go hand in hand, and indeed is suggestive of the view that one would never be a prostitute by choice but only because of, or linked with, drugs—assuming ACM-ing *is* prostitution. There is simply no sense of agency in these associations, other than the contradiction the good constable slips in by stating the models "allow" themselves to be trafficked. And of course they could not possibly show, or want to show, their bodies if they were not on drugs.

Contrary to these discourses is that ACM-ing is a freely-chosen occupation, even if the decision is constrained by structural economic alternatives—as all employment is. Certainly alternatives do exist, even if they are not as financially rewarding as cybersex-work, as millions of low-income women in other forms of informal sector employ-ment in the Philippines are testament.

The free, rational and un-coerced nature of the choice of low-income women to engage in cybersex-work forms the crux of the assertion that it is an act of agency, to achieve valued ends (Sen, 1999, in Gasper and van Staveren, 2005: 139), as identified and appraised by the individuals them-selves—most often to help their families. Sen considers "agency as the ability to set and pursue one's own goals and interests, of which the pursuit of one's well-being may be only one" (Peter, 2005: 19). This conception of agency and personal development is one of freedom—the expansion of choices, the freedom of individuals to do or to be, and to live the life that she values or has reason to value.

In facilitating cybersex-work, ICT expands the choices of low-income women, endowing them with the freedom to engage in this form of work, if they so desire, expanding their capability, the possibilities of "alternative lives", and the range of their freedoms (Gasper and van Staveren, 2005: 142). ICT has promoted a capacity for agency, a capacity to earn an income, which in turn enables the gurls to contribute to family expenses and to spend on herself, which are themselves freedoms. Indeed, in the case of cybersex-work, the ability to set and pursue the goal and interest of making money and the imperative of earning an income are privileged over and above how the means to achieve this may impinge on one's subjective well-being and sense of self.

A cybersex-worker's agency is concretely exercised in her entering into cybersex employment. The act itself is a product of her deliberations and negotiations with herself. This dynamic is found in the case studies. While the gurls may realize the economic empowerment that can be had from cybersex-work and the sense of freedom derived from the exercise of their agency through participation in this form of employment, at the same time, gurls may interrogate what their aims are, and vacillate between, on the one hand, how the work is degrading, and, on the other, how it does not touch the core of her being and how the person in front of the camera is not who she really is (*noli me tangere*). A denial of cybersex-work as sexual work because it is remote, intangible and impersonal, facilitates her ability to reconcile these.

Conclusion

We find a certain irony in that cutting edge technology of the 21st century, so essential for and indeed a product of modern capitalism, and potentially liberating, may create and facilitate a system of work that may be experienced as exploitative. But is it indeed experienced as such?

Being an ACM opens doors to gurls who are not, or do not want to be, prostitutes (in the classical, non-virtual sense) but who otherwise do not readily have many employment prospects. Indeed, if we are to agree that sex-work is work, and consider what may be poor/better/best work for young unskilled girls, then prostitution may well be better, at least in terms of providing more money, excitement, opportunity to travel or to meet a foreigner who may be a future spouse, and the gurls may have almost no direct supervision; but it comes at moral, social and possible health costs. Perhaps then what is "best" is being a digital "sex-worker", but without many of the risks of prostitution. These gurls perceive ACM-ing as an opportunity to work, and often at their own tempo, and without such risks.

Thus we have tried to portray not just how this industry works, and these gurls work, in a social and economic sense, but also sexually. While these gurls mostly present their sexualized bodies as products, largely they are not necessarily uncomfortable with this. They are "born" with a beautiful body, as *GurlofurDreams* noted, and work within a society that is globally recognized as erotic, and that places a good deal of emphasis on beauty and erotic capital, for whatever purpose. These ACMs, as women, consciously, socially, take advantage of those facts. They see their activities as work, as employing the only "assets" that they have, and may ever have. Certainly one could argue that, if these gurls had an education, skills and expertise, they would have more options (cf. Bernstein, 2007). That cannot be denied. But clearly some do have those advantageous characteristics, as the brief citations indicate: school teacher, salesgirl, manicurist, student, etc. Yet they choose, for one reason or another, to present their sexuality and to be paid for it.

They do not see themselves as sex-workers, and least as

prostitutes—and even if they did are we to condemn that as non-work? They perceive themselves as doing a job, as a performer, while also recognizing that middle class society at large disapproves of them. They attempt to negotiate a middle path, employing an unspoken discourse of represent-ation of sexuality, between women as sexually desired personae and crass tangibility. For them, sex is still real; the virtual is symbolic, unreal, untouchable—contrary to those authorities that conflate the two.

These gurls are not trafficked. They do not fear bosses, traffickers or slavers, but in fact fear the police. They are trying to earn a living using glocalized technology, against which there was, until recently, no existing law. Yet, for reasons to be fathomed, police occasionally raided these "dens of iniquity" and confiscated the capital, asked for bribes, and harassed gurls and bosses. Their pretence was that ACMs were/are forced into "prostitution", are trafficked, are sex-slaves, and ultimately, if all else fails, that drugs or under-age girls are involved. Ironically, while customers could not touch ACMs, the police could.

What ACM-ing brings to the fore are several issues, as we have identified in this paper. In so doing, we have directed attention to a contemporary use of digital tech-nology that connects the local and global economies (glocalization), and which has effected changes in sexual cultures. In this endeavour, we have attempted to open up research in several interlinked areas—economics, labour relations, sexuality, agency, globalization, law, and digital technology—and which call for new research into this industry and new theorizing of and research methods into the issues to which ACM-ing gives rise.

References for this section:

Agustin, L. M. (2005). Sex at the Margins. Migration, labour
    Markets & the Rescue Industry. London/NY: Zed Bks.
Attwood, F. (2009). 'deepthroatfucker' and 'Discerning

Adonis': Men and Cybersex, International Journal of Cultural Studies, 12(3): 279-294.

Benoit, C. & Millar, A. (2001). Dispelling Myths and Understanding Realities: Working Conditions, Health Status, and Exiting Experiences of Sex Workers. British Columbia, Victoria University.

Bernstein, E. (2007). Sex-work for the Middle Classes, Sexualities, 10(4): 473–488.

Frank, K. (2007). Thinking Critically about Strip Club Research, Sexualities, 10(4): 501-517.

Gasper, D. and van Staveren, I. (2005). "Development as Freedom – and as What Else", in B. Agarwal, J. Humphries and I. Robeyns (eds). Amartya Sen's Work and Ideas, pp. 139-163. Oxon: Routledge.

Garcia, A. C., Standlee, A. I, Bechkoff, J. & Cui, Y. (2009). Ethnographic Approaches to the Internet and Computer-Mediated Communication, Journal of Contemporary Ethnography, 38(1): 52-84.

Hochschild, A. (1983). The Managed Heart: Commercialization of Human Feeling. Berkeley, CA: University of California Press.

Holden, K. (2005). In My Skin: A Memoir. Melbourne: Text Publishing Company.

Hugh-Jones, S., Gough, B. & Littlewood, A. (2005). Sexual Exhibitionism as "Sexuality and Individuality": A Critique of Psycho-Medical Discourse from the Perspectives of Women who Exhibit, Sexualities, 8(3): 259–281.

Kibby, M. & Costello, B. (2001). Between the Image and the Act: Interactive Sex Entertainment on the Internet, Sexualities, 4(3): 353-369.

Liepe-Levinson. K. (2002). Strip Show: Performances of Gender and Desire. NY: Routledge.

Mathews, P. W. (1987). Some Preliminary Observations of Male Prostitution in Manila, Philippine Sociological Review, 35(3-4): 55-74.

Mathews, P. W. (2010). Asian Cam Models: Digital Virtual Virgin Prostitutes ? Manila: Giraffe Books.

Mathews, P. W. (this MS). I'm a Cybersex Gurl, and I wanna tell u my story... Warrior Publishers. (http://warriorpublishers.yolasite.com)

McKeganey, N. (2006). "Street Prostitution in Scotland: The Views of Working Women." Drugs, Education, Prevention and Policy 13(2): 151-166.

O'Neill, M. (1997). "Prostitute Women Now", in G. Scambler & A. Scambler (eds). Rethinking Prostitution: Purchasing Sex in the 1990s. NY: Routledge.

O'Neill, M. & Campbell, R. (2006). "Street Sex Work and Local Communities: Creating Discursive Spaces for Genuine Consultation and Inclusion", in R. Campbell & M. O'Neill (eds). Sex Work Now. Cullompton, Devon, Willan.

Peter, F. (2005). "Gender and the Foundations of Social Choice: The Role of situated Agency", in B. Agarwal, J. Humphries and I. Robeyns (eds). Amartya Sen's Work and Ideas, pp. 15-34. Oxon: Routledge.

Pertierra, R. (2003). Foreword. Pilipinas #40. pp. 1-2.

Schweitzer, D. (2000). Striptease: the Art of Spectacle and Transgression, J of Popular Culture, 34(1): 65-75.

Sen, A. (1999). Development is Freedom. New York, NY: Anchor Books.

Senft, T. M. 2008. Camgirls: Celebrity & Community in the Age of Social Networks. NY: Peter Lang Publishing.

Walstrom, M. K. (2004a). "Ethics & engagement in communication scholarship: Analyzing public, online support groups as researcher/participant-experiencer", in E. A. Buchanan (ed). Virtual Research Ethics: Issues and Controversies. Hershey, PA: Information Science Publishing. pp. 174-202.

Walstrom, M. K. (2004b). "Seeing and sensing" online interaction: An interpretive interactionist approach to USENET support group research", in M. D. Johns, S.-

L. S. Chen, & G. J. Hall (eds). Online Social Research: Methods, Issues & Ethics. New York: Peter Lang. pp. 81-97.

Weldon, J. (2006). Show Me the Money: A Sex Worker Reflects on Research into the Sex Industry. Research for Sex Work. 9. pp. 12-15.

Willman-Navarro, A. (2006). Money and Sex. What Economics Should be Doing for Sex Work Research. Research for Sex Work. 9. pp. 18-21.

http://en.wikipedia.org/wiki/Pornographic_actor#Legal_cha llenges (accessed May 30, 2010).

http://en.wikipedia.org/ wiki/Human_trafficking (accessed March 3, 2010).

Responses to Reviewers of
"Noli me Tangere (Touch me not):
When is sex-work not sex-work?"
by Paul Mathews, John Escobar, and Louie Navarro,
published in *Sabangan* (February 2015).

As noted previously, there were several reviews of our paper, with useful comments, to which were responded. The original paper, reviewers' comments and our responses were published together in *Sabangan*. Here we reprint our responses to selected commentaries:

~

I begin my responses to the reviewers of our paper with a generous thank you for not only taking the time to read and comment on this work, but also for providing valuable insights and avenues for further research, and thereby engaging in this new field of research of which we know so little.

As I concluded in my book, *Asian Cam Models: Digital virtual virgin prostitutes?* (2010) and from which the current paper in part draws, despite limitations, "*my research is only* *a beginning, which will hopefully spur others to address yet another form of exploitation of labour, and possibly of sexuality (cf. Agustin 2005), through fieldwork & interviews —both of which present their own empirical and theoretical challenges. **Let us begin**.*"

That book failed to spur the engagement that this subject requires; indeed, in some cases I encountered quite open opposition or even hostility to my raising the issue of ACMs—and not least from Filipinas and Filipino media in Australia.

Given that literally nothing academic had been written about ACMs in the Philippines, as a new industry and as a personal phenomenon, my aim in publishing that book at that time, warts and all, was to put the ideas "out there". Ironically, having by chance come across this subject area, what struck me most was the economic relations of production vis-à-vis the gender/sexual aspects, although the two can be related. The irony is that much of what has been said in the critiques to which I now respond, and elsewhere, focus largely on those sexual/gender aspects. While this is certainly a valid focus, it, alas, for me at least, is at the cost of losing sight of wider, economic and structural issues.

An example is that many ACMs live and work in poor areas of the Philippines, many in relocation settlements. As we would all probably know, there is often no planning about such settlements, as in Carmona in the 1970-80s, and more recently in another region that for ethical and safety reasons I cannot name. They are areas that have few employment opportunities, few amenities apart from basic services at best, with small lots and houses that residents can buy from the government via an installment plan after meeting certain long-term residency requirements.

The few jobs that are available usually go to males. Perhaps a best option for residents, then, is to commute daily to a job in the nearest large town, which would cost them about 20-25% of their salary and require long, tiring hours of travel. Thus one can readily appreciate that the advent of ACM-ing is a boon, particularly for females, and most especially for single mothers who make up a significant proportion of ACMs. It provides employment, enables (primarily) *women* to work, and to work *at home*. (Single mothers in particular are able to work inside their own house, or nearby, take care of the children at the same time, and do other household chores—as Leanne and Cristy said). Nevertheless, even here exploitation occurs in the nature of piece-rates by which they are paid, whereby 75% of gross takings are extracted before the model receives what can be a mere pittance.

A street scene from a relocation settlement.
Several ACM's houses are located in similar streets.

Thus, in an attempt to continue to raise these issues of economic exploitation and hardship, along with related issues of sexuality and gender roles, globalization, glocalization, the impact and use of technology, agency, etc, the paper under review was placed to encapsulate and promote some of the main points in the book, to reach a wider audience, and to engage scholarship in the relevant issues.

It is with this purpose in mind that I welcome the reviewers' comments; to each one I respond generally, followed where I feel necessary with brief dot points to explain, develop or acknowledge issues. But it must be noted that some of the questions and comments assume immediate and comprehensive knowledge and information rather than what is at times a patchy and incremental collation and accumulation of data, which is still unfolding.

I thus present pertinent comments and responses in the order in which I received the reviews:

As the **first** review by **Neil Garcia** states, the paper complicates the interpretive task, and lays the groundwork for future studies, and it does so because the diverse factors that converge in the phenomenon of ACMs challenge "the paradigm that has governed much of the mainstream discussion of female sex workers".

Garcia's paper provides some very insightful comments, well articulated, that are worth republishing in full here:

I find this article...to be entirely fascinating and informative. While admittedly preliminary, the authors are able, for the most part, to ask the right kinds of questions, to complicate the interpretive task, and to lay the groundwork for future studies in this exciting area of research. The phenomenal rate at which information technology has penetrated the various strata and corners of the Philippines is indeed evident in the complex and astonishing ways that cybersex as a form of profitable somatized virtuality may be seen to have permeated the everyday lives of ordinary Filipinos (such as those women who work as Adult Cam Models).

The disjuncture or "lack of fit" between the idea and the practice, or the discourse and the performance, is easy enough to anticipate: despite its myopic conservatism, the paradigm that has governed much of the mainstream discussion of female sex workers in this country has, after all, been most keenly defined (and delimited) by the telling choice of terminology: Prostituted Women. Unlike in the Global North, countries in the Global South (to which the Philippines belongs) have generally not seen the "alternative" kind of feminist rethinking of the allied issues of prostitution and pornography—namely, that far from being self-evident, they are, at heart, fraught questions implicating the utterly important matter of female agency, and as such require serious and complicated unpacking. Instead, the kind of feminist position that has dictated the terms of the debate in the Philippines has tended to essentialize these issues as purely and simply oppressive and misogynistic.

The article, by highlighting the self-understanding of its Filipina respondents (who work as cybersex models) presents a powerful argument against this orthodox view, although we must remember that perhaps it may not unproblematically do that: remembering how it actually unfolded in the feminist history of other countries, the defense of prostitution or pornography as the defense of feminine agency (as such may be equated with freedom on the level of "fantasy life" and the "imagination") may need to be more appropriately made by Filipina women themselves, within the context of a social movement (or moment), and not through the agency of social scientists' gathered and interpolated data.

In other words, while in principle it will be easy to appreciate this article's demurral against the mainstream feminist morality that absolutizes the social evil of all sex work, the lessons of the crisis of representation do bid us to be somewhat more cautious, and to register our own misgivings about the possibly well-meaning project (at the same time that we make the improbable wish that it be the Filipina women themselves who would—hopefully, some day soon—collectively make a stand against this form of self-defeating oversimplification of what can only be an irreducibly complex reality).

I do, however, agree that this kind of "reading" needs to be made at this time, especially since cybersex represents a radically different realm of subjectivity and experience that does confound traditional models of understanding (of such issues as sexuality, gender, and even agency itself)... I do not find it incredible at the least that the respondents of this study perceive their work to be relatively personally innocuous, in light of the fact that recent events in Philippine mass media itself prove this to be so, after all: as Filipinos know only too well, the lives and careers of horrifically "scandalized" actresses (like Maricar Reyes and Katrina Halili) did not exactly suffer, despite the fact that their intensely incriminating sex videos turned viral for a time. Reflecting on this, we realize that it is the dromology of digitality itself that has made this otherwise unthinkable thing possible: not only the plenitude but the sheer velocity—the unbelievable turnover rate—of digital images renders them uniquely ephemeral (and in that sense, inconsequential), in the long haul.

Nonetheless, another perspective beckons: there will always be exceptions to any rule, and now and then we do hear of Filipinas suffering immensely, and sometimes killing themselves, after being "shamed" by a leaked sex video. Moreover, we cannot so easily celebrate the psychic and financial "affordances" of the glocal space that cybersex work inaugurates, since this arrangement is not entirely devoid of power relations: this is still clearly a helplessly transactional world, and as such we still need to be alert to the inequities attending this material "structure." While it may indeed be possible to analytically distinguish desire from need—and to champion the possibility that despite or precisely because of their neediness, the poor and the disenfranchised have desires, too—we also cannot afford to reduce the situation to the happy triumphalism of unbridled desire that the possibilities proffered by virtuality so seductively dangle before our fascinated gaze.

I will not repeat here Garcia's fine insights. However, while he suggests and perhaps holds hope of defense of feminine agency to be more appropriately made by Filipina women themselves, within the context of a social movement (or moment), and with which I agree, I see little chance for ACMs themselves taking up this moment, and perhaps even less chance of other Filipinas doing so given the very cold reception my 2010 book received. Short of that "moment", or perhaps as a spur to it, I have since interviewed several ACMs in 2014, and who have been keen to tell their stories in this book, in which I must, to some degree and of necessity, interpose.

I was—and am—not immune to the "crisis of representation", but given that at this time no one had spoken, at all, spurred me to speak to enable others to do so. I will not here belabour the further points that Garcia makes, for I wholeheartedly agree with them: that cybersex confounds traditional models of understanding, the role of technology in affording glocal/global space and voice and its down-sides, and the linkages between need and desire.

Overall, Garcia has encapsulated some of the key theoretical issues that my largely empirical paper, as a mere conduit of the lived experience of ACMs, presents. It is hoped that such analyses will be as challenging of conventional wisdom as they are challenging.

The **second** review by Joseph **Ryan Indon** is equally interesting. As with the other reviews, he raises some interesting points and avenues of research such as how law-enforcement institutions are constantly looking for new objects of control and discipline in order to justify their continued existence and authority, which strikes a cord with recent (2014) interviews with ACMs herein, who essentially said, "...*there are many girlie bars, why don't they raid them?*"

Another interesting point Indon raises, but which my writings to date have not even begun to unravel, is that the denial of ACMs' agency and the rules and laws enforced on these women are manifestations of the continuing *male-based disciplining* of women in society; meaning, women who moralize over women-who-sell-sex are themselves subscribing to a patriarchal discourse of the world.

Indon is right to say my paper lacks "description and exploration of agency among the ACMs" and that the "researchers then went on to stamp their theoretical interpretations...."

As noted in my introduction, the paper drew on my 2010 book, as well as a limited number of interviews. Method-ologically, there was little else to draw on in terms of how to conduct on-line research, what questions to ask on-line or "in real", or with vulnerable or marginalized populations—(I find the limited literature on the latter very PC)—and within various time and confidentiality constraints. Even in this current book, in which several ACMs *are* interviewed at length, it has been difficult to draw out what they really think and feel, without knowing and being with these models for a long time. Although this book hopes to achieve some of this rich description, there is, as I repeatedly assert, a long way to go.

Similar to Garcia, Indon understands the issue of "how technology is reordering social relationships, as well as re-defining activities such as sex-work." In this he encapsulates one of the critical issues, that has yet to be unpacked, and which our current paper could only touch upon.

Many people may condemn the newly accessible sexuality, while accepting the notion of intimacy as difficult and problematic, and of technology as enhancing con-venience and efficiency. It illustrates that what clients are really buying is a few minutes of human contact within a society where personal contact is fraught with difficulty and ambiguity, using technological innovation to reinvent or even discover intimacy. It illustrates how it may be possible to be human in the 21st century.

Following on from this, Indon also makes the point about how such technology has its down-sides, which ACMs perhaps have not considered. These are very valuable avenues of research.

Overall, Indon concurs with Garcia that "a more nuanced understanding of sex-work and agency, away from the predominant moral and sexist discourse," is a start, and this is exactly what the paper intended to initiate.

One last note, however, is that regarding the point of trafficking, which perhaps needs clarification. While I do agree some ACMs *may* be trafficked, my experience (and that of several colleagues who are also familiar with ACM sites) shows no evidence of this. It would be naïve to think, as Indon suggests, that ACMs are more controllable because they are on-line; the counter point would be that access to the internet by ACMs would enable them to more readily alert authorities to their plight. Frankly, I don't know—not surprisingly given that we know so little about the industry as a whole.

But if we are to talk about trafficking, then the recent expose (*Curse of Cybersex: The Lost Children of Cebu*, by Katrin Kuntz) of young boys and girls engaging in ACM-ing would suggest not so much trafficking, but social/kinship "persuasion" and cultural/filial obligations. Often when we think of trafficking we think of bad guys in black suits or pirate gear, but it may well be fruitful to consider how certain cultural values and relationships in Philippine society "encourage" youngsters to do what they must or should do to meet filial obligations. Jonaz is a case in point. At age 19, having just completed high school in a provincial barrio, she worked as an ACM 7 days a week—*as the sole breadwinner* for her family of seven. The immense obligation she felt toward her family overrode any notions of propriety or self. Melinda also exemplifies this: As Jonaz once said quite unequivocally, "Don't put me in a situation of having to choose between family and a boyfriend." Melinda had to choose and she chose family. So, who has power, control, exploitation of others? What kind of piracy or "trafficking" are we dealing with? And, of course, what kind of "agency"?

This is where research into ACMs opens up questions about and avenues for inquiry into underlying socio-cultural and economic factors that have hitherto remained largely unquestioned, unexplored. Thus while we may think of ACM-ing as a (*sexual*) phenomenon worth exploring in itself, I see it as one of opening up questions about other issues and social phenomena. Hence we have only just begun.**[32]**

The **third** review, by **Elinor May Cruz**, begins by noting the importance of the paper's contribution in giving some voice in the techno-legalistic and moral debate resulting in the Supreme Court's decision on cybercrime. While it may well be more difficult to reverse that decision in future without legitimating "sex" on cam, it is hoped that this current discussion, and this book that gives even louder voice to ACMs, will eventually prevail.

The review then focuses on the researchers' reflexivity. By way of explication, in the beginning there was no research design; the topic was stumbled upon, and my interest, as the lead researcher and author, was mostly on the work relations and economic conditions of ACM-ing. I spent more than 12 months on-line developing knowledge of the industry and some ACMs with whom I generated platonic relationships. There was nothing to guide how this kind of work could/should be carried out; and anyone who has spent hours and hours alone on-line doing anything remotely like this will know how grainy the objective/subjective divide becomes, and indeed how engagement can become even addictive. It raises the question of who is eligible to speak about these, if one has never been on such sites?

Overall, in the heat of discovery, the design, the methodology, the reflexivity evolved—and hence how we imagined the contribution of the research to knowledge production also evolved, keeping in mind that at the time the law on cyber "crime" was not yet finalized.

While there are texts that address certain aspects of research that are pertinent to this type of research, I also wonder how much the technology—the spatial distance bridged only by digits—which the gurls themselves use for their own purposes, affect the researcher?

One also has to take account that these gurls were at work when most of the interactions took place; it was difficult to not feel intrusive into both their time and space, and they had little reason to tolerate me as a researcher. This required developing a very long-term and subtle form of enquiry. As the reviewer suggests, this methodology itself needs an expansive enquiry and elaboration. We agree. But it is a topic area that would take up a good deal of space, and time, and my felt urgency was to get the topic of ACM-ing into wider circulation to counter what self-acclaimed do-gooder NGOs and the media often erroneously portray.

As with other reviewers' comments, Cruz notes that chat excerpts would indeed be insightful; unfortunately they were difficult if not impossible to get at the time. I hope this book goes some way in fulfilling that need.

As to being a white male, probably "the typical profile of an ACM customer", I have no doubt this affects information given and gathered, questions asked, perceptions and expect-ations on the part of both parties. But so too does being a female, or a Filipina, middle class, or of a particular age. We have only to think of what we may not have learnt since Margaret Mead in Samoa (cf. Bucerius, 2013).

While each of us is positioned, and position others, I

have found over 20 years that Filipinas are quite forthright in revealing their thoughts. More encouraging is that I find this trait even more so in the last 10years and am quite amazed at how articulate they are of their own views and their willingness—and right!—to question. This doesn't necessarily de-position participants, but may well show a resistance to being positioned, and an ability to (re)position others.

In the end, while the reviewer raises a valid point, it is an issue that has not been satisfactorily addressed, and indeed I often think this issue has been hijacked by female researchers or feminists. Put bluntly, women do not have a monopoly on researching sex, gender or women. I am readily reminded what different kind of answers Lisa Law or Nicole Constable or Rosemary Wiss may have got had they been males, and what interpretations may have ensued.

Regarding ethics, I was acutely aware of this issue, and had to decide what might need to be circumvented in order to convey the inside knowledge I obtained. What swayed me to present examples of studios and gurls was the fact that these images are not "readily accessible online" in the Philippines, and I argue it was important to provide a visualization of the settings. While trying to describe some of the interactions and to illustrate points not readily available to the audience, especially those within the Philippines, it was deemed necessary to present visual images of a new phenomenon, and the images themselves, as examples, are rightly texts of the phenomenon which need to be included in (further) analysis, as Cruz rightly points out.

I take the point that presenting some gurls may perpetuate or reinforce an objectification of them; what I wanted to show was the studios, and especially the teddies and other props, but this was not possible without including the gurl/s.

Regarding consent, this is a difficult issue that pertains to methodology not only for on-line research but any ethnography. How many of us have done fieldwork and obtained written informed consent from our participants?

One could argue that people who present themselves in the public domain to some extent leave themselves open to being accordingly portrayed. On the other hand, because they *are* vulnerable, greater care and respect should be afforded them. What I did to those whom I have used in the paper and book was reveal my self as a researcher and attempt to disguise the participants' identities as much as practicable.

I find it odd that the methods section appears defensive rather than explanatory. It was meant to convey the complexity and bewildering number of methodological and ethical issues that Cruz and others in fact raise, and in a very limited space, which were still being worked through. It was—and is—simply a work in progress. I do indeed find it a bit odd that the methodology is read as defensive, for as I say, "...within a *preliminary* study of the *issues*, such a deficiency in methodology does not constitute an apology, but rather a call for further research and the refinement of appropriate methods."

In her third section Cruz makes some very pertinent points, with which I largely agree. Of particular interest and value is the idea of touch, and Cruz is *very* much correct in raising the issue that touch is more than physical; it is indeed an area that requires a lot more exploration, which I had some difficulty in drawing out from my informants—even though I had found some Filipinas more forthcoming on other issues. However, having said that, in more my recent 2014 interviews with several male and female ACMs I did explore this to some extent; while some of them indicated the emotional aspect of being "touched" and touching, more pervasive was their dissociation of feelings from their actions; time and again their emphasis was on the work and especially the money, a separation of self from the performance:

Cristy: "We have dignity that at least a customer don't touch us. So, yes, we sell our body, yes, but no body can touch us."

Leanne: "It's ok for us to show ourselves,...."

Cristy: "It's really about making money and perform-ing..."

The ACMs didn't care about sexual slurs made by customers because their focus was very much on making money, so they ignored comments. What they were more concerned about was *others*—neighbours, NGOs, media, politicians, etc—making judgements about them and their work, not the racial, sexual, denigrating slurs made by customers, or having to expose their nakedness. Thus for them it was *others* who problematized their work and selves, it was *others* who "touched" them.

For example, I suggested to these interviewees that ACM-ing is not prostitution—because clients can't touch them, the gurl is not real, the "sex" is not real...?

Leanne: "For you [it's not prostitution], *but not for me."* (ie. for Leanne ACM-ing *is* prostitution).

Another ACM's foreign boyfriend had a problem with this idea of "touching", although the ACM assured him, *"it's ok, it's only work",* and thus she maintains her sense of self dignity.

Even when interviewing these ACMs I became aware that I was possibly problematizing something that was for them not there.

This is not to say that ACMs do not experience emotional or psychological or other forms of "touch", in the short or long term, but rather to say it is an area that requires a lot more in-depth enquiry. Certainly other researchers may adopt a "victim" perspective and focus on those gurls who, for whatever reason, present as traumatized—as the Israelis did. I was certainly not remiss in encountering some models who, one way or another, were affected; for example, one transgender worked for 12 hours and had no prvts, and was clearly very distraught—touched?

But I also hasten to add a caveat that, in pursuing this

issue, how much we, as middle-class and perhaps western/ized scholars might impose our own interpretations and expectations? While my more recent interviewees, in person, may have conveyed, or wanted to convey, that they are not "touched" by being an ACM, should we interpret this as true or as some kind of self denial—false consciousness? Simply, the evidence I have to date suggests the ACMs are not traumatized, or "touched", because of their work, but it is an issue worth pursuing *if* we can move from assuming that any gurl—ACM, porn actress, masseuse, bar-girl, prostitute, or other sex-worker—*must*, of necessity, experience some form of regret, remorse, guilt or other emotional turmoil. Or even if we are to collect empirical evidence, are we to be like the Israelis who were selective—indeed seeking out—those who suited *their/our* agenda?

Similarly, the point Cruz makes with respect to how technology enables "conditions of possibilities, of new forms of oppressions and negotiations" is also important. It is an arena that we are still developing, and that could not be done justice in the short paper we provided and which was not so much even developing ideas but asking questions. Hence, trying to unravel if ACM-ing was pornography, prostitution, stripping etc was not an assertion, but a presentation of different avenues and ideas for future contemplation. As I said in the beginning, the paper sought to ask questions, not answer them, to describe, not necessarily analyze. The same can be said about the questions of choice, of agency. What I was being told, what I saw, countered the mainstream, populist, feminist, NGO traditionalist view of coercive sexuality—normative views that Garcia in his comments so succinctly encaptures and challenges. If the paper "glosses" over these it is because the paper seeks to ask and provoke, to enquire and challenge, not answer. As Cruz states, there is a "voluminous amount of data to draw on what the ACMs have to say about their experiences in this largely unexplored phenomenon" which the current paper of some 20 pages could not possibly even scratch. Thus, because there was nothing beforehand on ACMs, other literature on pornography, prostitution/sex work or stripping and exhibitionism had to be trawled for some insightful hints and possible comparisons.

A few other points by way of explanation:

• That ACM work is "not really a difficult job", and that structural factors that give rise to ACM-ing are just some of the many issues to arise from the paper. Perhaps this should have been phrased to make it clear that I was referring to the physical exertion and work conditions vis-à-vis someone who, say, is street vending in hot weather, noisy traffic, encountering various physical dangers, etc. Gurls at least have some comfort sitting in an often air-con room, relatively quiet and clean. However, in rethinking this issue I have since noted—and concur with other comments re: emotional, psychological, legal and social aspects—that it is not as easy as it may first appear. While the creature comforts may be better than street vending, begging or scavenging, or being subject to incessant loud music and late/long hours in a bar, ACM-ing also has it drawbacks, not least of which are health issues: sitting/squatting all day possibly leading to obesity, long hours, eye strain, anxiety about meeting a quota, fear of police raids, neighbourhood gossip, abuse from customers, and so forth. Some of these issues were revisited in 2014 interviews, leading to some interesting if not contrary findings (although in 2010 I did note several difficulties), indicative of the reflexive and changing nature of research. Indeed, it was the very comments by reviewers and others who engage in this debate that led in part to further research such that, in this case, highlight the difficulty of the job:

They all agreed, it was not an easy job; they have to do what others want them to do, and "we get tired waiting for customers...It's just comfortable." Nevertheless, it's not really easy money because they have to work long hours, buy cosmetics, act/perform, people abuse them, they have to buy and wear sexy or good clothes, and they cannot work during menstruation. In addition, if the PC gets hot, as it tends to do in hot weather over a 12-hour period, then the connection and operation can be slow, and the PC may have to be shut down. Heavy rain can also interfere with the internet connections; and of course brown-outs make it totally impossible.

• In the same interviews with my 2014 participants the idea that ACM-ing was "better" than prostitution also is strongly reinforced. For example:

Leanne: "I'm a prostitute as well, but I'm the smarter one than the one working in a bar."

Q. So an ACM is a prostitute?

Leanne: "Yes but not as worse [bad] as working the bars."

But here a careful reading of the issue—that one form of sex worker is "better" than another—is not an assertion, but an exploration, a query: if we take a particular position, then what, perhaps, might follow…? There was never any intention—nor meaning—of promoting one form of sex work as better, but rather an attempt to explore the intricacies of what may be a hierarchy within sex-work and thus to understand how ACM-ing might fit into that.

• Cruz's comment re: "'so what if ACMs are prostitutes?' confounds the issue all the more" begs the response so aptly presented herein by Garcia: we need to question "the paradigm that has governed much of the mainstream discussion of female sex workers". We need to look beyond the moralistic hetero-normative, public/private, Madonna/whore dualism that underpins most views of sexuality and sexual display; we need to look at other possibilities, of sex-work as work, regardless of any hierarchy within or across sex-work generally. Having raised the issue of what might be perceived by the gurls as a "better" form of sex-work, it became readily apparent that such an exploration or analysis could fall too readily into the Madonna/whore dualism, and hence to break free of that the question is posed: does it really matter that ACMs are prostitutes or that even prostitutes are prostitutes? It only matters because we still subscribe to and theorize through the Madonna/whore image, and that sex-work cannot be "real" work.

The other interesting feature of this issue is that women (in this case ACMs) themselves are passing some kind of moralistic judgement on other women. So what was that which Indon referred to?...: The rules and laws enforced on these women are manifestations of the continuing *male-based disciplining* of women in society; meaning, women who moralize over women-who-sell-sex are themselves subscribing to a patriarchal discourse of the world.

As convoluted as it may seem, the obvious answer to this is that patriarchy (men of course) have constructed a world/discourse in such a way that even feminism is a diabolical plot (by men) in which women must/do operate, and/or that it is a conspiracy that distracts women (or feminisms) from the real issues, and thus allows men to pay lip service to "feminist" claims of equality while retaining intact their inner most thoughts that women are second class denizens. No doubt feminist reaction to this paragraph will be a false consciousness type of theorizing rather than a reflective look at the empirical reality. And, the reaction to this last sentence is that it is simply a means of deflecting attention away from both the reality and the theorizing. So how to win, and who can win, and should anyone win at all? What is to be won?

This is not to discount the empirical, social, political and humanitarian aspects that being a sex-worker entails. It's easy for us, as non-sex workers, to say that one's sexuality or sexual behaviour doesn't matter because we don't have to worry that our sexual behaviour will negatively impact upon our lives in the myriad of ways sex-workers experience every day. When we say that it doesn't matter, or so what if someone is a prostitute, we may be trying to be supportive, but of course it's not as simple as that. By dismissing the fears and anxieties of sex-workers, we show a lack of understanding about what they may face in their work and lives. *But*, if we continue to categorize and pathologize such workers in moralistic, medical or deviant terms, we perpetuate their outsider status. If we continue to theorize that it somehow *does* matter because we need to categorize, then we continue to focus on the sex and the sex-worker as deviant rather than the work conditions and the occupation as work. In other words, *"so what if ACMs are prostitutes?"* challenges us to normalize sex-work *as work*, to provide sex-work with an economic dimension, which, if achieved, might go a long way to removing those very fears and anxieties that sex-workers may experience.

• Similarly, Cruz draws on the title of my 2010 book's title, "digital prostitutes", which she claims casts ACMs as prostitutes. In line with the very bafflement and complexity of what I was uncovering in that pioneering work, I was asking a question, and hence the question mark (?) in the title: "Digital virtual virgin prostitutes?" Indeed, there are 26 questions marks in our brief paper, including the subtitle, indicative of the paper asking questions, exploring, not asserting, of opening up avenues of research, and hence the paper must be read in that way.

Thus, rather than claims, we present issues as possible contentions to be explored and substantiated (or not).

• Why most/all ACMs on this site are Filipinas is explained in the earlier book. One reason is because amongst Asian countries Filipinas speak English. It is ironic that that ability is a legacy of Western colonization, which possibly provided Filipinos to benefit from English education, but also left open the possibility of exploitation, as we may witness in the ACM phenomenon.[33]

• Cruz notes our comment: "They [ACMs] attempt to negotiate a middle path, employing an unspoken discourse of re-presentation of sexuality, between women as sexually desired personae and crass tangibility. For them, sex is still real; the virtual is symbolic, unreal, untouchable contrary to those authorities that conflate the two."

"Crass" in the sense that it precludes delicacy and discrimination. That is, the gurls recognize they are sexually desired, for their confronting physical attributes. But they steer a course between being acknowledged as women and performers vis-à-vis simply engaging in physical sex, which refers to a common and misconstrued discourse and perception that, because ACMs present their sexuality they are willing to engage in physical sexual relations for money, to be "touched" without delicacy or discrimination.

Overall, Cruz raises some very insightful points that I hope I have spurred. Many of the criticisms are valid, largely because in a short paper the issues could not be dealt with, even in the earlier book of 168 pages, because of the novelty of the topic area and research methodologies. If my responses seem defensive it is only because the paper must be read as an initial foray into unknown territory, and one that has few answers but rather raises more questions. If I were to take any one of the important and valid issues that Cruz raises or others raise, each would constitute a paper unto itself. That was not the purpose of the paper. The purpose was to provoke an open discussion of issues, and the responses by the reviewers would suggest that goal has been initially achieved.

The **fourth** review by **Cheryll Soriano** also provides some very valuable insights and questions, primarily about methodology and ethics. At this point in time I do not have the answers to complex ethical questions, which I agree need further consideration.

Thus, in response to a few points, I can offer only the following by way of explanation:

• More extensive discussion/thick description of what

the girls truly think about what they do, in their own words would be good.

I wholeheartedly agree with this, so much so that this very book will largely consist of interviews, off-line and verbatim. However, at the time of writing the paper (and the initial book) based on mainly on-line discussions it was difficult to get extensive detailed information, and to include any such descriptions in a short space would also be difficult. I hope to do justice to this issue in this book.

• That ACM-ing "does not touch their core being," is a very good point, which at the time I was at pains to try to explore with some ACMs on and off-line, and subsequently in 2014 interviews. As I have mentioned previously herein, four ACMs interviewed in 2014 emphasized that they manage well to separate performance from their off-line self, but also there was a hint that I was problematizing an issue that they either did not want problematized or that I was belabouring an issue that was not a problem, yet two of the interviewees also seemed to be aware it was a problem for them already:

Kate and Ken, who are married and work as a couple on the site, said: *"...it's really about making money and performing...doing what we would do anyway,"* yet they also asked that I not make any judgement against them for their work, and that other people make judgements about them and their work.

Thus, while they may assert ACM-ing does not "touch" them, there are also hints that it can or does. But, as noted before, it may not be the actual performance that touches them but the moral judgements made by others—which may also include their clientele, as well as their own moral regard (which we may have imposed or problematized, or they have developed in relation to Westernization); but we don't know as yet.

Indeed, Leanne begins to suggest as much in subsequent YM correspondence. As noted in an earlier transcript, she seems concerned about her kids seeing her naked and being a cam gurl (*"i cant even imagine my girls can see me naked on the room and asking me wat im doing"*), but then in the next comment reminds us of two, perhaps contrary, things: *"we're just doing cyber not (just) to be in bars and also a stepping stone to get out of that job"*; thus, even if her kids do see her as ACM-ing it's not as bad as being a prostitute in a bar. Thus she elevates herself above "real" prostitutes, and subsequently reinforces the notion that her ACM job is a stepping stone, as if to imply two things, however one may wish to interpret that:

1. unlike "real" prostitutes, ACM-ing is only a stepping stone, and

2. that being a stepping stone, it's a choice made toward an end and not an end in itself—which again implies that non-virtual prostitutes/sex-workers "somehow" undertake their work as a definitive career.

Nevertheless, part of this moralizing, perhaps self recrimination, is a realization of socio-moral pressure, that affects not only herself but perhaps also her family and kids: *"i cant even tell to people wat is my job...where i get money...i had many classmates now and their suspecting me...if the school know im a cyber girl...what will happen to me?..."*

On the other hand, are we to read this as a moralizing discourse or as a practical concern: that Leanne has few or no qualms about ACM-ing, but is concerned with how to circumvent or allay suspicions, in order to survive?—*"that y im looking for other things to do...to survive"*.

• As an adjunct to this, Soriano raises the question, "Do these cyber-identities differ from identities of those involved in physical sex work?" This is a very valuable area, which I began to pursue in my 2014 interviews, highlighted in part by the following transcript from two ACMs off-line:

Q. So what do you think of these massage girls [who execute lingham, ie. masturbation on men]?

Leanne: "It's the same..." [ie. they're prostitutes].

Q. But they actually touch the man's penis, then they say they are not prostitutes...

Cristy: "Still just the same. They are the kind of prostitute that don't admit they are."

Leanne: "They hide it."

Cristy: "They tell themselves it's therapy, but actually... it's undercover."

Q. But they have a certificate, saying they are trained, they're professionals...?

Cristy: "Yes, but underlying [it] they are some kind of prostitute."

One of the key questions posed in my paper was, in fact, are ACMs prostitutes, and if so or if not, how do they understand their position?

• A point for clarification re: conducting on-line interviews while posing as a client. While I did ask questions of ACMs at times without revealing my researcher status, these were often general questions that even non-researchers might ask, such as the gurl's age, home province, earnings, how long they had been an ACM, etc. For other gurls with whom I became more familiar and desired elaboration of their details, I did reveal that I was researching ACMs, and did explain the outcome of such research. That they continued to provide answers, discuss issues and, for some, agree to meet in person would reasonably imply they had given consent. However, because they were/are vulnerable, and may not be fully cognizant of the implications of participating, I took the responsibility of ensuring their anonymity and explaining my purpose.

• The discussion of control needs to be juxtaposed with the seeming lack of control in terms of the percentage of their earning vis-à-vis the site and their boss, and their conditions of work, etc.

With this I totally agree, and indeed it was this issue that initially inspired me to write about ACMs. I have written another paper addressing this issue. Again, given the limited space of a Journal paper it was not possible to include all issues.

• On more tricky technical issues, if any client can do a screen capture, does this not make the girls vulnerable and imply a lack of control?

Yes, it certainly does, and unfortunately most of the gurls are not aware that their rooms, performances and selves can be not only captured as screen shots, but also recorded as videos. (As an aside, customers who engage gurls in private chats/ performances and allow themselves to be on reciprocal cam, can also be recorded. *AsianPlaymates* has recently posted a warning to customers about this, but no such warning to the gurls is evident).

Having said that, it raises the issue of non-prvt chats/performances as public. Soriano raises the point of access and intention to be exposed to the public. This particular site, like many others, is readily accessible for free to the public; the gurls know this, and in fact rely on its accessibility for clientele. One *could* therefore argue that these gurls operate in the public domain. These are not private chat-rooms, and are not governed by any protocols or mediator. The debate then is to what extent can the public, or a researcher, use public information? And yes, the girls *do* take a risk, possibly unbeknown to them, of themselves being passed on to others. This is a whole new and complex area that requires exploration.

• On legalities and ethics: The research was conducted, and the paper written, before the final decision on the Republic Act 10175—which includes some reference to anyone knowing of such activities also guilty of some ridiculous crime. Is the law retrospective?

Related to this, can one conduct ethical research on what the law considers as "criminal" activities. Again, this is an important question, but certainly there has been much research in the past on illegal activities (as far back as

Cressy's 1932 study of taxi-dance halls and Whyte's 1943 *Street Corner Society*, for example), as well as many others about drugs, a plethora on prostitution (where this is illegal), and other illicit activities. While I do the best to protect my informants, and will continue to do the utmost to do so, for me I will take my chances in pushing the envelope of knowledge and advocacy.

The **fifth** review by **Trina Joyce M. Sajo**, as with the other reviews, recognizes not just the originality and exploratory nature of the work, but also the complexity of a myriad of issues.

Nevertheless, there are a few points and comments worth noting:

• The methodology section quickly turns into a defence.

As I noted previously, it was not so much a defence but an explanation that this methodology was new to us and there was some attempt to pre-empt criticism for what could be mistaken as voyeurism or vicarious salaciousness. Researching sex/gender issues—especially by (white) males—has never been easy, and often studying these issues has been stigmatized; Kirby and Corzine (1981) "describe this as 'stigma contagion', whereby researchers on sexual deviance come to share the stigma attached to the stigma that they are studying". (cf. Lee, 1993: 9; Voss, 2012: 404; Hammond and Kingston, 2014). This could only be made worse by use of particular methods that suggest voyeurism, as in cases of researching strippers or ACMs. This is not a purely theoretical issue, for one reviewer to my paper about ACMs submitted to *Sexualities* snidely said: "*The article could be seen as a male buyer thinking it might be fun to try to turn his hobby into a publication.*"

Reflexive research is an evolving process; had I known then what I now know I would have conducted the research somewhat differently, as I have done for this book. I would take greater risk in revealing my purpose as a researcher, enlist a female co-worker to obtain different perspectives, conduct face-to-face ("real") interviews, engage in better "real" ethnographies, support action research, take greater care of anonymity, and get direct feedback from participants about what I have written; most of all, I would enable their direct voices to be heard through written texts and video. Some of these are now employed in this current book, but were not available in writing my 2010 book or the current paper.

• How did the Internet as a medium, and websites in particular, affect the quality of interviews, for example, and the quality of data uncovered?

Again this is an interesting question, and as I have noted previously, it would be a subject unto itself. There is now coming into vogue publications that begin to address these issues. Suffice to say, in retrospect and following further research, that I find the internet medium deficient in some ways; for ACM research, the gurls had, ironically, no tangible "real" person they could know vis-à-vis real life/time interactions in which people somehow can judge a whole person and their character; it was as though cam contact was *all* performance. In addition, the gurls were at work, to interview them in any sustained way could interfere with their ability to earn an income. The obvious answer to that would be to pay them for their time, but that raises its own problems: should researchers pay informants (although this has been done), and would any grant body provide the funding for what may seem a voyeuristic hobby? It also runs the danger of, from the gurl's point of view, conflating a research role with a potentially sexually-charged prvt performance role. Add to this is that such interviews would have to be in written text, which requires greater effort and possibly runs the risk of less elaboration and explanation than verbal interviews—and possibly all of it in English. Last, but not least, social science methodology has shown that respondents are more willing to tell the truth, or to lie, through mediating technology (ie. the phone, writing, surveys, and now the Internet) vis-à-vis face to face interviews in real. How can researchers check the veracity of the information provided?

So, yes, the technology no doubt affects the quality of data. How we address that is still evolving.

• The introduction of other ACM customers in the network of relations, the significance of which is not quite fully elaborated.

If we know so little about ACMs, we know even less about customers. Acutely aware of this, and not just for ACM-ing but also for other kinds of sex work (cf. Caldwell, 2011), I am now devising a means of trying to get some glimpse of this side of the ACM phenomenon.

• Does using glocalized technology mean that ACMs are actively using and appropriating technology, or is the author speaking of the Internet as an infrastructure domesticated in the Philippines and appropriated accordingly by the people? In the context of cybersex, is this glocalization process achieved by the medium predominantly, or by the users of the technology? Importantly, how is glocalization reflected in the lived experience of cybersex, which, I can imagine, would extend such experience onto real-life, offline settings?

These are very important and complex questions that the paper could not fully explore without extending its length ten-fold.

• The equivalence of cybersex with ACM.

I stand corrected on this and amended the paper where appropriate. However, it's an interesting point in that, interviewing non-ACM informants few knew what cam modeling was, but once "cybersex" was mentioned they immediately "understood". Interesting, too, is that many media reports also use the term "cybersex" when in fact they are explicitly referring to ACM-ing; an example is in my paper: "'The reason why the models usually allow (*sic*) themselves to be trafficked in the Internet for *cyber sex* is because they don't have alternatives', a police informant said." Similarly, some of my 2014 informants also used the term: *"... you're doing cyber inside the house..."*

• Finally, Sajo questions if it is necessary to publish another article that does not bring anything strikingly new from previous work?

Another article? There has been only my one book prior to the *Sabangan* paper, and it was poorly received. I wonder what that might suggest? The poor publicity of ACMs necessitates the reaching out to a wider audience and opening the debate about a topic that people seem to want to ignore. As Garcia so succinctly states in his review: cybersex confounds traditional models of understanding. If my paper simply raises that issue to a wider audience, even with all its limitations with which I readily concur, then it *is* worth publishing.

The **sixth and final review** by **Rosemary Wiss** provides a broad contextualization of the web cam industry (in the Philippines), and where our current paper may be located within it. This is useful in contextualizing ACM-ing and our paper within wider debates over sex/gender, trafficking, technology, globalization and historical, economic and performance issues. But I feel that this is in fact the very problem of such a critique—we seem to be still stuck in old ways of looking at new things, as Garcia suggests, and in doing so impose scholastic frameworks around people and their actions, as well as draw on scholars' experiences in Cebu or Puerto Galera or elsewhere to frame our views, questions and critiques. But it seems these academic perspectives and words are the tools some of us are still stuck with.

This may be evident in the way in which the inaugural issue of *Sabangan* was constructed, with, perhaps, little guidance on how reviewers could, or should, approach our paper and develop their responses. In other words, several of the reviewers' critiques present as classical peer-review assessments and suggest numerous avenues of what could be or should have been done without acknowledging that in some 20 pages all the paper could do is raise and explore briefly a range of issues.

Thus, within this traditional academic framework Wiss' comments and suggestions have some validity and usefulness; but stepping out of that constraint, I found ACMs and ACM-ing refreshing and challenging. It is thus from outside a traditionalist framework, in part, that I respond to Wiss' comments. Here I am selective in responding to the more salient comments and questions by Wiss; some of the other points duplicate those raised by previous reviewers and to which I have already responded. Besides, several of the points Wiss makes would each be a paper unto itself:

• The "article shows a lack of commentary on research by feminist and sexuality studies scholars in the adjacent fields of commercial sex work, sex tourism, trafficking, pornography and the Internet,..."

Yes! If I were to spend another 12 months delving into the sex/gender/feminist or other theories of the above, it would substantially delay the publication of an exploratory study that is trying to get the subject matter on the socio-political and academic agendas. Apart from one of the primary aims of the paper being to "get the message out there", and that I am not an expert in all fields, my interest was in the economic/piece-rates and labour situation of ACMs. More importantly, to tie up the study with existing studies could detract from its freshness, its daring to challenge, to provoke a rethink of ideas and approaches. Partly out of necessity, partly from design, I wanted to get away from traditionalist views and ways of treating sexual phenomena.

• "...Mathews criticizes discussions of sex work that are founded on 'economic necessity',... Despite critiquing such economic rationalist assumptions, Mathews readily reinserts a rational subject in reaction to notions of Filipinas as irrational, uninformed, psychologically disturbed, situationally coerced and structurally constrained."

This passage asserts that, to posit sex work purely in terms of economic necessity robs sex workers of agency to act in terms of how they might meet that necessity. Much of the literature on economic necessity/poverty simply assumes that this reified condition is *sufficient* cause or motivation—that there is an uninterrupted, linear, causal relationship between economic conditions and sex work—that leaves no room to ponder how else women (and men) may meet their needs, one of which is sex work, and how they may come to decide that course of action. But in making that choice they are then moralized, unlike someone who may choose to beg, sell trinkets or engage in other ("legitimate") activities.

So, yes, I critique economic/rationalist assumptions, but also acknowledge that sex-workers do consider their economic condition as a factor in their decision to engage in sex work, but it is not the only factor, and the relationship between their condition and their choice of work is not as straightforward as economic rationalist might simplify and argue.

• "In contemporary gender studies the term performance usually evokes Butler (1990) but Mathews doesn't reference her or what he takes this term to mean. Instead his paper fluctuates between representing web-cam girls as voluntarily choosing their sexualized performances and naturalizing their sexuality as innate, and thus subject to both innate self-expression and their own 'sexual liberation'."

Perhaps then someone should ask *them*—and not Butler, who is by no means without criticism—what *they* mean by performance, rather than imposing Western scholastic interpretations beforehand. From my 2014 interviews:

Alex assured her boyfriend that she didn't mind doing the performance,...

Cristy: "It's really about making money and performing..."
Cristy: "You make your own salary,...it depends on...your performance."
Cristy: "You have to learn how to perform and always change your performance."
Leanne: "I'm an ACM, you know it's all about performing."
Cristy: "You just act, perform, like an actress,..."
Ken & Kate: "If the customers believe it, then we have good acting, a nice performance."

It is all too easy to get bogged down in debates about what is/is not performance and hence what is real/unreal, the "true" or acting/performing self. These gurls and guys didn't seem to have a problem repeatedly using and referring to the term "performance", and separating that from their "real" selves. If everything is "performance", then who is the real me? Do we run the risk of naturalizing this notion of performance, and all behaviour as simply performing? As earlier sociologists would say, we play roles—but if every thing we do is a role, then who is the "real" me?

I am fully aware of Butler's work, but not tied to her positioning and psychologizing people's behaviours or motivations, and least of all that of women from other cultures. The importance of culture in structuring the meanings of behaviour, not least of which is sex-work, is not only commonly absent in studies, but it is also frequently overlooked in international discourses which continue to privilege Western categories, subjects and experiences. I deliberately avoided Butler not only because she obfuscates rather than clarifies, but because she psychologizes and reifies an action into a concept. "Performance" is a question-begging concept and we have more to gain by addressing questions about it than by foreclosing them through reference to an intellectual "authority".

• "In relation to the commercial sex industry in the

Philippines, while prostitution is numerically dominated by domestic clientele, its most infamous form has involved foreigners as it signifies the foreign exploitation of Filipinas and therefore the Philippines. This history includes militarization in the Asian Pacific region...Military bases, international sex tourism, and the subsequent sexualization of Filipinas as an industry form the conditions of the new web-cam commerce. That such a trajectory can be represented as a utopia of freedom, choice and self-expression, produces an origin story that does not have a history. In so doing it ignores the structural constraints, or the conditions in which agency occurs, in which Mathews claims he wishes to embed his study of ACM agency."

I have never denied that history and the consequent structural constraints; I am often at pains to pull up students and others regarding comments that sex-workers or poor people could find (other) work. Nor have I declared that ACM-ing is an economic panacea. What I am saying is that, within those constraints noted by Wiss and others, which have historical roots, cam gurls *do* make choices; they are not simply robots. The choices may be limited, constrained, but they *are* choices. Perhaps this issue should be taken out of feminist ideologies and placed within a philosophical debate? Perhaps the issue, too, is that some people vis-à-vis cam gurls have a tremendous problem coming to terms with the fact that millions of gurls/guys have made a decision to engage in sex work, amongst which ACMs may be included:

Leanne: when her boss and friend asked her to be an ACM, she felt it was OK to do so, and that taking off her clothes on cam was "no problem, I'm open minded. I'm not a virgin, so it was ok for me."

But it is odd that Wiss says that *numerically* Filipinos exploit Filipinas, but then hones in on foreigners as exploiting Filipinas—and the *infamy* of that—and therefore *ipso facto* the country. It is, again, an issue of focusing on outsiders and the sensationalist, and simply ignoring the *numerically* predominant exploitation, including that by *mainly female* bosses of ACMs (who are often friends or relatives of the ACMs!). It readily reminds me of the 1960s-70s surveys about Filipina sexuality, where it was found that two-thirds of Filipinas were not virgins at the time of marriage, and went on to discuss this issue, *totally* neglecting the other one-third who were virgins. So, how much has been written about the numerically predominant local Filipino men "exploiting" Filipina sex workers...?

In the passage, "it signifies the foreign exploitation of Filipinas and therefore the Philippines", Wiss seems to treat Filipina ACMs and Filipinas in general as the personification of the Philippines. If one exploits Filipinas, so Wiss appears to argue, one is *ipso facto* exploiting the Philippines. I find this proposition odd; but even if we accept it, what then are we to make of the neglect of the domestic and numerically larger exploitation? Is there a qualitative difference that overrides the quantitative factor? If so, how and why? Is it in fact a matter of some scholars, in their own way, "exploiting" Filipinas and the Philippines as well, inasmuch as they are using the case of ACMs/sex-workers and other instances of infamy, engaged it seems only by foreigners, to propagate their particular ideology? Is it in fact true that Filipinas, and in particular Filipina sex workers (or ACMs), represent the Philippines? Is there not more to the country than just female sexuality? To pursue Wiss' argument runs the danger of perpetuating the view of the Philippines as a sexual playground for foreigners, when in fact it could be argued it's more of a carnival for the local men, as perhaps Estrada's and Bongbong's chicaneries might represent. This is not to discount the importance of sex tourism and the like, but to bring to bear some balance, if not shift from a guilt-laden post-colonial mentality.

Perhaps equally profound, however, is, if we accept Wiss' argument that by exploiting Filipinas, men (presumably—suggestive of a feminist dimension to the argument vis-à-vis a purely politico-colonial one) are exploiting the Philippines, then does this also apply to other countries such as the USA where there are a large number of sex-workers and even ACMs? Or, what country is being exploited if an American travels to Germany and engages a Colombian or French migrant sex-worker?

• "By a process of repetition, which is the very basis of performance, in this case of scholarly assertion, ACM work represents choice."

And I will repeat it here yet again and again and again until the voices of ACMs are heard, as my 2014 informants articulated:

Leanne: "We choose that work [ACM-ing]..."

Cristy: "Some models, especially single gurls, work in cam because they want to marry a foreigner..."

Kate: "I knew I had to take my clothes off and touch myself,..."

They also stressed that they make a choice to work as an ACM.

Melinda plans to also work as an ACM in her spare time and, hopefully, with her own PC.

Jonaz's aunt had an old computer and asked if Jonaz would work for her. She first worked from her own home....she would assure her boyfriend that she didn't mind doing the performance, that it was only her job.

Paris: "After a few months I decided to work as an ACM... Soon I moved to my aunty's house, [and] I bought my own PC and was my own boss."

Alex had returned to work as an ACM, with her own PC and earning as much as 20,000 pesos a month. At an hour-long interview with an incompetent Israeli TV crew, with myself present, Alex was asked a range of questions of which the themes of sexual exploitation, objectification, victimization and trauma reoccurred.... She did not provide the interviewers with the gender-bashing responses they had hoped for.

I have repeatedly said that all ACMs whom I have encountered have chosen to be an ACM, for a range of reasons, and within the socio-economic, gender/sexual structural constraints that the world and history have developed and imposed—just as we all make choices within those constraints; some of us have greater choices and fewer constraints.

If I am to be criticized for repetition, and therefore by implication making a rhetorical case for agency, then perhaps the same could be said of the often one-eyed feminist cry that women are historically and socially and gender/sexually constructed and *therefore* are unable to make genuine choices—spurious logic—while men seem to not experience such predisposing factors and can make choices. That being the case, I choose to be King!

This argument is not about choice, it's about an ideological stance that women generally take that females cannot make free choices. It is my repetition of this *availability of choice* and *capacity to choose* that irks simply because it is so embedded in some discourse/s that women cannot choose. It's an ideological position about inequality, which I fully acknowledge and empathize with; but in-equality does not mean an inability to make choices, it means an inability to make *more* choices. If repeating this ad nauseam is performance then perhaps it is because it needs repeating, for the alternative is to silence the voices of all minorities, and continually cry, and perform as, victim.

We are all subject to our own histories, including the reviewers herein, from which it would seem some do not, themselves, reflect upon, but continue to throw up their arms and ring their hands and cry what a miserable world we live in, how oppressed we are, and it's all the fault of men.

Hammond & Kingston (2014: 332) explore that Feminist methodologists have argued that knowledge is contextually specific and the researcher's biography affects what they find out, and, therefore what we know (Stanley and Wise,

1993). Research and critique are not undertaken in a vacuum, and researchers cannot claim to be neutral, detached or objective from the social world they study: our thoughts, feelings, experiences and behaviours are influenced by wider society and our own individual biographies, which can affect not only research findings (Hammersley and Atkinson, 2007; Mason, 2002) but also the perception and critique of others' research.

Perhaps, then, instead of a fatalistic victimology mentality we could perhaps step back and acknowledge our constructions and work to change them, as I have done, by taking this initial step of voicing concerns and conditions that ACMs have articulated to me. Indeed, speaking for women itself has a history. By speaking for third-world women, or any sex worker for that matter, Western scholars (myself included) assert their own right to participate in the State; so, isn't that exploitation of others? Thus, I am no longer simply and purely the medium through which fieldwork was conducted but part of the story (Maher 2002: 316). But how do we escape that ? Do we in fact want to escape it and not be part of the story?

• "Mathews indicates that staged intimacy is part of the girls' business, with the girls asking the men as 'friends' to send them money and goods. Mathews puts quotation marks around the word 'friends', yet he doesn't seem to critically reflect on his own position as a 'friend' to some of the girls he gave gifts to."

"When analyzing the web-cam studios Mathews notes that one of the consistent features were teddy bears or toys as props. These are indications of the girls' youth, 'but also pander to the customer's fantasies by projecting themselves as subservient, juvenile females who need care or mentoring'. This is a role Mathews seems to have claimed as in his role of 'consoling and counseling' the girls."

Here I take strong objection to the imposition of my role—which seems to suggest a primary or singular role (as well as smacks of Butler's psychologizing of role and behaviour)—of being a consoling or counseling agent. At no time did I identify with such a role or mission, or set out to undertake consoling or counseling. It so happened that on several occasions—and indeed on 3 occasions in one night— I encountered gurls, with whom I had built rapport, in some distressed state about various things, and even some visibly crying. It would be only natural as a human and as a researcher to ask why they are upset, and to respond via the technology in the best way I could. What else was I to do— simply tell the gurls I am not interested, that I don't care, and disconnect (DC)?

Unless you are *there*, you can't see what you *would* do, and when you *are* there, you can't always see clearly what to do. What would *you* do? What did Dr. Wiss do when confronted by such situations in Puerto Galera?

I had built a relationship of mutual respect with these gurls, a relationship of friendship and trust to some extent— however that may be interpreted by them or me; they knew I would not take them into a prvt show, as I had told them so, and as in any friendship I was prepared to—and did—draw boundaries; but nevertheless we had built some level of rapport and knowledge of each other as much was practicable, and indeed so much so that these gurls were willing—even wanting—to talk to me about their problem/s. Indeed, on several occasions the gurl herself initiated the conversation. For example, "Trina", who was (and still is) a very feisty model, suddenly, without my prompting, began asking me about her appearance, her body image, her intellectual ability (taking pains to show me her graduate certificates), and asking me why guys in real don't like her, as well as telling me all about her dog and pups, again taking time out to fetch and show them. Is this all performance? Or is there some level of rapport, some kind of friendship or in the least acquaintanceship?

The fact is that, despite their poverty and problems with

their kids, themselves, health, kin and debts, ACMs can and do use ITC to reach out. ITC was formerly local and kin/friendship based (ie, cell phones), and largely limited in its use within domestic or national parameters; even for those who could use a PC frequently, contacts were/are primarily local or kin based, even if kin are overseas. Now, however, for ACMs with ready access to the internet and frequent contact with "wealthy" foreigners, ITC has become global. Although spending money on ITC detracts from money on real immediate needs, it is possibly compensated with a wider network of "kin"/*kaibigan* (friends) on whom one can call. Thus, what the internet has done is to enable virtual kinship, making the global local.

Some ACMs develop, to varying extents, "friendships" with clients, whatever that may mean or involve for each. But it is known that some gurls do call upon these geographically distant friends for money in times of crises, or perhaps the pretence of crisis. I long ago argued (Mathews, 1992) that having many children is somewhat like investing in lottery tickets, in the hope that at least one of them will eventually "pay off" by getting a good job, having a good marriage that would help her parents, or even marrying a foreigner and being able to remit money to the parents or even have them also migrate to a richer country. There are many cases where this has occurred to continue the faith and hope.

As with children, an extended kinship network also offers opportunity, or at least the potential, for landing a good job or indeed any job, marrying upward, or being able to call on for assistance in times of need. So, the wider/greater that kinship, the greater the potential.

Thus, instead of being culturally and kinship bound, relying on kinship or local patronage, ACMs extend their circle of kinship to outsiders, even to strangers, who become pseudo—virtual—kin. The case of Leanne's 2 year old daughter getting sick exemplifies this. In the past people like

Leanne would borrow (*utang*) from kin, friends or patrons to buy medicine or to visit a doctor, go to a "free" public hospital, or go to a local *hilot*, or, by default, allow the kid to continue to be sick and, with minimum capacity to intervene, ride out the sickness episode. Now they turn to "extended kin" for immediate help, making sickness and other hardships have a dollar value rather than more a socio-cultural value and meaning.

I encountered several instances of this, apart from Leanne pleading for 1,000 pesos for her sick daughter, among other crises noted in her story. Melinda also asked for financial help for her sick daughter and father, her daughter's school needs, and even in person when I was in Manila for her own medical expenses. Her friend, Jonaz, also sought a "gift" of 2,000 pesos for her own medical expenses; while Jonaz, without asking directly, hoped I would contribute to her father's medical expenses.

Thus, through their children—and it would seem mainly female children—the "lottery" of life was paying off in some cases; but what differs from the occasional foreigner meeting up with a poor peasant girl of the barrio or slums, or even the many bar-girls who snag a foreigner husband, is that ACMs are reaching out across the globe, even being proactive in seeking foreigner "kin" without necessarily meeting them in real. And this is not necessarily a relationship of love or potential marriage, but one of "monetary friendship", of friendship or virtual "kinship" that is underpinned by a principle of often unrequited debt.

If it is all performance then are these gurls simply performers in real? Who is the real girl?

Was Leanne just performing when she and I chatted on YM on July 16 2014 (and subsequently)? She was no longer able to work as a cam gurl because of her school, family and other work commitments; perhaps she was telling me her plight to evoke sympathy and elicit financial support, although she knew by now that I would not send her anything.

Or perhaps she just wanted someone to tell her problems to—and not for the first time—to which I tried to respond positively, sympathetically and with hope, as a friend:

Leanne: paul wait im in verry deep deep problem first i dont have connection and also a verry though [tough] schedule at school wid my 9 subject for 25 units and also having a part tym job on my aunts bussiness for my baon [food; lunch] and milk for the kids ...behind of [besides] my dizziness all da tym aswell...i dont get enough sleep na

Me: I was worried about you with the typhoon.

Leanne: sum of the trees and roofs are flying last hour...signal no.3....ok now here....hope Jonaz is fine aswell....hru [how are you?]

Me: yea i think she's flooded...lives near a river

Leanne: cant [you] msg her still? Shes not answering yet?

Me: no fone ....and her roof leaks

Leanne: i just had a very fully liaded sched [laden schedule]...plus a job on my aunt

Me: just organize yourself....a time for this, time for that....

Leanne: uu [yes] [it] help for my baon and babys milk

Me: least u have a job, that's good.

Leanne: im just borrowing aunts PC now.... for me to be able to do my projects....assignments...coz i still dont have connection....at home

Me: ic

Leanne: i know how ofc [of course] [how to use MS Word]....its just my tym....im working aswe....aswell....on aunt now

Me: yea i know...its hard, just have to be super organized, I guess.

Leanne: just to continue schooling i owe her a lot na ....i have 7am to 8pm at school....4x a week

Me: that's 13 hrs a day !

Leanne: and my half day is twice only

Me: yikes 6 days!

Leanne: my s [schedule] mondays and half day

Me: Mmmm, they don't make it easy dba [do they]

Leanne: need to work at aunt...i wanted to rest na nga [really]...coz i feel dizzy still

Me: try to eat well and sleep 8 hrs a day Leanne

Leanne: having hatd [haven't had] tym sumtym to cope on the lectures...coz hard to read and think...wen dizxy...i need to wake up 5am...how is that 8hours of sleep ...was thinking to stop [school] na lng

Me: but then u waste all that money and effort.

Leanne: i owe a lot of money na....to evrybody

Me: try to get to the end of semester 1 naman.

Leanne: if gods will...gods grace dba...im getting streesed wid my research na thats a big problem

Me: u stress too much L, try not let things upset you...

Leanne: i just wish im not poor

Me: me too...that I am not poor, and yr not poor...but now L, yr lucky, bc Jonaz's house is down in the typhoon,...so u have a house dba and safe...

Are Leanne and I simply performing? To what end? Leanne neither asked nor expected anything from me other than to listen, as millions of friends do. Is this *all* performance? If so, then who is the real Leanne or Paul?

I will not separate my humanity from my research. If that is a problem for theory or methodology, then you deal with it, because I don't have a problem with it.

But it does leave me to wonder if only female researchers can be "friends" with female participants? I could suggest that what underlies this question of a male researcher being friends with female participants, and especially ones who present ostensibly as sexual, is a certain phallocentrism, as well as a moralistic hint that ACMs are, just perhaps, sexually "promiscuous" or "fallen women", and that my friendship had an ulterior diabolical motive. I knew my relationship to these gurls, but I didn't know the relationship of others to them, and hence my caution of referring to some clients as "friends".

What this whole debate raises is what Burke (2014) encapsulates: The study of sexuality generally, as a stigmatized subject, has an impact on who can write about it, what they can write, and where that writing is published. How does this impact on what we know, what we can come to know from different (male/female or other perspectives), what we can ask, how we can overcome these barriers, and larger questions about positionality in the academy and the field. If only women are permitted to legitimately research and write about sexuality/gender then this leads to possibly less diversity demographically, a factor that may reduce the potential for challenging existing and developing new frameworks and methods. If we take this curtailment to a ridiculous conclusion, then we could argue that only sex-workers can speak about sex work. But who gives only women the right, the legitimacy to research and talk about sex work/ers? Well, no doubt in a diabolical plot, men of the patriarchy give such women that privilege, such that we now have subordinate woman talking about even more subordinate women, and so who is to believe her?

Burke (ibid: 72) goes on to say that justifications for studying sexuality should not be necessary—such studies are "a lens into the social world deserving of inquiry that can help answer questions about workplace practices, power relations, workers' rights and health, and the reproduction of inequality."

But it is not just about who can write of sex workers, women vis-à-vis men, but also about the sex workers themselves. No matter how much we may see, or want to see, sex workers as victims, we continue to define them as sexual, as seductress. Feminist theories reduce women's identity to a single trait, contrary to Butler's notion of performance wherein identity is made up of several performing traits and hence none are real (ie. if prostitution is performance, then where is the victimization—or is that also performance?) These theories simply essentialize and fail to move outside the phallocentric imaginary, in which all women are reduced to a vagina, to potential or real prostitutes and to their sex acts. Not only does this reify an image of the prostitute as sexual, and as subordinate, it also sustains the myths and norms of the sex industry, of potent men and submissive women, rather than transforming (Scoular, 2004: 345).

Just as Kingston (Hammond and Kingston 2014: 335) found her identity as a female sex work researcher may have labeled her as "different", as sexually liberal, it seems I also, as a sex-work researcher, may be labeled as "different", perhaps suggesting that I have an ulterior motive, of my research camouflaging an easy way to meet "loose" women and maybe using my status to obtain sex or free sex—a bizarre notion in the Philippines where one can go into a bar or visit a massage place and buy sex cheaply—or be willing to pay for sex, a view that not only critics may think but also importantly think that is how ACMs may perceive me; and of course the converse, that all such gurls are willing to sell sex. Yet as we have seen, all of the ACMs interviewed concurred with what Cristy articulated: "*I really have to know him deeply*", that they would not have sex for money. As Zurbriggen (2002: 336) suggests, participants might assume that because the researcher is studying sexuality she must be sexually interested or available (2002: 262), or, if male, willing to pay for sex, or like Zurbriggen, in my own case with Paris (the *bakla*), being available for sex. In some cases male researchers have identified assumptions and expectations made about them as men researching sex and sexuality—assumptions made about their interest in their topic, or perversions that they may have (which were considered to have ultimately led them to research their topic) (Hammond and Kingston, 2014: 337). That being the case, then perhaps I am a voyeur!

All this highlights an assumption that all men are sexual predators, and that all women can be bought, and that ACMs are loose women who can be bought more cheaply. It is pure phallocentrism.

• "Privileging a 'native voice' in sex work will not however be a permanent escape from hegemonic power because they arise from it."

Yes, but then what? Are we not to make a start, are we not even to allow a native voice? Short of auto-ethnography, are we all to stand by, muted by academic protocols? If I didn't publish this or similar work, then what would we know, where and when would we begin? Just as do-gooder NGOs proclaim that sex-workers should be rescued, but offer no alternatives, critics readily offer only criticism and no solutions. While criticism certainly has its place in highlighting deficiency, it must also be tempered with constructionism.

• "Admitting the girls present their 'sexualized bodies as product', Mathews naturalizes the commodification of their services."

This is purely an economic argument about an economic principle, piece-rates. If anything, it denaturalizes the commodification of (sexual) services by arguing that capital takes a human subject and objectifies her/him as labour power, as commodity. Indeed, this is my main bone of contention in the whole ACM phenomenon, of how labour (and emotional labour) is commoditized and naturalized by capital(ism), and in particular through piece-rates.

• "Mathews states he never revealed his identity as a researcher."

A careful reading of the script will show: "To *customers* I never revealed my identity as a researcher..." and "To some of the ACMs with whom I became familiar I *did* reveal my identity as a researcher, and raised the possibility of my doing research on their activities."

In general:

As I stated in the beginning, and in my book, I did not set out to answer questions but rather to ask them, and to describe as best I could at that time some of the data I obtained by various means about ACMs and ACM-ing. Where I do put forward some questions, suggestions, issues, they are simply that—exploratory comments about a new phenomenon, which, despite it having some connections with a range of other factors such as sex tourism, military bases, prostitution and other forms of sex work, economic and labour conditions, sexuality and gender, technology and globalization, etc, is a new phenomenon and *may* challenge the way we do and need to think about these issues. How ACM-ing challenges them I am, at this stage, unsure; but what I am sure of is that if we persist in squeezing this new phenomenon, or others, into the same old boxes, by asking the same old questions and taking the same old views— theoretical and ideologically based—then we will end up with the same old tiresome responses. So, the question is, how *should* we think about ACMs and ACM-ing?

While I thank the reviewers for their contributions, insights, questions and directions, most importantly it is to be recognized that by such contributions we have begun to open up a frontier that often has been hijacked by moralists and media who have drowned the silent voices of ACMs. If the paper has achieved even some articulation of their situations, then I have no regrets.

Ultimately, as Garcia notes, my paper set out to address two things: 1. simply to document this phenomenon and open debates about it; 2. to ask the basic question, is ACM-ing some form of sex work (or more narrowly, prostitution) ? Where does ACM-ing fit into the scheme of things, given the great role that ICT takes in this, and the internationalization of ACM-ing? While phone-sex, porn movies and other similar activities also engage technology, then what makes ACM-ing different, if at all, and what is the significance of the differences and similarities? And how do we go about framing and researching these issues?

For example, Amy Flowers (1998) explores the connections between disembodied communication, the manufacture of fantasy and expressions of intimacy. She argues that disembodiment is a central defining feature of phone sex, as with other forms of mediated sex such as ACM-ing and porn movies. She frames her discussion of the phone sex industry in terms of classical theories of the relationship between modernity, technology and alienation, insightfully noting that, "In a society where intimacy is problematic, people find creative ways to use the very aspects of communication that have been are assumed to be alienating" (ibid: 2). The relationship between technological convenience, isolation and desire is a promising tension around which to explore contemporary expressions of sexuality without being rendered in terms of a simple dichotomy between "real" intimacy and "artificial" technology or virtuality in which disembodiment is perceived as negative and "artificial intimacy" as a self-evident problem. Presumably, those who "manufacture" fantasies for the purposes of arousal are contributing to the production of a sort of false intimacy. But what makes something artificial— the process of manufacturing it? This line of reasoning implies a possible "natural" intimacy or realness that is out of step with most contemporary theory. (cf. O'Brien, 1999: 267-272).

As with phone sex, ACM-ing has the potential to "disembody" participants, even though they may actually see one other (at least one-dimensionally), and indeed, for both customer and the gurl, "embodiment" of some kind is critical in their presentation of their sexuality; some kind of embodiment is in fact what customers are paying for. But in what sense then is this one dimension embodiment, and is it the same as pornographic films?

For the gurls, while they rely on their embodiment, they may also disembody themselves, by presenting their actions as mere "performance", just as porn stars might do. In deed, one could argue that some sex-workers in real may also disembody themselves, even though they engage in physical, "real" sex.

If our paper—and this book and my previous book— have managed to problematize these and other issues, not least of which how we approach embodiment and sexual behaviour, then they have achieved their purpose.

References cited for this section.

Bakeries, S. (2013) Becoming a "Trusted Outsider": Gender, Ethnicity, and Inequality in Ethnographic Research. Journal of Contemporary Ethnography, 42(6): 690–721.

Burke, M. (2014). Positionality and pornography. Porn Studies, 1(1–2): 71–74.

Caldwell, H. (2011). Long-Term Clients Who Access Commercial Sexual Services in Australia. Masters Thesis, University of Sydney.

Flowers, A. (1998). The Fantasy Factory: An Insider's View of the Phone Sex Industry. Phil'a: U of Pennsylvania.

Hammersley, M. and Atkinson, P. (2007). Ethnography: Principles in Practice (3rd ed). London: Routledge.

Hammond, N. and Kingston, S. (2014), Experiencing stigma as sex work researchers in professional and personal lives. Sexualities, 17(3) 329–347.

Kirby, R. and Corzine, J. (1981). The contagion of stigma: Fieldwork amongst deviants. Qualitative Sociology, 4(1): 3–20.

Kuntz, K. (2014). spiegel.de/international/world/how-a-city-in-the-philippines-is-combatting-the-plague-of-child-porn-a-958390.html

Lee, R. (1993). Doing Research on Sensitive Topics. SAGE.

Maher, L. (2002). Don't leave us this way: Ethnography and injecting drug use in the age of AIDS. International Journal of Drug Policy, 13(4): 311–325.

Mason, J. (2002). Qualitative Researching. London: SAGE.

Mathews, P. W. (2010). Asian Cam Models. Giraffe Books. E-book: www.smashwords.com/books/view/447769

Mathews, P. W. (2015). I'm a Cybersex Gurl, and I wanna tell u my story. Canberra: Warrior Publishers.

Mathews, P. W. (2017). Cam Models, Sex Work, and Job Immobility in the Philippines, Feminist Economics, 23(3): 160-183.

Mathews, P. W. (2015). Piece-Rates as Inherently Exploitative: Adult/Asian Cam Models As Illustrative. Journal of Marxism and Interdisciplinary Inquiry.

O'Brien, J. (1999). Book Review of Flowers, A. (1998). The Fantasy Factory: An Insider's View of the Phone Sex Industry. Sexualities, 2(2): 267–272.

Scoular, J. (2004). The 'subject' of prostitution: Interpreting the discursive, symbolic & material position of sex/work in feminist theory. Feminist Theory, 5: 343-355.

Stanley, L. and Wise, S. (1993). Breaking Out again: Feminist Ontology & Epistemology. London: Routledge.

Voss, G. (2012). Treating it as a normal business: Researching the pornography industry. Sexualities, 15: 391.

Zurbriggen E. (2002). Sexual objectification by research participants: Recent experiences and strategies for coping. Feminism and Psychology, 12(2): 261–268.

PART 3

The Structure of Sex-Work Services in the Philippines and Labour Immobility

According to Weitzer (2009) and Heyl (1979), it is rare for Western sex-workers to experience substantial upward or downward mobility, although some girls may experience temporary mobility. Changing levels requires contacts and a new set of work techniques and attitudes. Occasionally, an upscale worker whose life situation changes (e.g., because of aging, drug addiction, financial crisis, health or family factors, etc) is no longer able to work in that stratum and gravitates to the street. But transitioning from street work to higher levels, especially the top echelons, is quite rare because most street workers lack the education and social and perhaps language skills associated with upscale work. If a move does take place, it is usually small or lateral within a domain or segment.

In this section I undertake a comparative exploration of several forms of sex-work, and suggest different reasons for a lack of occupational mobility *within* the sex industry of the Philippines, as well as consider the interplay between economics and segments of the sex industry and Philippine culture.

While I acknowledge that sex-workers do consider their economic condition as a factor in their decision to engage in sex-work, it is not the only factor, and the relationship between their condition and their choice of work is not as straightforward as economic rationalism might simplify. By comparing street sex-workers, bar girls and masseuses with ACMs, in terms of their lack of occupational mobility within

180

the sex industry of the Philippines, we show the fallacy of a common perception that all sex-work is and all sex-workers are the same. It is assumed that because ACMs present their sexuality on cam they are prostitutes and therefore willing to engage in physical sexual relations for money, to be "touched". But I show that, for ACMs, as with other types of sex-workers, there are several structural and social factors that mitigate against job mobility between them, even though there may be some economic gain if they did so—and thus economic motives may be attenuated by other factors.

Thus, in what follows I provide an overview of 3 types of sex-work in the Philippines (street workers, bar girls, masseuses) to suggest how they each perceive their own type of work and that of others, and I suggest reasons why they may not move from one type to another. I then show that, because some ACMs do not necessarily perceive their work as prostitution, they are unwilling or unable to move to other forms of sex-work, even though the economic rewards *may* be greater.

Sex-work commonly has been organized according to similar principles across different times and cultures. A general socio-economic "hierarchy" suggests that at the bottom is street prostitution, followed by brothels, bars, and clubs. Call girls and escort agencies occupy the middle to high positions, and kept women the top rungs.

While this structure is in fact more complex, it has rarely been questioned or analyzed, and appears to be underpinned by certain socio-moral undertones. The criteria for such a structure are seldom enunciated and, as I suggest, are in fact problematic. To use a primary criterion of income or pricing can fall short, for an independent street worker could, theoretically, earn more than a brothel worker who splits her income with the brothel owner and may also have to pay other expenses.

Thus a popular perception and assessment of different forms of sex-work may have derived not from economic criteria, but from moral judgements: street workers "do it" in rather unpolished places, perhaps quickly, and standing on the street they are open to public scrutiny (ie. the public domain), whereas escorts present a more refined and largely discreet presentation (private domain), with brothels, bars etc somewhere in between. If only things were that simple: some brothel and bar girls also are escorts, and vice versa. Further, such a structure is based on Western experiences and analyses, with scant regard to third world socio-economic and cultural factors.

The structure of sex-work in its various forms *in the Philippines*—of which there is a dearth of information—is very complex in detail, but it can be broadly categorized as below. However, it will be evident these categories are not exclusive, in that girls could shift from one category to another. Thus in the following categories a freelancer or street worker could also be, either simultaneously or temporarily, an escort; or a bar worker could also freelance outside her formal work hours; and bar workers or masseuses could do escort work for the bar or parlour. If we use the statistical concept of "main source of income" or "main activity", we may avoid such a conundrum, but avoiding that does not reflect reality.

Thus, rather than using either economic or social/moral criteria, I use the idea of public versus private domains, or what Ronald Weitzer (2009: 222) refers to as a segmented market between the indoor and street sectors. Within each domain is the criterion of *the extent to which these sex workers present themselves as providing sex as their primary service*—and hence introduces a subjective element of how girls may perceive or experience their work. This structure does not *necessarily* reflect earning capacity and income, but may suggest capacity or incapacity for occupational mobility *within* the sex industry, as well as a publicly constructed and hence socio-moral "hierarchy". Such segmentation may also be marked by major differences in working conditions, risk of victimization, job satisfaction and self-esteem.

The public domain consists of 3 categories of sex-workers who undertake solicitation in streets and parks. In each of these categories workers present themselves as providing either sex as their main service, or another service such as massage, with sex as an additional and optional service:

1. Street workers whose only activity is selling sex.

2. Street workers, who may hold some official masseuse accreditation and permit, and who *ostensibly* do massage, but whose focus is in fact prostitution, ie. selling sex.

3. Street workers who hold some official masseuse accreditation and permit. They work with or for a massage parlour and in fact provide massage; sex is *additional* and *optional*.

The private domain consists of 9 categories of sex workers who undertake solicitation in bars, parlours, hotels, via the internet, etc. In each of these categories, other than brothels, workers present themselves as providing primarily a service other than sex, with sex as an additional and optional service, although such service may hardly be subtle.

4. Brothels*

5. Bar girls (Guest Relations Officers (GROs) and dancers), who work for "girlie" bars, and who provide "companionship" or "entertainment".

6. Escorts/Call girls* (other than bar girls/GROs).**[34]**

7. Massage parlours, where workers provide massages at various levels of competency, but also various forms of sexual services are available.

8. Live porn shows and porn movies*

9. Strippers*

10. ACMs (who problematically cross the public/private domains).

11. Phone sex*

12. Masseuses who work in/for a hotel and who, by all

official accounts, do not provide sexual services, but sex *may* be additional and optional.

* No information is available on these, or they generally are not available or are limited in the Philippines.

Within these categories of sex-work, the women experience degrees of supervision. While prostitutes who work as freelancers or street walkers have no supervision, women who work in bars are supervised by a manager (*mama-san*)—particularly in terms of what they can and cannot do. For ACMs, their bosses may not micro-manage a gurl's work, but rather rely on piece-rates as a control mechanism: if the gurl underperforms during a work period this will show up in her periodic tally. However, in some cases bosses do micro-manage by constantly checking on a gurl's productivity. Similarly, masseuses lay some where in between. Depending on what the arrangement is, they may be expected to achieve a quota of clients, or monitoring may rest essentially on piece-rates and hence their own efforts. However, if they are *assigned* customers they have little control over how much work they can do.

Outlining this structure enables a better understanding of the location of ACMs, and enables exploration of the features of several categories to understand if the workers experience mobility between them, and if not, why not. In particular, I argue that ACMs rarely move to other forms of sex-work. But this argument is largely anecdotal, as no studies of the sex industry as a whole have been undertaken. The argument is also based on how ACMs express their perceptions of their own work and that of other sex-workers. Essentially, because ACMs do not identify as prostitutes, they find it difficult within themselves to want to move into other forms of sex work. Also, some of the reasons they took up ACM-ing vis-à-vis other forms of sex work constrain their mobility. Similarly, other sex workers are faced with particular obstacles to become, for example, ACMs or qualified masseuses.

Here I detail only street workers collectively who are popularly considered to be on the lowest rung of sex-work, bar girls who probably are the largest group, masseuses within massage parlours, and ACMs, who are the focus of this book. Also, I do not address the possibility of mobility from a secondary to a primary segment of work, as simply almost all these sex workers have very limited education or officially recognized skills.

1. Street workers:

While this type of sex-worker can be found in particular areas of major cities and towns, they have never been well documented.

The are 3 subcategories in this classification:

(i) Those girls who make little or no pretence of providing primarily a sexual service. It includes freelance girls who work outside or inside some bars but are not employed by them, as well as college students in some places. Prices are variable and negotiable, ranging from 300-500 pesos for a short time, to 1,000+ pesos [at USD$1 = 40 pesos], depending on the sexual activity. They keep all of their income, but they may informally share it with a "companion" who serves, like a pimp, to procure clientele or accompany and support the girl.

Some of these girls have "pimps", although we need to be careful to distinguish these from a Western idea. These males, many of whom are transgenders who are themselves available for sexual engagement, do not control or own the girls, but intermediate for them in transactions, often because they are related to the girls. The girls are not duty bound to hand over all or most of the earnings to such intermediaries, but may provide some kick-back to them. Philippine society and culture, and the notions of *utang* ("debt") and reciprocity are too complex for a simple financial transactional model.

For example, street workers can be encountered mostly

at night along Quezon Blvd in the north of Metro Manila, and in Zamora Street in Makati, in the south, amongst several hotels and entertainment (girlie) bars.

The Quezon girls stand in the shadows of this busy boulevard, which also features a number of entertainment girlies bars, pubs and karaoke bars, and approach motorists who slowly cruise by. They offer most sexual services (masturbation, fellatio, full sex), often performed in some darkened street or enclave, in the client/s' car. Some may go to a client's home or hotel with him.

Fees are negotiated beforehand and vary from girl to girl and depending on what the client requires, and in some cases how many clients are involved, and what value the girl may place on herself—her age, beauty, charm—and what value the client may place on these characteristics.

Usually the time spent with a client is not of concern, but is usually understood to be for a short time of 1-2 hours. An overnight engagement would command a higher price, of perhaps 2-4,000 pesos.

Prices can start at about 500 pesos, and may go to about 2,000 pesos, but these are negotiable for the above reasons and because of strong competition and, in some cases, the dire need of some of these women to earn money.

Little is known about who these women are or where they live, although they must live within easy commuting distance if not in the immediate area. Their situation leaves them open to being seen by local people who may know them as neighbours, to physical abuse or robbery, and to police surveillance.

Their ages range from, ostensibly, 18 to the 30s or 40s.

Their clients are largely Filipinos who, mostly, are wealthy enough to own a motor vehicle, as few foreigners frequent this part of Manila.

Apart from Quezon Blvd, girls can be found in other areas, but local knowledge is required to know where and to be able to readily identify them. For example, on one occasion I was passing through a busy intersection in Cubao, on foot, in mid-afternoon, and was approached by a girl who was selling clothes and miscellaneous items. She asked if I was interested in sex, and introduced her 18 year old friend who was doing nothing other than waiting for sexual customers. Following her cue I engaged them with some questions, amongst which was if the first girl, rather than her friend, was also available, to which she replied in the affirmative. This encounter led the two girls to show me where the sexual activities took place: this was a nearby tenement of sorts, with numerous rooms of Dickensian quality and almost match-box dimensions—large enough for a mattress on the floor and a small cubicle containing a non-flushing toilet, tap and bucket.

The price was 700 pesos for straight sex with a condom (and an extra 100 pesos if she took off her bra); no time limit was discussed, as it was assumed that once the client had satisfied himself the transaction would be complete. She also indicated that a "tip" of about 20-50 pesos had to be provided to the young man who showed us to the room, and who clearly earned much of his income as a cleaner, escort and guard.

This encounter and others with several girls on Quezon Blvd suggests that many of the girls hold other jobs, probably of a menial nature, and undertake prostitution as a "sideline" to supplement their income.

In contrast, Zamora Street—a short (300-meter) one-way stretch of road occupied by about 20 girlie bars and several hotels of quite reasonable quality—offers greater diversity and luxury if not sophistication. The street is a major shortcut through to several major roads, one of which leads to the more central part of Makati city, the prime business centre of Manila about 2-3 kilometers away that also houses many large 4-5 star hotels. Makati is also near several residential areas of mixed quality, and from which many of the Zamora girls come.

In this street there is a range of sex workers. At this point I will focus on street workers, who include quite a few transgenders. They are aged generally between 18 and 30, and walk up and down the street and nearby side streets, occasionally stopping for a while on the sidewalk at particular locations—all within viewing distance of the local police outpost. While some are available throughout the day, the larger number of them can be seen from about 5pm to 3am.

Two street workers (left), & three masseuses in uniform.

A single street worker in Zamora Street (below).

They approach men, mostly foreigners, walking by, asking them if they want a girl or suggesting thinly veiled offers for a massage. These girls often work in twos or threes and make no pretence of being available to go to a client's hotel.

Unlike the Quezon girls, they are usually well dressed in alluring clothes and cosmetics, and their prices start at about 1,000 pesos for full service and perhaps a time limit of 1 hour. They may try to entice a client by offering 2 girls at a discount. Several hotels in the area warn guests about these girls, suggesting they are not real masseuses and are likely to rob or assault clients and/or infect them with STDs. [35]

Some girls are newly arrived in Manila from the

provinces and relatively inexperienced, and thus amateurish in their approaches and in sexual or massage service. For example, a client told me that he took an 18 year old girl, new to Manila, to his hotel room on the understanding that she would engage in full service for 1,000 pesos for one hour; but in the hotel room she had to be strongly convinced to remove even her bra, declared that she was a virgin and therefore would not engage in coitus, and was not adept at fellatio, even though she declared she had performed fellatio before in her home town. She had arrived in Manila only a few days earlier and needed money to sustain herself until she obtained a factory job for which she had already applied.

Similar street venues exist in other cities of the Philippines, but have not been well observed or documented.

(i) a. Students are a subcategeory of the above. Some of the street workers are students specifically seeking money for their school needs. It was rumoured that in one provincial city students seeking money for sex could be found loitering near their college.

In the 1980s, in Ermita, Manila, one particular place was the *Manila Rendezvous*, which was renown for meeting college students who were willing to go, as "companions", with mostly foreigner clients. This semi-open air establishment was large, with music and a dance floor, alcohol, and commonly accommodated over 400 girls seeking clients with whom they would spend anything from a few hours to a whole day/night, and even several days.

The girls would sit at tables in pairs or groups, and usually an interested male would approach a particular group and ask to join them. In taking up a "date" with a man, she would commonly stay with him for several days, often travelling around the country with him, and negotiate a monetary reward to meet her "school needs" for the time she spent with the client. (The general fee at that time was about 300 pesos a day, equivalent to about 2,000 pesos today).

It's not known if the *Manila Rendezvous* still exists (I last visited it in 2005), or if other places have arisen in Manila, or similar places exist in other Philippine cities.

(i) b. Freelance girls who work outside or inside bars

Somewhat similar to street workers are girls who are freelancers but work particular areas around or in bars. If the bar is a girlie bar then they are not permitted inside or too near because they would detract from the bar's own girls' capacity to attract clients.

Such girls are not as numerous as they used to be in the 1980s-90s, particularly in Ermita (the main red-light area of Manila, which was largely shut down by Mayor Lim in the early 1990s). However, some still ply their trade in Angeles City, Olongapo, and even smaller provincial towns such as Surigao City. They may work alone or with a female companion, and usually do not have a pimp, nor are they directly linked to a massage parlour.

Loitering near girlie bars, and on occasion inside non-girlie bars/restaurants, they approach men passing by or who are entering or leaving the bars, asking if the potential client would like a girl. Their strategy inside the bar is a little more subtle: they will sit near a man or group of men, perhaps ask to be bought a drink, engage in friendly conversation and be quite physical toward a man who shows any interest. If they are successful then she and her client will go to the latter's hotel—although some hotels will not allow them to enter. In that case she will attempt to persuade the client to rent a room in another nearby cheap hotel for several hours (what is called in Taiwan a "love hotel" but has no similar nomenclature in the Philippines, but which are now beginning to sprout up in various cities).

An example is the case of Richard, who went to one of the few remaining bars in Ermita after its shit down, directly across from his hotel. The bar provided a venue for music and pool, and food and alcohol was served by attractive young waitresses who were not available for sexual services. As Richard took his seat a young woman, Mary, who had followed him in, sat very close to him and within minutes was in intimate physical contact with him. Her story later unfolded along these lines: that she had a sick 1-year old baby, who at that moment, unbeknown to Richard, was being cared for by her husband immediately outside the bar door, and she needed to earn some money to buy medicine for her child. Richard took her back to his hotel room, where she insistently and somewhat desperately negotiated a 2,000 peso fee for about 2 hours of her engagement. They arranged to meet later that evening at the bar.

When she did turn up she introduced Richard to two girl-friends, and instructed them to look after Richard, as she had to attend to her baby. With these two girls Richard settled into the bar for a drink and food, but was immediately approached by several other girls who clearly knew that his two companions were prostitutes and knew that Richard had earlier been with Mary. Later, Richard and his two new companions went to another similar bar in the area, where he observed several more girls attempting to solicit clients, including himself.

(ii) The second category of street sex workers consists of girls who may hold some masseuse accreditation or permit, and who *ostensibly* do massage but whose focus is in fact prostitution. However, many of these girls work usually in association with rather than for a massage parlour: they must carry and display their "masseuse accreditation", and they *may* wear a semblance of a parlour's uniform, but they work on the street to solicit clientele, and operate very much like street workers not at all associated with parlours or massaging. Often these girls carry in their handbag some massage "equipment" such as oils. In taking up their offer for a "massage", the girl will lead a client to a massage place, or, preferably go with him to his hotel. Prices start at 300 pesos for a massage, and 1,000+ pesos for sexual activity. The girl will keep almost all of the income.

(iii) The third category consists of girls who hold a masseuse accreditation and permit, and who *do* provide massage, and sex is *additional* and *optional*. These girls work with or for a massage parlour, wear the parlour's uniform, and solicit clientele on the street. Prices start at 300 pesos for a massage, 500 in the client's hotel (the hotel receives 200 pesos if the girl goes there in her uniform, because hotels often have their own masseuse), and prices for sexual activity, usually masturbation, may start at 1,000 pesos. The worker receives only 90 pesos for the massage of 1 hour, but additional income from sex is hers for she simply does not inform the parlour of any sexual activity.

The workers of these 3 categories work on public thoroughfares, and generally charge the lowest prices of all sex workers. They look for quick sessions, seeking as many clients as possible and for the minimum amount of time spent with any one client, (although time-keeping is not overly rigid except in the parlours). However, these girls are open to the possibility of being an "escort". Essentially (i) and (ii) sell sex (including "full service", ie. intercourse) as their focus occupation; the third category differs in that they provide sex as something additional and optional. While most of these latter girls only provide "hand-relief" and do not allow clients to touch the masseuse, there are exceptions: In one encounter, Christine, a qualified masseuse in uniform, provided a good massage then negotiated full service for a *total* of 2,000 pesos, with no specified time limit. She paid nothing to the hotel because she changed from her uniform to civilian clothes, and paid nothing to the massage parlour with which she was associated because her boss did not know of her transaction.

For the street worker (i) who provides sex only, her mobility is limited in that she must complete an accredited

Course in massage and obtain an official identity or permit to work as a masseuse. Many of these girls work locally, near their home, as they have family responsibilities or can not afford extensive travel to tourist venues. Most of their clients are Filipinos.

The second and third types of worker tend to live within commuting distance of tourist areas. While some of them are quite young (18-22), others are older. They *could* take up being a bar girl, but they may value their independence, the *possibility* of higher rewards without sharing with an establishment, or be reluctant to dress in a bikini or provide full service, or they may lack the performative or "teasing" abilities required of a bar girl or ACM.

2. Bar girls:

Dancers and GROs probably constitute the most common type of sex-worker, and operate in established and usually licenced "girlie" bars of varying sizes and sophist-ication, which can be found in most major cities such as Zamora Street in Makati, Angeles City, Olongapo, Cebu, and among scattered girlie bars of Cubao/Quezon City and even in remote cities such as Surigao. It is a very complex system because there are usually 2-3 categories of girls (dancers, GROs, and waitresses) who work in such bars, and because of the specific operation of each of the establish-ments in terms of how they employ/pay workers, how many girls are employed, what services the bar provides, what girls are allowed to do, and how customers procure a girl of their choice. They also differ in terms of the clientele for whom they cater such that the larger city venues (Cebu, Makati, Angeles, Olongapo) attract foreigners, whereas more localized less sophisticated venues (eg. in Quezon City) cater for mostly local Filipino men. In addition, the girls are required to be registered with local health services and undergo mandatory periodic health checks, which may incur an expense for the girls or for the business, or may not always be met.

"Girlie bars" are, as the name might suggest, bars of varying size (from about 60 x 60 feet to some as large as a modest house, and some with 2nd floor facilities) with various seating arrangements (although in principle essentially the same) for clientele who can gaze upon and flirt with many girls in bikinis (see examples below). The venues are usually very dark, even though strobe and crystal ball lights are on (no pun intended).

Many of the bars have some kind of raised stage or catwalk on which the girls dance, some quite high and central, while several bars may instead have a sunken stage, often with choreographed dance shows. In all the bars it is mandatory for each customer to buy a drink.

"Bar girls" are the essence of the business: dressed in only bikinis they generally "dance" (ie. gyrate to their own interpretations of the music) to *very* loud music on a small stage that may be equipped with dance poles. Commonly, several of the girls take turns to dance to three tunes before being allowed to have a break, during which time they are expected to approach customers and *overtly* flirt with them, attempting to have the customer buy them a "lady's drink" (commonly a soft drink or low alcohol drink) at a mark-up price of 400-600% (eg. 390 pesos vis-à-vis a bottle of beer at 150 pesos, which itself compares with the outside retail price of 25 pesos). If they are successful then they get a percentage of the cost and are allowed to remain with a customer until she finishes that drink. They are then required to return to the stage to dance.

If they are unsuccessful in procuring a lady's drink, then the *mama-san* will berate them and/or the customer, and make the girls try other customers, or dance. However, if it is evident that a customer is keen on a particular girl (or girls), and shows signs of staying and buying more drinks for himself (and perhaps his male companions) and there is likelihood he will take the girl out of the bar for the night, the *mama-san* may relax her vigilance, although she will still commonly pressure the customer to buy drinks, particularly lady's dinks, and this will be encouraged also by the girl/s herself.

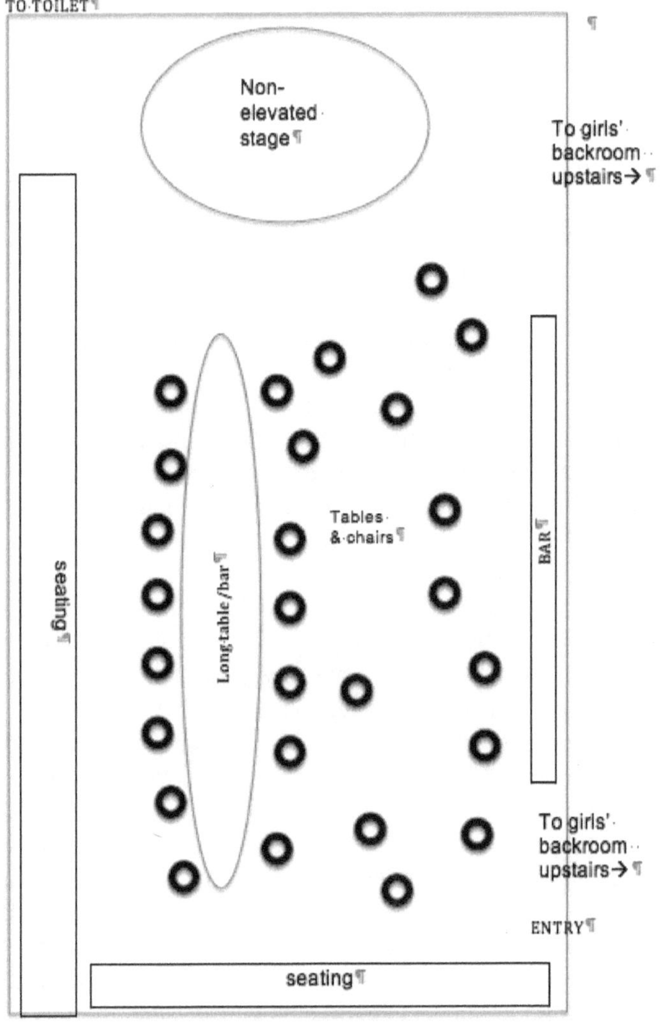

Floor plan of bars in Zamora St., & in Angeles City (below).

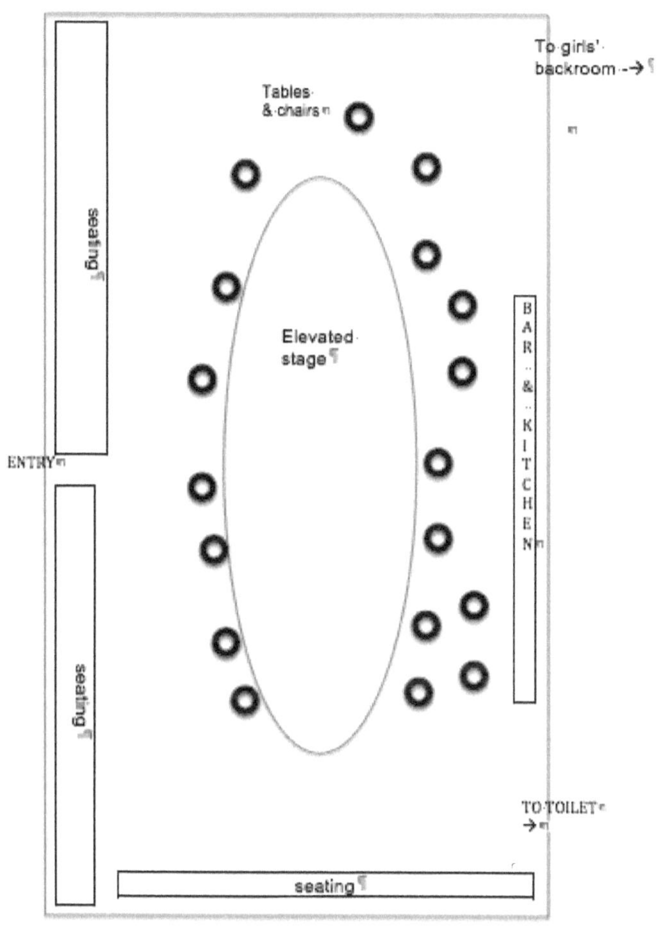

In other bars, apart from the foregoing roles that girls perform, they may also be required to participate in choreographed musical shows. In such venues it is mandatory for each customer to buy at least one drink for himself.

In contrast, GROs may be dressed in sexy attire or a

uniform, or general civilian clothes. In some places they double as waitresses, while in other places there are designated waitresses (who may or may not be available for sexual liaisons), or the *mama-san* will also double as a waitress.

The role of the GRO is to meet and greet customers, to generally pamper clients, often by touching them or providing an ad hoc massage (for which one has to give a "tip"), offering themselves for sexual liaisons, encouraging drinking and especially the purchase of lady's drinks for themselves or other girls, and, importantly, to facilitate the meeting of a client with any particular girl he may be keen to meet. Most GROs *and* waitresses are also available for sexual liaisons.

Thus, very quickly after entering such an establishment a client may have several women, both GROs and bar girls, talking to and pampering him, so much so that some of the women will engage in foreplay, often moving to a rear and dimly lit seat where direct sexual contact can be undertaken. Here negotiations also occur about taking any of the girls out of the bar.

The income of bar girls varies according to the arrangement under which they are "employed". In some places they *may* get a minimal salary (360-460 pesos a day), supplemented by commissions from lady's drinks, tips, and escorting with a client—who is required to pay a "bar fine" for that privilege. In other establishments girls may get no salary and must rely on commissions, tips and sexual liaisons. However, some are provided with accommodation or food—although this is not always free.

Similarly, GROs rely almost entirely on commissions, tips and liaisons, in addition to the good-will of bar girls to share their income from the liaisons that GROs have facilitated. While in some places they may get a minimal salary, they (and/or waitresses) may also get a commission on all drinks a customer buys and whom they serve; thus at the end of their shift, perhaps at 10pm, they ask customers to pay their bills so as to record their entitlements to commissions. All these girls therefore largely work on a piece-rate/commission basis and are thus severely subject to the quantity of custom and their ability to solicit clients, as well as restricted in their ability to moonlight. Thus their monthly income fluctuates, although it must be "sufficient", in some sense (of which we know almost nothing), for them to remain in the job, or they have no alternative.

Commonly all these girls work 9-12 hour shifts, often 6 days a week, are not permitted to leave the premises during their work hours, nor take a day off work without prior arrangement.

Should a customer wish to have a sexual liaison with a bar girl or GRO, he can do so in three different ways. First, he can pay about 2,000-3,000 pesos to the *mama-san* to take the girl to a private room for 1-2 hours. The girl receives only a proportion of this, but she may ask for a tip from the client.

Second, the customer can arrange with the girl to meet him after work; but this is forbidden. If she is caught out she may lose her job and/or be fined up to 7,000 pesos. Nevertheless, it is a common practice, although it can be difficult if she finishes work at 5am. Often, if a girl is able, she will spend a few hours or overnight with a client and return to work the following day, but they greatly prefer if the client is in a hotel some considerable distance from the bar where the girl works so as not go be seen by other girls who may inform on her.

For example, Peter, an American customer at one particular Zamora Street bar, was quickly surrounded by 9 GROs and bar girls shortly after entering the premises. He was enticed into a back, corner lounge seat of the general bar, where several of the girls engaged in open foreplay with him, and others exposed their breasts, etc. At one point, Skye, a bar girl, intervened by taking both Peter's pants and her own bikini down and simulating sex. The *mama-san* persisted in asking Peter to buy lady's drinks for all 9 women (totaling over 3,000 pesos), to consume more beer, while one girl massaged him and asked for 500 pesos for doing so, and others begged for a tip so they could buy some food. (Several other experiences suggest that many of these girls are frequently hungry).

Peter arranged to meet Skye at 10pm that night, after she finished work. She took the risk and went to his hotel for the night, for which she asked 2,000 pesos. She then arranged to take 3 days off work in order to spend time with Peter, with him covering all her incidental costs and giving her a few more thousand pesos. Several weeks later Skye took a week off work and travelled with Peter to a beach resort. Again Peter paid all costs, provided spending money, and in the end paid 4,000 pesos to Skye for "loss of income".

In Angeles City the work conditions and proscriptions are similar to those bars in Zamora St., but procurement of a bar girl varies slightly. In Angels the bars are larger and some have large, elevated stages that accommodated 20-30 girls at a time. Each girl displays a number; the customer informs a GRO that he would like a particular girl/s to sit with him, in which case he must buy her a lady's drink. One client, George, followed this procedure, only to find out that the girl of his choice was a "cherry-girl" (virgin), which quickly became known to the *mama-san*. She berated the girl, saying that she could not work in the bar if she was unwilling to go with clients—which in all bars is mandatory.

Third, the "official" method of organizing a liaison is to pay the *mama-san* a "bar fine" of 2,000-3,000 pesos, of which the girl may get a small proportion. The fine is to compensate the business for the loss of the worker; it is a flat rate that allows the girl to be away from the bar for a few hours or days. However, if she is on a salary, she does not get paid for her absent days.

In the two latter arrangements clients also have to

negotiate directly with the girl a payment for her services, which can vary from 1,000 to 10,000 pesos, in addition to any incurred costs (food, travel, gifts, etc), particularly if the client asks the girl to accompany him for several days, and thus she becomes an escort. She is free to keep whatever the client directly pays her.

These bars derive their income in large part from bar-fines and highly inflated drink prices, while keeping costs down by paying no or minimal salaries. Their main costs are salaries (if paid), payments to management, security and a DJ, high licencing and electricity fees, possibly fees for the girls' health checks, and possibly some "agreement" with local police and officials. But on closer inspection of some these bars, particularly in Zamora St., it was evident that, in some cases there were 50 girls and very few customers throughout the night, and thus while the business may have low labour costs its income was also low, while other costs were high. This would seem to suggest that such businesses may be venues for money laundering or other illegal activities.

In contrast to the foregoing description of bars that tend to be larger, well established and urbane in the larger cities with fifty or more girls, there are also smaller rather un-polished establishments, with perhaps only 4-6 girls. While the prices may be cheaper, the establishments are of poorer quality and serve mostly local, Filipino clientele. To take a girl to a private session is not only cheaper but also circumscribed by time limits.

Some of these girls, particularly in provincial towns such as Surigao, may approach customers and offer private shows, or short-time sex in an upstairs room. For example, my companion and I in Surigao were looking for an accept-able bar to have a drink; as we approached one establishment at 7pm, a young girl, in her late teens, began to negotiate a private show at the cost of 1,500-2000 pesos, with no particular time limit. This show would entail, as she said, dancing naked and "touching". Although she worked at the bar as a dancer, the bar was not yet opened at that hour.

While most bar girls have only a high school education, the qualities that are required of them are to be young, usually 18-25, attractive, able and willing to "dance", willing to wear skimpy bikinis, and an ability and willingness to intimately flirt with and ultimately have sex with clients. If a girl becomes an escort for several days the rewards can be quite good, apart from the fact that she does not have to work in the bar for that time. However, such a relatively lucrative income may last only a few days, and be infrequent. One bar girl, for example, had not had a client for several weeks, even though she was popular in the bar.

Recruitment into the occupation may be through friends, or by responding to advertisements posted outside the establishments. There are minimal financial costs in being a bar girl: uniforms/bikinis are supplied by the business; cosmetics may have to be paid for, and girls may have to contribute to health checks. Perhaps the two biggest "costs" are that of becoming infected with an STD which would require her to cease work and pay medical expenses, or becoming pregnant, which would require her to cease work for some considerable time. Quite a large number of bar girls have children, but in order to return to sex-work they need to maintain their attractive appearance and hence often do not breastfeed their children.[36] This places an added financial burden on them to buy milk formula, as well as having health and reproductive implications, apart from having to leave their children in the care of relatives for the long periods of their employment.

Another "cost" is that of social stigma. In their local area of residence a girl may be suspected of being a bar girl because she leaves home every evening and wears cosmetics (as some of the ACMs noted). She may also have to hide her occupation from her family, commonly saying that she works in a restaurant or hotel. Indeed, Skye eventually stopped being a bar girl because she found it increasingly difficult to fabricate to her children the work she did.

Contrary to other studies that suggest prostitutes find difficulty in marrying or having a long-term partner, many of the girls I met did have, at least in the past, a partner. Indeed, it was often because their partner had left them that they took up sex-work to support a family, rather than their partner leaving them because they were sex-workers. In addition, it is possible for a girl to return to her hometown, where her occupation is not known, and marry, for it is not uncommon for various sex-workers to migrate to a large city to undertake sex-work.

For bar girls, occupational mobility into other forms of sex-work such as a masseuse can be restricted by their education level and financial capacity to become qualified, and also the time required to attend classes for up to 3 months, as well as their own acknowledgement that they are not good at massage.

When asked why they do not become ACMs they indicated they didn't know much about that work, other than it was illegal, and had little idea of how to go about working as a cam model. Many also said they did not have a PC or the technical knowledge to engage in the work—even though bar girls are of about the same age as ACMs—or did not know anyone that could introduce them to that line of work. We met only one GRO who previously had been an ACM.

Others, however, took a different position. Skye, for example, said, *"It's embarrassing to play with myself, why would I do that when I can have real sex, the real thing!?"* Skye was not only referring to *real* sexual activity, but also implying that bar girls formed real relationships, becoming the client's girlfriend, even if only for a short time, and which could also provide opportunity for a more permanent relationship. Thus bar girls perceive ACMs as crass, simply displaying "publicly" their naked body like porn stars, without any real but only ephemeral relationships.

3. Massage parlours:

This category is constituted by three types of parlours and workers:

(i) Where parlours and their workers make little pretence about providing full sexual services, which may be built into a (fixed) price.

(ii) Where workers do massage, and sex is additional and optional.

(iii) Where workers do massage, of which one form involves genital stimulation (*lingham*, ie. hand relief) as part of a "therapeutic" massage package.

(i) In the first type of parlour the girls tend to be youngish (18-24) and not found in all cities or locales, thus this description draws on the experience of Zamora St., Makati. Here the girls stand on and traverse the main street and surrounding side streets, as I have briefly described in the category of street workers (ii). While they do not wear a uniform they are, nevertheless, registered with the local government as masseuses and licensed to operate in the area of Zamora St., and have undertaken some training (of dubious quality) in massage. Although they may also be "associated", or claim to be associated, with a massage parlour, they do not need to be officially qualified, but must be able to perform a reasonable massage, and be willing to engage in sexual activities.

They commonly work in on their own, in pairs or in small groups of 3-4. They approach potential customers by asking if the men want a massage, and hand out a business card, on the back of which is handwritten their own personal cell phone number and name.

In taking up an offer for a massage with such a girl, there are two options: first, the client can accompany her to a nearby massage parlour with which she is familiar and pay

300 pesos plus 50 pesos for room rental (as a fee to the business because she is not officially employed by that business) for a 1 hour massage. The massage is likely to be poorly done, and cut short by the girl offering various kinds of sexual liaison, from masturbation, fellatio to full service.

The second option is that she can go to a client's hotel room for only 300 pesos, and where, again, negotiations take place for any extra service. One client explained that he took such a girl to his room in expectation of a professional massage, in the least. He explained that she was not at all adept at massaging, and would engage in only limited sexual activities, even declaring that she didn't know if she was a virgin (a misunderstanding that may have been due to a language problem). He paid her 1,500 pesos for a poor massage and limited sexual engagement.

(ii) The second type of parlour we have already touched upon regarding street workers. While one can walk into such a parlour and receive a massage, with sex as additional and optional, one can also be solicited by streetworker masseuses affiliated with such an establishment and who usually wear a uniform. This type of parlour, and their workers, blur the boundaries between the first and second types in that workers *may* be nude during the massage, may allow them selves to be touched, and in some cases engage in full service.

These girls—from age 18 to some older women of about 40 years of age—wear distinct uniforms that identify them as masseuses linked to nearby massage parlours, and carry a local government certification badge, which certifies they have completed a massage course (again of dubious quality), and work for and are registered with a massage immployer. They commonly work in small groups of 3-5 and locate themselves at particular places along Zamora Street, almost shoulder to shoulder with other street workers. While no pimps were evident or spoken about, occasionally a girl may mention that her employer/manager of the massage parlour sometimes comes out to check on the girls. While fear of losing their job and possible official accreditation may drive these girls to work diligently, what also motives them is, from my impressions, the sheer need for money.[37]

Like the other street workers, they approach potential customers by asking if the men want a massage, and hand out parlour business cards, on the back of which is hand-written their own personal cell phone number and name.

In taking up their offer one again has two options: for 300 pesos one can go with a girl of choice to the massage parlour where she works and receive a reasonable massage in which the client is fully naked, but the girl remains clothed.

The premises vary in quality, from the dark, poorly furnished, shabby establishments in which rooms are barely large enough for two people and a massage table, and in which doorways are covered only with thin curtains, to more elaborate, bright clean rooms with doors.

While the price in Zamora Street is rather uniform at 300 pesos for a one hour massage, one encounters additional costs: 20-50 pesos for the rental of the massage room, about 100 pesos for a (cold) shower if one chooses, and even more for a spa, plus a tip of 100-200 pesos to the girl. Many times I asked these girls on the street what the price included, such as a "happy ending"; on all occasions, without fail, the girls tended to giggle and deny such an activity, but added that I should try a massage to see...

During the massage the girl or client may suggest "extra service", ie, masturbation ("happy ending"), the price of which is negotiable but usually is about 1,000 pesos, all of which the girl keeps. Choosing this option there is the strict edict that the client must remain very quiet, as the parlour is ostensibly for massage only, and the client can not caress the girl, although some may allow some degree of fondling.

Of the 300 pesos for the massage, the girl receives only

90 pesos, although she may receive a small percentage of charges for showers and spas. Conversely, she may have to give a small amount of the 1,000 pesos to the business.

The second option with such a masseuse is to go to the client's hotel room, but the price for a massage in that case is 500 pesos. Several girls explained that some of the hotels do not allow masseuses in uniform to provide a service in a guest's room because each hotel has its own masseuse, and thus outsiders would detract from her income and possibly the hotel's reputation. Thus the additional 200 pesos was paid directly to the hotel.

However, these masseuses are willing to go to their massage parlour and change from their uniforms into civilian clothing and thus enter the hotel with their client as a friend, and thus charge only 300 for a one hour non-sexual massage. Needless to say that, like the events at a massage parlour, negotiations can take place about extra service, which can range from masturbation to full service—given now that there is no need for discretion. One client's experience best exemplifies this: he engaged such a masseuse, Christine, who was in uniform, who changed her clothing and returned to his hotel room as a "girlfriend". There she provided a professional massage, while she was naked also, and then negotiated further service. For 2,000 pesos she engaged in *full* sex, foolishly without a condom, for about 90 minutes, although no time factor was ever of any concern.

One of the striking features of the foregoing venues and types of sex-workers is that in some places (eg. Cebu, Quezon City, Olongapo, Zamora St.) the number of girls outnumber the available clients. Zamora Street exemplifies this: while there are several large hotels in the vicinity with foreign guests, there are also about twenty girlie bars, each employing 30-50 or more girls, in addition to about 200 street workers as well as the availability of walk-in massage parlours. In other words, there hardly seems sufficient potential custom to warrant so many girls persisting in their endeavours, amongst which competition for clientele is very strong, as can be seen in street workers of the various kinds standing almost shoulder to shoulder.

(iii) In the third type of parlour, girls are accredited masseuses, based on a 2-3 month course, and present more discreetly their service as "purely" therapeutic. In those parlours that provide *lingham* as the only "sexual" service, the girls do not wear a uniform, and do not remove their clothing, nor are clients permitted to intimately touch the girls. This is the highest level of massage in those establishments, costing 1,200 pesos for an hour, of which the girl receives about 200 pesos.

Generally, prices start at 300 pesos for a massage, and prices for sexual activity may start at 1,000 pesos. Massage prices are based on an increasing scale that takes account of the time (30-120 mins), the type of massage, and the sexual service provided.

In each of these parlours the girls work on piece-rates rather than salary, but have no discernible costs, as uniforms and other necessities, where applicable, are provided by the business. While clients can choose their masseuse, ordinarily each masseuse is allocated by the receptionist.

The masseuses in these establishments are generally a little bit older than bar girls, but still in their twenties or early thirties. Whether these girls were once other types of sex-worker is unknown, and whether they would be willing to take up other types of sexwork is equally unknown, although we have encountered the occasional bar girl who had been a masseuse. On the other hand, those masseuses who provide only *lingham* as part of a therapeutic package are adamant that their activity is not sexual, and they hold other forms of sex work, including ACM-ing, in very low regard.

4. ACMs:
The final type of sex-work to be discussed is that of

ACM-ing, which introduces the notion that, while, ACM-ing may be sex-work of some kind, it is not, according to our informants, prostitution. As an adjunct, ACM-ing also interrogates how technology-mediated "sex" affects not only conceptual notions of sexuality but also the self identification of ACMs.[38] Perhaps equally problematic is that I have placed ACM-ing in the private domain because cam models neither sell "sex" nor promote their availability "on the street", in public. On the other hand, ACMs could be positioned in the public domain because, arguably, they not only do sell "sex", but do so through a public medium, a virtual street.

But granted they can be placed in the private domain, I locate ACMs between strippers and phone sex because, while they are similar to strippers in that they present their sexualized body, they do so virtually, and unlike phone sex, their sexual presentation is visual, audio and textual. But since the fundamental criterion is to what extent workers primarily sell sex, then one could argue strippers directly sell, in real, their sexuality, whereas ACMs do the same but virtually, in addition to providing another service, that of chatting. But it is the technological mediation, the virtuality, that problematizes the sexuality. On the other hand, phone sex, although also virtual, presents sexuality only in audio form, and it is the client who largely constructs the sexuality—which raises the question of whether or not phone-sex workers are selling sex, or the imagination of sex.

I have already outlined how ACM-ing is structured, their work conditions, the gurls' perceptions of ACM-ing as a job, and their insistence that it is not prostitution. This brief allows us to understand ACMs' views of other forms of sex-work and hence their unwillingness or inability to take up other forms of sex-work.

The ultimate goal for some ACMs is to set up their own business, and possibly become a boss. For this they require a decorated room, a PC (16,000+ pesos), internet connection

(1,000 pesos a month), reliable electricity (about 1,000 pesos a month per household), and a Paypal account. Since they will not be paid for at least the first 15 days they also require some cash reserve (about 300-500 pesos per day).

Bosses—most of whom are women—achieved their position in different ways. Both Cristy and Ray and been (and continue to be) ACMs, who earned enough capital to set up several PCs each. Both Jonaz and Melinda also had bought PCs and each were contemplating employing another model so that the business could run 24/7. Other bosses, such as those of *Avril*, Chelsea, Paris and Jonaz, were middle-class and therefore already financially capable of providing the capital. The attraction of this cottage industry for bosses is, in keeping with Philippine socio-economic behaviour, to have a "sideline" business. ACM-ing in particular allows this with minimal outlay for an existing bedroom in their house, and for a PC which, as an asset, can be sold if necessary. In some cases it allows a boss to work as a model and hold other jobs; and, significantly, enables bosses as "employers" of piece-rate workers to earn income without themselves having to do anything or be on the work site—for piece-rates, as I have said, shift responsibility and risk to the worker and therefore models do not require close monitoring. In addition, on-going expenses are minimal, depending on the arrangement with the models: in some cases the models are responsible for at least a portion of the internet and electricity costs, while there are no licences, health checks or recurring registration fees with the site. The downside is that ACM-ing is illegal (since 2013) and considered by some as immoral and therefore discretion must be maintained within the community.

Occupational Stasis
While we can not assert that ACMs do not move into other forms of sex work, their insistence that they are not prostitutes and that they prefer not to be touched by clientele

would suggest that they are unwilling to take up other forms of sex work. Because ACMs with whom we talked did not self-identify as prostitutes, they were adamant that they would not engage in real sex, even for large amounts of money. Leanne and Jonaz pointed out that a *mutual relationship* was required, involving liking one another and respect, to enable them to have a sexual relationship in real. However, Cruz and Sajo (2015: 9) in their interviews with 10 ACMs claim that 7 of them had worked in the conventional sex trade, and that they "kept a revolving door between the offline and online worlds, switching to one source of money or the other depending on available opportunities and the briskness of transactions."

Other reasons for not taking up alternative forms of sex-work rested on socio-moral grounds, as the gurls' foregoing articulations have illustrated:

Ken: "If you work in a bar many people know you're a prostitute, but if you work on the cam...."
Cristy: "...you can hide your self, you're doing cyber inside the house. You can hide it."
Ken: "No one can know...."
Leanne: "you're working as a cam gurl; your neighbour can't know it."
Ken: "But if you're working in a bar..."
Leanne: "...your neighbours can see you, wearing makeup, always going at night, they will think you're working in a bar and that's bad [immoral] for them that you're working in a bar."

Other, structural, factors that led, in part, to them becoming ACMs and to remaining in the job is the *in*convenience of other kinds of work, and conversely the convenience of ACM-ing. Single mothers in particular are able to work inside their own house, or nearby, take care of their children at the same time, and do other household chores. As Leanne said, *"If you work in a mall you have to leave kids somewhere, that's a problem, who will look after them if I am not there?"* But even if they are not single mothers, they may not have the education or performative ability to get alternative work. Part of this structural constraint is that many ACMs live in relocation settlements or slum areas that have few employment opportunities. Nevertheless, ACM-ing is not "easy money".

While these adverse work conditions may account for what appears to be a "high" turnover of cam models, it is impossible to measure. Because any one cam model can have up to 4 screen names on a site, and be registered with several other sites with the same or different screen names, it is not only difficult to identify the gurls but also to keep track of how long they remain in the job, or if and when some may return, often with a new screen name or two, and impossible to know what they do when they do leave. Only a handful of original gurls since 2009-10 can be currently identified as remaining on *AsianPlaymates*.

The small number of gurls who left ACM-ing and with whom I was able to maintain contact have followed several options: they took up college studies (Leanne, Jonaz, *GurlofYrDreams, Avril*), returned home to their province (*Avril*, Joy) and/or took up other unskilled jobs, such as Leanne who helped her mother sell vegetables, Melinda who worked in a fashion boutique for a while, Jen who was supported by her husband and worked in a café, or one or two gurls who did in fact have formal qualifications and may have taken employment using those skills. In addition, as far as I know, none of the ACMs had engaged in other forms of sex-work prior to being an ACM, even though there was opportunity to do so, which may suggest that ACM-ing is not only a first choice for them, but often an only choice.

While my sample is a small proportion of the thousands of gurls who are or have been ACMs, the strong views articulated by the 100-plus gurls with whom I conversed—

and the many more bar girls and masseuses who had never been cam models—would suggest that ACMs generally do not become other types of sex-workers, and vice-versa. These views are driven by strong socio-moral perceptions, that may well override economic imperatives. When asked at what point would they work in a bar or do sex in real—if their PC was broken and their children were hungry and they could not get a job, would they become a bar girl or street worker?—Leanne and Cristy responded:

Leanne: "Still not. I can work with a boss again, ask them to let me work there until I earn a lot."
Cristy: "No, I don't see myself working in a bar, because I know I can do some thing [else], other little job...."

PART 4

Clients ?

The literature on sex-work has traditionally ignored customers, but this has begun to change in recent years (eg. Caldwell, 2011). Even fewer studies have explored the experiences of customers during or the meanings they attach to paid sex encounters, but some recent analyses of data from the Internet shed light on this dimension (Weitzer, 2009: 224-225).

As in any commercial relationship, customers of sex-workers would seem to far outnumber the workers who service them; but this may reflect a Western scenario, for as we have seen in the Philippines, street-workers, masseuses, girls in bars and ACMs, may well outnumber the available clientele, particularly non-Filipino clientele, at any one time or locale.

Nevertheless, a sizeable number of men have bought sex, whether in their own country or another, and it would seem that millions patronize ACM sites (see endnotes #1 and #2). Much of the literature suggests that customers patronize sex-workers for different reasons, amongst which are some of the following:

1. They desire sex with a person with a certain image (eg. sexy, raunchy, etc), or physical appearance (eg. race, physique, transgender, large or small breasts, etc).

2. They are unsatisfied with the sexual dimension of their relationship with their current partner, if they have a partner.

3. They have difficulty finding a partner for a convent-ional relationship.

4. They find engaging a sex-worker as transgressive conduct, as risky, thrilling, or sporting.

5. They wish to avoid the long-term obligations or emotional attachment involved in a conventional relationship.

6. They seek a limited, quasi-romantic, and emotional connection in addition to or instead of sex (ibid: 224).

While these reasons could apply to men (and women) who connect with ACMs, we do not know at this point if such reasons do apply, given that the connection is virtual, or if there are other reasons.[39]

Leanne, for example, said clients go to ACMs because they want a *Filipina*, not a Westerner, that they like the Filipina appearance and attitude, which would fit with #1 above in addition to an (erroneously) assumed Filipina docility, loyalty, domestication etc, but also young and sexy.

Another reason, not included in the above list, is that they also want to help Filipinas, and they perceive that taking an ACM into a private chat, or simply chatting with them in public or private without any sexual performance and giving them some payment, achieves this.

Leanne also suggested that some clients have no girlfriend/wife (as per #3 above), or that it's difficult to have a relationship in their country because white girls are jaded and demanding, expensive, always wanting gifts, eg. cars, jewelry—which might fit #5 above.

Clients also go to the *AsianPlaymates* site in particular because there are too many guests at other sites, or *AsianPlaymates* is easy to navigate and familiar to them, as may be the case with several other sites.

My own limited conversations with some clients in public chats would suggest that some may visit ACM sites to vicariously engage is quasi-romantic/sexual relationships, as they may be too old or physically challenged to engage in real relationships, particularly with young girls and especially Asian girls whom they may prefer.

While some such customers may fit the foregoing

description, there may well be others who fit the notion of "beggar"—a term that ACMs use. That is, a customer who does not log on using a screen name, and hence is unable to take a gurl prvt, or customers who do log on with a name, but rarely if ever take a gurl prvt. In either case, they may be simply unwilling to spend a small amount of money, or vicariously enjoy the sexuality of the gurls. Sometimes these "beggars" do not even engage in free public chat with the gurls, while others will do so, but often in order to entice the gurl into revealing more of her body, commonly with promises that he will take her prvt if she does so. In some cases the male client will reveal himself to the gurl via his cam and publically chat with her while masturbating. See the stories of Kate and Cristy for examples.

Other clients are, as Cristy noted, simply "psycho"; but unlike non-virtual sex, ACMs can readily kick them out of a public chat or prvt performance because the girls don't rely on public chats for money, and because they don't have a supervisor they simply don't have to put up with some of the shit clients engage in. Gurls will do many things, like poo and piss etc, but are ready and able to draw the line.

However, labeling these men/women clients as voyeuristic or vicarious tells us what they do, not necessarily why.

One of the appeals of cyber-sex, as well as phone sex or other technologically mediated personal engagements, is that people who would not otherwise have, or dare access, non-virtual sex services, are given free range of self expression without having to brave a bad neighborhood, seedy establish -ments, or be recognized patronizing them. They, too, can first develop relationships without being shy, without fumbl- ing or feeling inadequate, projecting a persona with which they are comfortable, and thereby possibly build their self esteem. Or, they may be unable to afford to go to the Philippines to meet in real. (One client was saving up to go to the Philippines, and even publically proposed marriage on-line; the gurl turned him down). Thus self esteem can also be shattered on-line.

Or, clients may not meet in real because they may not know what to expect regarding a gurl, her family, the culture, or think they are too old for a young girl, or maybe unwilling to take a chance that the gurl may reject him once she meets in real. Others are simply physically too ill to visit another country and thus may reminisce and live, in this instance, vicariously.

But having said that, we really don't know for what reasons customers visit ACM sites. What we do know, to some extent, is that very few gurls meet up with clients. Amy Flowers (1998), too, indicates that phone-sex operators almost never meet with clients. As Flowers suggests, the allure of virtual-sex (fantasy) does not lie in the hope that the girl will come to life; in fact, it relies on the serenity of the client's knowledge that she will *not*. If she were to come to life, with her would come the ambiguity, danger and difficulties of a real relationship. She is desirable only as long as she remains abstract, in some sense, as virtual, as unreal, as a performer, and as performance. With reality she achieves imperfection.

As Goffman (1963) points out, if a client is socially isolated or stigmatized, he would not seek out someone similar, but rather a pretty girl, for he does not want to be further stigmatized through association with another stig-matic, nor, perhaps even meet in real as that would reinforce his stigma and challenge his notion of himself. Thus just as a gurl is desirable only as long as she remains abstract, so too may a client.

Thus few men visit cam models in real, other than perhaps to (attempt to) have sex with them, as we saw with Leanne and Jonaz, on the assumption that ACMs are loose women, easy pick-ups, "stand-bys". Such men would appear never to have visited the Philippines previously; had they, then they would more likely know how and where to access sex workers, as I described in the preceding section. However, like "beggars", they may also think that accessing a cam model provides them with some sense that they are not buying sex, or that they do not have to pay for the sex, perhaps even that ACMs are not prostitutes—an odd notion that seems contrary to the men's penchant for treating ACMs as standbys.

References

Caldwell, H. (2011). Long-Term Clients Who Access Commercial Sexual Services in Australia. Masters Thesis, University of Sydney.

Flowers, A. (1998). Fantasy Factory: An Insider's View of the Phone Sex Industry. Philadelphia: University of Pennsylvania Press.

Goffman, E. 1963. Stigma. London: Penguin.

Weitzer, R. (2009). Sociology of Sex Work. Annual Review of Sociology, 35: 213–234.

CONCLUSION

I began this book for two reasons. As an anthropologist I was acutely aware that the voices of ACMs had never been heard, and this was reinforced by comments from fellow academics and reviewers of our paper, as outlined in Part 2. Such an imperative was only borne out more forcefully by the events that took place with the misfit Israeli TV crew, as explained in Part 1.

Purpose aside, the book may seem like a motley collection, but there is method to my madness. Following the Introduction and a note on methodology to satisfy academic critique and introduce ACM-ing to neophytes, Part 1, as I said, gives voice to ACMs. Here, however, we run into a conundrum as to how the gurls see their work, and most especially in relation to an earlier (abridged) paper in Part 2 in which gurls did not see their work as sex-work, and most especially full-service prostitution. I continue to wonder if these two differing views are really different, or a result of methodology and circumstances, given that the paper presented in Part 2 was a first foray into the complex issues.

And complex they are, as can be seen by the reviewers' comments and questions, and my attempt to respond to them. Attempts indeed, for we have a long way to go. But go where?—that is my concern: that we will simply recycle old discourses, old paradigms, squeeze to fit the phenomenon and the lives of ACMs into existing pigeon holes. Garcia is very insightful in this regard.

While this Part and the book overall argues that being an ACM provides opportunity to gurls who are not, or do not want to be, prostitutes, but who otherwise have very limited employment prospects, such an argument seems to me to run into a "development" discourse, one of economic-necessity, rather than take, also, another direction: that of agency—

agency within structural restraints, as we all must bear, and has been the bane of sociology since (and before) the discipline's establishment: to what extent does "society"/ structure impinge upon the individual, his/her choices, abilities, capacities, and to what extent can the individual resist, use, manipulate, accommodate, appropriate, break free from, etc etc those restraints. Thus ACM-ing provides gurls an opportunity to earn *some* income, in a way that is both economically and socially "convenient" to them, and in some way they choose this. That "some way" is the problematique.

For this and several other reasons ACMs are unwilling and/or unable to move into other forms of sex-work, and, conversely other sex-workers advance their own reasons for occupational immobility. How these notions, and inabilities, fit with economic theories need to be pursued, or alternatively, existing theories need to be informed by this new phenomenon and expanded to incorporate it.

We then moved on to Part 3, which has a long story behind it, but essentially draws on the notion as explicated in previous parts: that if ACMs are not, or do not perceive themselves as, sex-workers, then where do they lie in any kind of structure that, rightly or wrongly, construes them as such? Even if they do recognize themselves as sex-workers, why do they not occupationally take up other forms of sex-work, and conversely, why do other sex-workers not take up ACM-ing?

This part arose after my submission of a paper similar to that in Part 2 to the Journal *Feminist Economics,* which wanted more of an economic slant, eg. what was the occupational mobility of sex-workers in the Philippines. (Economists seem to lead rather sheltered lives). In addressing their concerns I realized that, after 25 years researching the Philippines, nothing of any substance had been written about the structure of sex-work there. Certainly there has been various ethnographies (Constable, Law and Wiss readily come to mind), but nothing sociological about its socio-economic structure. Calling on my own experiences and those of friends and colleagues, Part 3 attempts, in a very simple way, to try to address this shortcoming—and no doubt, as another pioneering work, will draw comments. I welcome them.

By summarizing with broad brush strokes the sex industry in the Philippines—which cannot do justice to its complexity—I suggested various categories in which sex-work, including ACM-ing, my be placed. Although different sex-workers encounter obstacles to employment mobility, not all obstacles are either economic *or* social/cultural. While some forms of sex-work may provide more money, excitement, travel or marriage opportunities, they may incur some moral, social and possible health costs. Some forms of sex-work, such as massage, do not necessarily evade these drawbacks, despite protestations of legitimacy.

Finally Part 4 on clients falls very short of a whole picture. As much as we would like to give voice to sex-workers, we should, indeed must, give voice to mostly, but not exclusively, men who, just as sex-workers may "sell sex", buy "sex". A myriad of questions arise: do men "buy" sex, buy "sex", how do they feel about paying for sex? What is their attitude during the sexual engagement, commanding, submissive or otherwise? What are their economics?

We have only just begun.

ENDNOTES

1. Not the real name of the site. I have taken care to disguise the identity of the participants.

2. The site is one of 14 clones owned by the parent Company. *AsianPlaymates* had 3,450 registered models in 2014, and in 2010 had a daily average of 17,000 hits by clients. There are over 50 sites worldwide that for the most part present Asian gurls. They are owned by a small number of companies, and are open 24/7.

Another popular site claims to be the largest webcam site on the Internet and in the top 300 websites on the Internet by US traffic, having over 15 million registered members, and over 100,000 registered models worldwide. It claims more money is spent on its site than on any other webcam site in the world.

It is estimated that about 30,000 Filipinas are involved in ACM-ing at any one time.

3. Hilary Caldwell, a PHD student at UNSW, is currently researching women who buy sex. Apart from exploring various facets of this phenomenon, her pioneering work argues that perhaps more women than we realize do buy sex. If accessing ACMs is a form of buying sex, then knowing the gender of clients may go some way to substantiating Caldwell's argument.

4. Cruz and Sajo (2015: 18) make the point that cybersex "Cybersex laborers help create values by making transactions through Western Union or other money transfer facilities. Although probably negligible in value compared to the growth and size of remittances from overseas labor that enter the country annually, remittances are a key driver of domestic consumption which is fundamental to the Philippine economy. Payments made from cybersex are part of this overarching structure. In this regard, cybersex's monetary transactions contribute to national revenue since they use the same financial tools that are facilitating the resources to keep the national economy buoyant. These instruments do not discriminate the motivations behind financial transactions, as long as the operational and security protocols are followed by senders and receivers."

However, an obvious rejoinder to this point might be: should we then encourage income from say drug activities or even trafficking?

5. Sherry Turkle (1995, *Life on the Screen*) explores the idea that on-line services make it possible to integrate our multi-faceted post-modern selves with our sense of central self. The multiple selves that emerge in disembodied communication are linked to a central self and are not distinct entities; although details and physical descriptions may vary, core elements of character, humour and personality remain constant. Here, in Leanne's case, bridging the performative self as an ACM and her real "moral" self—and as we shall see with both her and Cristy regarding how their cam activities do affect how they see themselves, their self regard, and what they will do—the "central self" as a woman, mother, righteous, moral, etc, takes precedence.

6. By this time the reader will probably be nodding his/her head in "the know" or with disapproval; and while what I say here may seem defensive (damned if you do, damned if you don't), the truth shall be told. I never suggested to or expected from Leanne, or any ACM, sexual favours. The fact is that I had long ago realized that ACMs are not "loose" women, that just because they engage in virtual sex does not mean they readily engage in real sex. Indeed, this whole thesis emphasizes that. Besides, why bother to force the issue when one can, in the Philippines and elsewhere, readily meet with a non-virtual sex-worker? With Leanne, I was after a story, as this book unfolds, and she was a key informant, confidante and assistant—as it in fact turned out, for she did introduce me to several other ACMs.

7. Leanne was not the only one to make reference to despair or suicide. Melinda commonly did, and another ACM whom I briefly met on line had a YM caption-message of *"I want to kill myself really don't know what to do now I don't understand my life."* She told me her mother had died (or was dying) and she had a big problem of related expenses. She was herself a mother of two children, aged 7 and 4; at the age of 23 this meant she had become pregnant at age 16.

8. Here Leanne is referring to my asking her long ago to assist me with finding ACMs and do interviews with them, in Olongapo or Manila, and inferring that such assistance would or could involve "companionship". While she later said on-line and in person several times that she would never be a "real" prostitute, here she seems to have succumbed to economic imperatives and contemplated the possibility of— and the apparent regret of not—engaging in non-virtual sex work. But also, this comment could be construed as opening the possibility of her engaging in a sexual liaison with me in order to gain my financial support.

9. One ACM I conversed with on line told the story of being married to a foreigner, who soon after the birth of their child left for his home town in the USA. He refused to get a divorce, or couldn't be bothered to do so, which left the girl unable to move on with her life. While she could get an annulment, this was very expensive. Better not to marry *diba*.

10. I say this not because I personally condemn prostitution, or of men engaging prostitutes—indeed, quite the opposite. I suggest that some men, even though they do engage prostitutes, may hold some guilt or resentment about it. In addition, it is not uncommon among "men's talk" to deny having engaged with a prostitute except perhaps as a lark, as part of a boys' night out, for to suggest that one frequently or even occasionally engages sex workers can be construed in several ways, one of which is to suggest the men are inadequate in personal and sexual relationships with women. The "masculine" view is that one should not have to pay for sex—interpret that as you please! Thus, men cheating an ACM by getting the girl to provide some kind of free show, mitigates their having to pay for sex, and indeed may enhance their sense of sexual self-worth by simply being able to trick a woman, a Filipina, and "get" free "sex".

11. Unfortunately, in this case, Ann's body, as with other ACMs, can be construed as capital—in the sense of something that can be used for the production of goods or services. I will not indulge here in a Marxist or feminist debate about the body as capital or as labour/labour-power.

12. This was to the effect that Jennifer's German boyfriend got drunk with the alleged killer, an American serviceman, and the former flirted with the latter, and subsequently when the American and Jennifer went to a hotel and had sex, the German boyfriend, who presumably was on drugs, was hiding in the room.... But because Jennifer was seen to have a boyfriend, the American didn't realize Jennifer was a TG. At one point Ray joins the conversation, saying that it was when the American guy had sex with Jennifer he discovered Jennifer to be a transgender and could not accept it. So, they all agreed, the American killed Jennifer because he was shocked that she was a TG. However, the three informants agreed that Jennifer in fact had a vagina, having had a sex change, which raises the question of how the American came to know that Jennifer was a TG.

13. I certainly do not condone "Mr. Big's" exploitation, particularly the piece-rate system of payment that underpins the industry and in particular the whopping 50% proportion of payments the site reaps. But neither do I like or condone GMH or Ford, Rockefeller or Gates or any other big/exploitative business; but we live in a world of capitalism without which…Well, we could get philosophical and ideological. In practical terms, for the historical moment, this *is* the system we have, without which people may well be worse off. What we *can* do is temper its worst aspects until something else comes along at our instigation.

14. Dr. Mathews conducted the initial netographic work and was subsequently assisted in fieldwork in the Philippines by John Escobar and Louie Navarro, who also contributed to the writing of the paper. I take full responsibility for errors and omissions.

15. Many of these autobiographies and case studies are similar in approach and intent to the studies of drug users, gangs, and other "deviants" that made for popular sociological reading several decades ago. The studies are of interest because of the details they provide in domains that have traditionally been understudied and/or pathologized.

16. The distinction between identity and character/performer may seem artificial, but such a distinction may be necessary for a gurl if she is to maintain her dignity. It protects her from insult, the clients' usurious sexuality, and from her own "callousness" toward clients. When identity and performance are linked, separation may become problematic, yet a gurl's ability to separate the character/performance from her real identity/self can be critical, helping the gurl to distance her (real) self from mercenary sex acts and the manipulation/ control by clients. Optimally, it allows her to be unaffected in her private life, though this may not always be the case in actuality (cf. Cruz and Sajo, 2015, 2015a: Cybersex as Affective Labour: Critical: Interrogations of the Philippine ICT Framework and the Cybercrime Prevention Act of 2012. http://link.springer.com/chapter/10.1007/978-981-287-381-1_10/fulltext.html and Exploring the Cybersex Phenomenon in The Philippines, EJISDC (2015) 69(5): 1-21.

17. This term was used by several ACMs, and occurred in several screen names. We can only speculate that some ACMs (as with some teens and magazines) use "gurls", because it plays on "curls/girls/guys" in an attempt to be non-sexist. It would appear to be a kind of post-modernist or at least trendy use by girls and teens to make girls seem different from other generations and supposedly equal to boys, but because it plays on "curls/girls" the term still identifies them as female. So "gurls" uses the U (or GU) from guys, which rhymes with girls and curls. The significance of this for ACMs (and perhaps generally for girls in the 21st century) is that gurls are like guys, taking a more proactive (sexual) role, which they reflect in the language they use. Other explanations are possible.

18. While many gurls at this site came and went, I managed to develop conversational or "pen-pal" type relationships lasting weeks or even months with several gurls, and with about thirty others for shorter periods. Many of the conversations were intermittent, during which I would initially ask how old they were and their names (common questions asked by many customers), which province they came from, about their family, when they started as an ACM and in particular at *AsianPlaymates*, their previous work and educational history, and eventually moved to asking questions about their work and work conditions, how much they earned, what they thought of customers, and the occasional vignette. Often we would exchange private email addresses and correspond by that means, and for a few gurls I sent them a birthday or Christmas gift. Overall, I developed relations of friendship. Reciprocally, I encouraged the gurls to ask me any questions they liked, and we exchanged information about our daily lives.

19. For a full account of methodology, see Mathews, 2010.

20. We have no way of knowing if clients are male or female; the site presents itself through its various texts as largely heterosexual, and thus we assume most customers are male and heterosexual, although the site does present transgenders. On this basis I refer to clients as males, unless otherwise indicated.

21. The site changed its format and mode of operation in late 2013, such that it is not always possible to see other customers' names. Besides, both customers and gurls can engage in private conversation within the public chat domain.

22. The implications of two-way visual technology are at this stage speculative. Obviously the gurl can put a face to a screen-name if the client uses his webcam. Perhaps more importantly, she may see how the client is responding to her actions and conversation. More in line with mutual cyber-sex, each of the parties can visually and virtually engage in "sex".

23. Participants use a range of cyber-text, as noted earlier in this book.

24. While participants may like to believe that their communication and relationship with a particular ACM is unique, that he is special, the fact is that at the end of the "line" an ACM has a very different view and agenda.

25. It was very difficult to get a picture of a gurl's room without her being in it. While these pictures may perpetuate or reinforce an objectification of them, what I want to show and emphasize is the studios, and especially the teddies and other props; thus I have attempted to attenuate any objectification by blocking certain sections of the pictures. What swayed me to present examples of studios and gurls was the fact that these images are not readily accessible online in the Philippines (because the site is blocked in that country), and I argue it is important to provide a visualization of the settings. While trying to describe some of the interactions and to illustrate points not readily available to the audience, especially those within the Philippines, it was deemed necessary to present visual images of a new phenomenon, and the images themselves, as examples, are rightly texts of the phenomenon which need to be included in (further) analysis.

26. Personally, I applaud the imagination and innovativeness of these Pinays. Rather than denigrate and prosecute or persecute them for "lurid" activities, they should be praised and honoured for not only their artistic presentations—just as the appropriation of the jeepney has been—but also for their valour in addressing their poverty and familial survival in a country where the government and the selfish moralistic middle class can do nothing but pour scorn and persecution.

27. In a paradoxical fashion, in the space where exotic exchange takes place, hegemonic gender roles are both upheld and contested (Liepe-Levinson, 2002). The women are still objects, but are also now free to display their sexuality and take satisfaction in the attention they receive. *Jazzy, Sheena,* Chelsea and others are examples. Indeed, one could argue that the whole ranking system for these gurls on this site pandered to the cultural position of women (*and* young, unskilled women, *and* Filipinas), and to a sense of vanity that is often assigned to women. Yet, ACMs were, in an act of empowerment, able to appropriate that space.

28. This paper was written prior to the passing of the Philippines' *Cybercrime Prevention Act*, which possibly further problematizes this issue.

29. While some may critique this reference as dated and foreign to the Philippines, the point is that an esteemed Court decreed that prostitution involves partaking in a real act, not the portrayal of an act. Somewhat similar are laws about indecent (sexual) assault, that require the persons to be physically present in time and space.

30. By this I mean that, unlike other possible jobs that involve heavy manual labour, or being in the heat and dust and noise common to many jobs in the Philippines, gurls can work at home with air-con or fan, in a quiet and clean environment, without much heavy physical exertion, and hence in some ways it's a more "convenient" than easy job. However, in other ways it can be a difficult work, both physically and emotionally: ACMS have to do what others want them to do, and *"we get tired waiting for customers... It's just comfortable."* They have to work long hours, buy cosmetics, act/perform, people abuse them, they have to buy and wear sexy or good clothes, and they cannot work during menstruation. In addition, if the PC gets hot, as it tends to do in hot weather over a 12-hour period, then the connection and operation can be slow, and the PC may have to be shut down. Heavy rain can also interfere with the internet connection; and, of course, brown-outs make it totally impossible.

31. Under (pre)existing Filipino laws ACMs are not classified as prostitutes, but when detained or their activities are closed down they are assumed to be involved in human *trafficking*—which essentially means prostitution. According to one police informant, the Philippine National Police (PNP) would sometimes use the law (RA 9208), wherein one paragraph refers to ACM-ing as internet pornography. Other times, however, the PNP would use the Revised Penal Code and categorize the models as prostitutes (vaguely and broadly defined)—which runs counter to the spirit of RA 9208, which categorizes them as victims.

Among continuing contestation, the Philippines' *Cybercrime Prevention Act of 2012* was *in part* implemented in 2013, in which "The willful engagement, maintenance, control, or operation, directly or indirectly, of any lascivious exhibition of sexual organs or sexual activity, with the aid of a computer system, for favor or consideration" is considered a crime. But it is still not clear if this means ACM-ing is prostitution or pornography.

32. For me, such articles raise more questions than they answer. I agree of course that children should be legally protected and kept out of the cam model industry. But the authors of such articles are always big on moralizing and hand-wringing and utterly bereft of concrete solutions for the young women/men engaged in sex or modeling work. It is their lack of interest in even conceiving of possible alternatives for cam models which, for me, suggests that their concern isn't really genuine.

What if the cam model industry in the Philippines was to be somehow shut down? What will the young women employed in the industry do? As unpalatable as it may be to financially comfortable bourgeois moralists, perhaps the industry may be, for such young women, the best of a limited set of options. If such moralists have no alternative to offer, then perhaps they should just step aside and let these young women get on with their work and lives.

What may be actually driving such moralists is, to paraphrase Agustin, an urge to control not only the sexuality of working-class women, but of all women.

And another thing: why do bourgeois journalists and moralists find cam model work so objectionable? Why is it *intrinsically* more offensive than other low-status, low-paying and hard laboring work? A maid sells her gender/sexuality perhaps just as much does a sex-worker—one doesn't find too many male maids....

33. As an aside, it has been more recently (2014) noted that several other (new?) sites present Asians from other countries (eg. Vietnam, India), apart from a long-standing Japanese site for which one needs to be able to speak/write Japanese. ACMs also exist in a number of countries, including the USA, Romania, and most recently discovered, Columbia.

34. In many countries freelance sex-workers may advertise their availability for in- or out-calls; the latter may include accompanying a client for a few hours, over night or several days to social functions etc—which may include sex—and therefore are "companions"; or they may simply offer sex (and massage). Brothel workers also can undertake *ad hoc* a similar role. Such freelance escorts are rare in the Philippines, and brothels do not exist. Rather, "escorts" in the Philippines are mostly bar girls who may accompany a bar client. However, this remains a conceptual grey area. There are, however, call-girls/escorts available through agencies, although not many, and of which I know nothing about.

35. These advisories serve at least two purposes: 1. To give some legitimacy to the hotels and area as attempting to be respectable; 2. To help limit the incidents of bad experiences which could locally and internationally reflect on the area and its businesses.

36. One other factor to take account of is how girls give birth. It is not uncommon for girls to undergo Caesarean incision, which, in the Philippines, often entails a vertical rather than a horizontal cut, and which leaves a discernible scar; this may mitigate their ability to attract clients.

37. An astute reader will pick up on this statement as a contradiction to other assertions that girls engage in sex work for reasons other than economics. The fact is, we don't know, because few if any have been asked. But, one way out of this is by recognizing that economics is more than money, it is also about weighing up the pros and cons, of strategies, of (moral) principles, and of agency and capability. If we reduce everything simply to dollars, then we reduce all human behaviour to a mercenary status.

38. Although technology-mediated sex is not new, as phone sex and porn movies have existed for many years, ACM-ing differs in that it is visual, textual and audio vis-à-vis phone sex, and interactive and live vis-à-vis porn movies.

39. I attempted to run an anonymous survey by approaching several ACM site owners to use their email database. None of them replied, from which we can only assume they are not interested or have much to fear....

ABOUT THE AUTHOR & OTHER WORKS

Dr. Paul Mathews is an anthropologist and sociologist who has worked on Philippine issues for 30 years, and also spent 2 years in Taiwan. He has written extensively about Philippine society and culture in such areas as health, gender relations and sexuality, values, and economic development. He is currently freelancing, following a Research Fellowship at the Australian National University. He is Secretary of the Philippine Studies Association of Australasia, & former Managing Editor of *Pilipinas*, A Journal of Philippine Studies.

Other works by this author

Books and refereed book chapters

Cheng, Y-Y., & Mathews, P. W. (eds). Policy and Practice: Education & ESL in Taiwan (due for publication 2015).

Kumar, A. & Mathews, P. W. 2011. Research and Writing Skills. NY: Lulu Press. ISBN: 978-1-4466-0560-8

Mathews, P. W. 2010. Asian Cam Models. Giraffe Books. (Reissued as an E-book, Warrior Publishers, 2014). https://www.smashwords.com/books/view/447769

Lee, S-H. K. & Mathews, P. W. 2006. Travellers in Taiwan. ISBN 0-646-46836-7. In English and Mandarin. http://www.smashwords.com/books/view/458374

Umali, J. (with P. Mathews). MY RIDDLE BOOK. 170 all-time riddles & jokes. https://www.smashwords.com/books/view/456860

Kumar, A. & Mathews, P. W. 2002. Globalization and Local Knowledge: The Politics of Health Beliefs in South Asia. Delhi: Atma Ran & Sons & University of New Delhi.

Mathews, P. W. & Boon, H. 2001. Annotated Bibliography of Alternative Medicine. Sydney: UWS. 143pp.

Mathews, P. W. 2000. Filipinos in Canberra: Networks and Social Support. UWS Monograph. 53pp. + Appendices. ISBN: 0 646 43415-2

Mathews, P. W. et al. 1997. Integrated Language & Learning Practices in the Humanities. University of Western Sydney.

Mathews, P. W. 1995. Filipinists in Australia: Directory & Bibliography. Department of Political & Social Change, RSPacS, ANU. Canberra. For the PSAA. 380pp.

Mathews, P. W. 1994. "Compadrazgo: Culture as Performance", in Cultures and Texts: Representations of Philippine Society. Eds. R. Pertierra & E. Ugarte. University of the Philippines Press. QC. Pp. 47-79.

Mathews, P. W. 1992. Directory of Filipinists in Australia. Philippine Studies Association of Australia. Canberra.

Mathews, P. W. 1992. "Surigao By-Passed", in Turner, M. M., May, R. J. & Turner, L. R. eds. Mindanao: Land of Unfulfilled Promise. New Day Publishers. Quezon City. Pp. 87-96.

Mathews, P. W. 1987. Male Prostitution: Two Monographs. (a) Some Preliminary Observations of Male Prostitution in Manila. (b) On 'Being A Prostitute'. Australian Book Co. & Distributors: Sydney. 98pp.

Mathews, P. W. 1982. The Things We Do For Money: Everything You Always Wanted to Know About Taxis But The Driver Wouldn't Tell You. Australian Book Co. & Distributors: Sydney. 128pp.

Articles in refereed journals

Mathews, P. W. The Social and Economic Value of Children in Philippine Society, Philippine Sociological Review, 34(1): 37-55. 1986.

Mathews, P. W. Some Preliminary Observations of Male Prostitution in Manila, Philippine Sociological Review,

35(3-4): 55-74. 1987.

Mathews, P. W. On 'Being A Prostitute', Journal of Homosexuality, 15(3-4): 119-135. 1988.

Mathews, P. W. Medical Idioms as Legitimate Responses to Family Planning, Social Analysis, Vol. 31. Pp. 103-125. 1992.

Mathews, P. W. The Language Debate—The Case for Pilipino, Asian Studies Review, 15(3): 131-132. 1992.

Mathews, P. W. Family Planning and Community in the Philippines and Bali, Philippine Studies, 40(4): 435-463, 1992.

Mathews, P. W. There Ain't No AIDS in the Barrio: The Politics of AIDS in the Philippines, National Aids Bulletin, pp. 47-49. 1993.

Mathews, P. W. Compadrazgo: Culture as Performance, RIMA, 28(1): 35-58. 1994.

Mathews, P. W. A Note on the Politics of AIDS in the Philippines, Journal of Contemporary Asia, 24(1): 95-100. 1994.

Mathews, P. W. Social Control in Non-Allopathic Therapeutics, J of Social Inquiry, 5(1): 17-36. 1995.

Mathews, P. W. Church, Religion and Fertility in the Philippines: The BRAC Study Revisited. Philippine Studies, 44(12): 69-104. 1996.

Mathews, P. W. Introduction, in Nation-Building: The Case of the Philippines, 1896-1996, Pilipinas, special issue #27. 1996. Pp. vii-ix.

Mathews, P. W. Voodoo as a Medical System, Journal of Social Inquiry, 7(2): 24-40. 1997.

Mathews, P. W. Land Rights for Gay Whales: Political Correctness or Ideology Under the Mat? J of Social Inquiry, 8(2): 64-83. 1998.

Mathews, P. W. Review article: Philippine Gay Culture: The Last 30 Years. Binabae to Bakla, Silahis to MSM. By J. N. Garcia. Asian Studies Review, 23(3): 407-412. 1999.

Mathews, P. W. Hierarchy of Medical Resort in a Philippine

Barrio, Pilipinas, #34, 2000. Pp. 111-149.

Mathews, P. W. & Kumar, A. An Exploratory Study Of Alternative Medicine Use In Western Sydney. J Social Inquiry, 11(2): 17-37. 2001.

Mathews, P. W. & Colbourn, A. Filipinas' Experience of Migration in Western Sydney, Pilipinas, #39. 2002. Pp. 76-89.

Mathews, P. w., Whitty, M., Sheaves, F. Using Alternative Therapies: A Survey from Western Sydney, J of Social Inquiry, 13(2): 22-42. 2003.

Mathews, P. W. & Nocheseda, E. I. Manifesting Palaspas: Palm Leaf Art in Philippine Life and Culture, Pilipinas, #41, September 2003. Pp. 18-45.

Mathews, P. W. Transgendering Sexuality in the Philippines, Pilipinas, #46. 2006.

Mathews, P. W. & Loong, N. Lost in (Third) Space: How I Lost My Ethnic Identity, Journal of Social Inquiry, 15(2). 2005.

Mathews, P. W. Learning English in Taiwan: A Comparative Commentary, Tung Nang Institute of Technology J of Linguistics, 2005. Pp. 367-372.

Mathews, P. W., Owen, C., Ramsey, W., Corrigan, G., Bassett, M. & Wenzel, J. Assessment of a Peer Review Process among Interns at an Australian Hospital, Australian Health Review, 34: 1-7. 2010.

Owen, C., Mathews, P. W., Ramsey, W., Phillips, C., Corrigan, G., Bassett, M. & Wenzel, J. INTERN CULTURE. INTERN-AL RESISTANCE, Australian Health Review, Sept. 2011.

Mathews, P. W., Recabar, J. & Navarro, L. Noli me Tangere: When Prostitution is not Prostitution. Sabangan (Crossroads), Issue #1, August 2014.

Mathews, P. W., et al. Time spent on health related activities associated with chronic illness: a scoping literature review. BMC Public Health (in press 2012).

Cheng, Y-Y., Guey, C-C., Mathews, P., Kiyonaga, K., &

Shibata S. English as a Foreign Language in Elementary Schools: The Case of Taiwan. Shumei University Journal #9. Pp. 44-81. 2012.

Cheng, Y-Y., Guey, C-C., Mathews, P., Kiyonaga, K., & Shibata S. English as a Foreign Language in Junior High Schools: The Case of Taiwan. Shumei University Journal #10. Pp. 19-65. 2013.

Mathews, P. W. (2017). Cam Models, Sex Work, and Job Immobility in the Philippines, Feminist Economics, 23(3): 160-183.

Mathews, P. W. (2015). Piece-Rates as Inherently Exploitative: Adult/Asian Cam Models As Illustrative. Journal of Marxism and Interdisciplinary Inquiry.

Conference and working papers

The Value of Children in the Philippines. Staff/postgraduate seminar, UNSW, 1986.

Compadrazgo. Staff/postgraduate seminar, UNSW, 1987.

Rent Capital & Petty Commodity Production. Staff/postgraduate seminar, UNSW, 1987.

Medical Idioms As Legitimate Responses to Family Planning. Third International Philippine Studies Conf., Manila, July 1989.

Surigao By-Passed. Conference on Mindanao, ANU, 1989.

Medical Idioms As Legitimate Responses to Family Planning. Seminar Program, ANU. 1990.

Church, Religion & Fertility in the Philippines. 4th Int'l Philippine Studies Conf, ANU, 1992.

Church, Religion & Fertility in the Philippines: Values, Action & Development. ASAA 9th Biennial Conference, Armidale, July 1992.

Religion, Church, Fertility & Development. Anthropological Society Conference, Melb. 1993.

The Discourse of Family Planning & Nationalism in the Philippines. PSAA/PSC Seminar Series, RSPAS, ANU. Sept. 13, 1995.

Are They Serious ? The Discourse of Family Planning and Nationalism. 3rd International European Philippine Conference, France. April 1997.

Illness & Medical Resort in Surigao, JCU/PSAA Centennial Conference. July 11-13 1998.

Does Family Planning Mean being a "Proper" Citizen in the Philippines? 6th International Philippine Studies Conference, July 10-14, 2000. Manila.

Transgendering Sexuality in the Philippines. 7th International Philippine Studies Conference, Leiden. June, 2004.

Mathews, P. W. GAS: GROUPS, ASSESSMENT, SALVATION. Teaching Methods (of English) in Taiwan. 1st Annual English Conference, Applied English Dept., Tung Nan Institute of Technology, Taiwan, June 17, 2005.

Mathews, P. W. Double-Speak as Discourse. International Symposium, "Applied English Education: Trends, Issues and Interconnections", March 9 2007, I-Shou University, Taiwan.

Mathews, P. W. Return to Eden: Education in Taiwan. I-Shou University English Dept's Seminars. Inaugural presentation, October 2006. Taiwan.

Mathews, P. W. Noli me Tangere: When Is Prostitution Not Prostitution. 10th Women in Asia Conference, ANU, Canberra. July 2010.

Mathews, P. W. Noli me Tangere: When Is Prostitution Not Prostitution. Sociology Seminar, ANU, Canberra. October 2010.

Mathews, P. W. Report on time use amongst chronic illness sufferers, Menzies Institute of Health and Policy, University of Sydney. 16 August 2011.

Mathews, P. W. Adult/Asian Cam Models (ACMs) in the Philippines: Health Implications and Advocacy. 12th Social Research Conference on HIV, Hepatitis & Related Diseases (HHARD), "Silence & Articulation".

National Centre in HIV Social Research, UNSW, April 12-13, 2012.

Invited Presentations

Guest speech, Rotary Club/Surigao Heritage Centre, 2000.

Discussant, 1st Annual English Conference, Applied English Dept., Tung Nan Institute of Technology, Taiwan, June 17, 2005.

Works of fiction

Mathews, P. W. My First Riddles. Hamlyn: Sydney. 1974. 45pp.

Mathews, P. W. My Second Book of Riddles. Hamlyn: Sydney. 1975. 45pp.

Mathews, P. W. Collected Poems. Stockwell: London. 1976. 24pp.

Book & Film Reviews

Beyond Marxism. (Allen & Patton, eds). Mankind, 14(2): 130-131. 1983.

Cruz-na-Ligas. (Lagmay). Philippine Studies, 35(1): 134-135. 1987.

Fertility and Kinship in the Philippines. (Yu & Liu). Philippine Studies, 35(1): 130-133. 1987.

Urbanization & Migration in ASEAN Development. (Hauser, ed). Philippine Studies, #35. Pp. 538-540. 1987.

Open Cut. (C. Williams). Mankind, 17(1): 63-64. 1987.

ASEAN-U.S. Economic Relations: An Overview. (Kintanar Jnr. and Loong-Hoe, eds). Philippine Studies, 36(2): 264. 1988.

Babaylanism in Negros: 1896-1907. (Cullamar). Journal of Contemporary Asia, 22(4): 565-568. 1992.

Babaylanism in Negros: 1896-1907. (Cullamar). The Review, 13(1): 113-114. 1989. (Asia Studies Assoc. of Australia).

Angry Days in Mindanao. (Schreurs). Journal of

Contemporary Asia, 22(4): 568-572. 1992.

The Emerging Gospel. (Torres & Fabella, eds). Landas. 1989.

Sociology: Themes and Perspectives. 3rd Ed. (Haralambos).

Perspectives in Sociology. 3rd Ed. (Cuff et al).

In Praise of Sociology. (Marshall).

Dimensions of Australian Society. (Graetz and McAllister).

Every Student's Guide to Sociology. (Kellehear).

ANZJS, 27(3): 437-438. 1991.

Socio-Economic Determinants of Health Systems in India. (Kaifi). J of Contemporary Asia, 23(2): 278-280. 1993.

Phenomena & their Interpretation. (Bulatao). J of Contemporary Asia, 23(4): 570-575. 1993.

Remittances and Returnees. (Pertierra). J of Contemporary Asia, 23(4): 570-575. 1993.

The State, Economic Transformation and Political Change in the Philippines. (Doronilla). Journal of Contemporary Asia. 24(2): 238-240. 1994.

Artisans and Entrepreneurs in the Rural Philippines. (Rutten). Philippine Studies, 42(1): 124-28. 1994.

Methodology for Population Studies and Development. (Mahadevan & Krishnan). J of Contemporary Asia, 24(2): 240-241. 1994.

Politics and Society in the Third World. (Kamrava). Journal of Contemporary Asia, 25(1), 1995.

The Politics of Agrarian Reform in the Philippines. (Putzel). Pilipinas #25, 1995. Pp. 105-107.

The Process of Development of Societies. (Alexander). Journal of Contemporary Asia, 1995.

Environmental Politics, (Krishna). J Contemporary Asia. 1996.

TXT-ING Selves, (Pertierra). Pilipinas, #40, 2003. Pp. 73-4.

Other outputs

Bayot ! A 20 minute edited video compilation of (July 2000) fieldwork data on transgenders in Surigao. (Non-peer reviewed).

Introduction, in Surigao Across the Years, by J. Almeda. 2000. Surigao Heritage Centre. Philippines.

Mathews, P. W. "A System Tailor-made for Cheats", The Australian, Sept. 5. 2007. P. 44.

Mathews, P. W. "Staff Shortages are of their Own Making", Letter to the Editor, The Australian, October 14, 2009. P. 26.

Editorship of scholarly journals

Mathews, P. W. & Ugarte, E. Nation-Building: The Case of the Philippines, 1896-1996, Pilipinas, special issue #27. 1996.

Mathews, P. W. Editor, Asian Studies Association of Australian e-Journal, 1998-current.

Mathews, P. W. & Aguilar, J. Editors. Special Philippines Issue, Asian Studies Review, 1999.

Mathews, P. W. Australian Editor, Pilipinas, 1995-2002.

Mathews, P. W. Managing Editor, Pilipinas, 2002-2008.

Connections

Connect on LinkedIn.

Homepage: http://drpaulmathews.yolasite.com/

Editing & Proofreading services available:

dr-mathews-editing-proofreading.yolasite.com/

Galleon Consultancies: GalleonConsultancies.yolasite.com

Books by Warrior Publishers:

The Magical Shahua and fifty shades of fur... P Mathews
smashwords.com/books/view/949920 ISBN 9781082326448

A Tale of Two Families. P. Mathews.
ePub 9780463250174 Amazon pback: 1980979049; 978-1980979043 smashwords.com/books/view/822236

I Can Never See My Self. Sanitee T'Chong.
ISBN: 9781370673988 Amazon pb: ISBN-13: 978-1093912999 smashwords.com/books/view/738824

The Habitus of Fertility: A Tale of Two Families. P. Mathews.
ePub 9781370755837 smashwords.com/books/view/775568

Are They Serious? The Discourses of Family Planning, Bio-Citizenship and Nationalism in the Philippines. P. Mathews
smashwords.com/books/view/681248 ISBN 9781370152902

Education and EFL in Taiwan: Policy & Practice. P. Mathews. (ed).
ISBN 9781370464418 smashwords.com/books/view/718304

Male Prostitution: Two Monographs. P. Mathews
https://www.smashwords.com/books/view/662166

Samantha Guimoi & The Trinity of Terror. S. T'Chong.
smashwords.com/books/view/444048   9780646571478
amazon.com.au/Samantha-Guimoi-Trinity-Terror-Sanitee

Naked in a Nipa Hut: I'm a Cybersex Gurl & I wanna tell you my story... P. Mathews.
smashwords.com/books/view/579749 ISBN 9781310141461

Asian Cam Models: Digital Virtual Virgin Prostitutes? P. Mathews.   smashwords.com/books/view/447769

MY RIDDLE BOOK. 170 all-time riddles & jokes. Jhenna Umali. smashwords.com/books/view/456860

TRAVELLERS IN TAIWAN Reflections of Formosa. Shi-Hui Lee & P. Mathews.
smashwords.com/books/view/458374
ISBN: 97813 113 49897; 97813 111 22759 (Chinese)

The Can: Benny & The Gems. B. Roberts & P. Mathews
https://www.smashwords.com/books/view/598910

DAZE OF OUR LIVES. Bruce Roberts & Paul Mathews
https://www.smashwords.com/books/view/619690

Complementary Therapeutics. A Selected Annotated Bibliography. P. Mathews & Heidi Boon.
ISBN 9781311871466 smashwords.com/books/view/602281

Directory of Filipinists in Australia & Bibliography. P. Mathews & A. Fisher.
ISBN 9781310766961 smashwords.com/books/view/621655

Collected Poems...& Philosophical Essays. Paul Mathews.

Princes of Beauty: Boy Prostitution in Sydney. P. Mathews.
ISBN 9781311368256 smashwords.com/books/view/639594

The Things We Do For Money! Everything you always wanted to know about taxis but the driver wouldn't tell you. P. Mathews.   smashwords.com/books/view/658100

***Mabait*: A Foothold in Life. Paul W. Mathews**
smashwords.com/books/view/927160 Amazon paperback.